Superintendent Performance Evaluation: Current Practice and Directions for Improvement

Evaluation in Education and Human Services

Editors:
George F. Madaus, Boston College,
  Chestnut Hill, Massachusetts, U.S.A.
Daniel L. Stufflebeam, Western Michigan
  University, Kalamazoo, Michigan, U.S.A.

Other books in the series:

Superintendent Performance Evaluation: Current Practice and Directions for Improvement

edited by

I. Carl Candoli
Austin, Texas

Karen Cullen
Cornell University

Daniel L. Stufflebeam
Western Michigan University

KLUWER ACADEMIC PUBLISHERS
Boston/Dordrecht/London

Distributors for North America:
Kluwer Academic Publishers
101 Philip Drive
Assinippi Park
Norwell, Massachusetts 02061 USA

Distributors for all other countries:
Kluwer Academic Publishers Group
Distribution Centre
Post Office Box 322
3300 AH Dordrecht, THE NETHERLANDS

Library of Congress Cataloging-in-Publication Data
Superintendent performance evaluation : current practice and
   directions for improvement / edited by I. Carl Candoli, Karen
   Cullen, Daniel L. Stufflebeam.
       p.   cm. -- (Evaluation in education and human services)
   Includes bibliographical references and index.
   ISBN 0-7923-9891-2 (alk. paper)
   1. School superintendents--Rating of--United States.   I. Candoli,
   I. Carl.   II. Cullen, Karen.   III. Stufflebeam, Daniel L.
   IV. Series.
   LB2831.762.S87   1997   97-2392
   371.2'011--dc21   CIP

Copyright © 1997 by Kluwer Academic Publishers

Printed on acid-free paper.

Printed in the United States of America

Contents

Executive Summary

Every school district needs a system of sound superintendent performance evaluation. U.S. school district superintendents are and must be accountable to their school boards, communities, faculties, and students for delivering effective educational leadership. Districts and their communities are not being served well, however, by the present evaluation systems. This is unnecessary as well as unfortunate since the field of education has issued definitive standards for designing and conducting sound evaluations of personnel and programs.

To assure that they are evaluated fairly, competently, and functionally, superintendents need to help their school boards plan and implement evaluation systems that adhere to the evaluation standards. This summary outlines some of the problems and deficiencies in current evaluation practice and offers professionally-based leads for strengthening or replacing superintendent performance evaluation systems. Boards and superintendents are advised to make superintendent performance evaluation an integral part of the district's larger system for evaluating district needs, plans, processes, and accomplishments.

General Characteristics of Current Superintendent Performance Evaluation Practice

The current practice of superintendent performance evaluation can be characterized as follows:

Prevalence and Importance

1. Nearly all school boards regularly evaluate the superintendent's performance--79 percent annually and 7 percent semiannually.
2. The extent to which boards and superintendents perceive performance evaluations as contributing to the overall effectiveness of the superintendency and the school system is inconclusive.

Purpose

3. Among the commonly stated evaluation purposes are to clarify superintendent and board roles, inform the superintendent of the board's expectations, assess performance with standards, identify areas needing improvement, improve educational performance, improve superintendent/board communication and relations, improve planning, aid in the superintendent's professional development, inform personnel decisions, assure accountability, and fulfill legal requirements. These important purposes clearly require pertinent and dependable performance evaluations.

Criteria

4. While nearly 87 percent of superintendents have job descriptions, only about half are evaluated according to the job description criteria.
5. Criteria used to evaluate superintendent performance include traits, qualities, skills, processes, and outcomes.
6. The evaluation criteria used most frequently are superintendent/board relationships, general effectiveness of performance, and budget development and implementation.
7. Superintendent evaluations leading to terminations are often grounded in personality factors rather than sound assessments of performance and accomplishments. While boards must choose superintendents with whom they can feel comfortable, the bottom line concern must be with selecting and supporting superintendents who deliver effective leadership.

Models

8. Twelve main models for superintendent performance evaluation were identified that reflect 3 main orientations: global judgment, judgment driven by criteria, and judgment driven by data.
9. None of the models meets well the Joint Committee's *The Personnel Evaluation Standards.*
10. However, the models driven by criteria showed the most promise, with the strongest ones keyed either to explicit duties or to a printed rating form.

Evaluators

11. More than 90 percent of superintendents are evaluated by board members, often with data input from the superintendent.
12. Input from other stakeholders, such as peers, subordinates, constituents, teachers, and students, is solicited in no more than 10 percent of school districts.
13. Many school board members are not adequately trained to evaluate superintendents.

Assessment Methods

14. The prevalent methods are unvalidated rating scales and checklists, often lacking in objectivity.
15. In general, there is a lack of validated superintendent performance evaluation instruments that may be adapted to particular school district circumstances.

Reporting Methods

16. For nearly half of the superintendents, their evaluation is discussed with them at a meeting of the board and superintendent.

Obvious deficiencies in present superintendent performance evaluations include insufficient focus on job-performance criteria, inadequately trained evaluators, weak evaluation models, and technically inadequate methods. Given the important purposes of superintendent performance evaluations, it is vital to correct these deficiencies.

Standards for Sound Superintendent Evaluations

An appropriate place for boards and superintendents to begin the needed improvement process is to adopt the accepted standards for sound personnel evaluations. These have been professionally defined and provide specific, technical advice for defining the parameters of a sound evaluation system; assessing the adequacy of evaluation processes, data, conclusions, and reports; training the evaluators; and organizing a working evaluation system.

The national professional associations of school administrators and school board members along with 12 other professional associations defined, through their standing Joint Committee, the standards for sound educational personnel evaluation (also another set for program evaluation). This work is authoritative, since the Committee is accredited by the American National Standards Institute as the only U.S. body recognized to set standards for educational evaluation. *The Personnel Evaluation Standards* are designed to help educators develop, assess, adapt, and improve systems for evaluating educational personnel, including teachers and support personnel as well as administrators. Unfortunately, school districts have been slow to implement the Standards. All school districts are strongly encouraged to formally adopt the Joint Committee Standards as the policy basis for all their educational personnel evaluations.

The Standards posit 4 basic values for the personnel evaluations of all school districts, with each value defined (much more specifically than can be shown here) by several standards.

Propriety standards require that evaluations be conducted legally, ethically, and with due consideration for the welfare of the evaluatees (e.g., superintendents) and of their clients (students and community). The 5 Propriety standards are Service Orientation, Formal Evaluation Guidelines, Conflict of Interest, Access to Personnel Evaluation Reports, and Interactions with Evaluatees.

Utility standards are intended to guide evaluations so that they are informative, timely, and influential. The 5 Utility standards are Constructive Orientation, Defined Uses, Evaluator Credibility, Functional Reporting, and Follow-up and Impact.

Feasibility standards require evaluation systems that are easy to implement, efficient in using time and resources, adequately funded, and politically viable. The

3 Feasibility standards are Practical Procedures, Political Viability, and Fiscal Viability.

Accuracy standards require that the obtained information be technically accurate and that conclusions be linked logically to the data. The 8 Accuracy standards are Defined Role, Work Environment, Documentation of Procedures, Valid Measurement, Reliable Measurement, Systematic Data Control, Bias Control, and Monitoring Evaluation Systems.

Use of the Standards in Evaluating Existing Superintendent Performance Evaluation Models

Our background study applied the details of the 21 Personnel Evaluation Standards to identify the strengths and weaknesses of 12 different models, believed to account for most of the models currently used to evaluate superintendent performance. The models are grouped according to how evaluation judgments are made, as seen in the following list:

Models Based Mainly on **Global Judgment**
- *Board Judgment* (Individual and collective board member judgments, presented to the superintendent usually once per year)
- *Descriptive Narrative Report* (Board's end-of-year written report, which may include a section by the superintendent)
- *Formative Exchanges About Performance* (Periodic formative discussions between board and superintendent)
- *Stakeholder Evaluation* (Annual or less frequent assessment based on querying of stakeholders)

Models Driven by **Specified Criteria**
- *Printed Rating Forms* (Usually annual rating of superintendent performance by board members on a structured form)
- *Report Cards* (Usually the board grades selected dimensions of superintendent performance on an annual report card similar to that used with students)
- *Management by Objectives* (Quarterly, the board and sometimes an outside evaluator assess superintendent performance against preestablished performance objectives)
- *Performance Contracting* (Annual assessment is in terms of a contract specifying expected outcomes, often including student gains, and consequences, such as financial rewards)
- *Duties-Based Evaluation* (Annual, in-depth examination by board members of the superintendent's performance in fulfilling defined duties)

Models Driven by **Data**

- *Superintendent Portfolio* (Usually twice a year board examines performance using accountability records compiled by the superintendent plus stakeholder input)
- *Student Outcome Measures* (Annually board judges superintendent performance based on trends in student outcome measures)
- *School and District Accreditation* (About every 5 years, board judges superintendent performance based on the school district's self-study and judgments by an accrediting body)

When compared to the 21 Personnel Evaluation Standards, no model is sufficiently strong to warrant its continued use without substantial modification. In improving or replacing their evaluation systems, school districts should be careful to build upon the current models' identified strengths and to avoid the identified weaknesses.

The pervasive strengths of the models include regular evaluation by the board, ease of use, low cost, acceptability to board members, wide range of criteria, flexibility to respond to changing district needs and circumstances, criteria keyed to district priorities.

The pervasive weaknesses were unclear and/or inconsistent application of criteria; ambiguous basis for judgments; vulnerability to bias and conflict of interest; lack of credible monitoring and review of the evaluation system; inadequate provision for stakeholder involvement; criteria, duties, and/or performance objective used are out-of-date, superficial, and/or not keyed sufficiently to job requirements; failure to consider the work environment.

Toward an Improved Model for Superintendent Performance Evaluation

The assessment of existing performance evaluation models against standards of sound personnel evaluation supports the need for better models and provides some useful leads for development. Accordingly, CREATE constructed a new model designed to

1. meet the requirements of *The Personnel Evaluation Standards*

2. build on the strengths of extant superintendent performance evaluation models and avoid their weaknesses

3. embody and focus on the superintendent's generic duties

4. integrate established evaluation concepts, including the basic purpose of evaluations (to assess merit and/or worth), the generic process of evaluation (delineating, obtaining, reporting, and applying information), the main classes of information to be collected (context, input, process, and product), and the

main roles of evaluation (formative input for improvement and summative assessment for accountability)

5. provide for adaptation to the wide variety of school district settings

Superintendent Duties and Required Competencies

It is recommended that school districts adopt an approach to superintendent performance evaluation focused on superintendent duties and needed competencies. Accordingly, the district should clarify the enduring generic duties of the superintendency, use these each year to define the coming year's accountabilities, and also clarify the competencies needed to effectively administer the district. Figure 1 provides a general framework identifying both the generic duties and the required competencies. The broad duties of the superintendency (based on an analysis of actual superintendent positions) are listed on the matrix's vertical dimension. The horizontal dimension lists the main competencies required to perform these duties (as derived from the 1993 AASA standards for what superintendents should know and be able to do). The x's in the intersecting cells suggest what particular superintendent competencies are needed in fulfilling given duties.

The General Outline of the Proposed New Model

CREATE's draft model is designed to help school districts delineate particular superintendent duties, evaluate fulfillment of the duties, provide direction and support for improvement, and make informed personnel decisions.

All superintendent evaluation should be driven by adherence to the professional **standards** of sound evaluation plus ongoing, effective **communication** between board and superintendent and, as appropriate, with district personnel and constituents.

Also, the superintendent's performance should be evaluated within the larger system of school district evaluation. This includes **context** evaluation, which examines district and student needs, community climate, public expectations, and statutes and policies, plus **input** evaluation, which examines district and campus plans and budgets. The board can use district-level context and input evaluation information in determining annual superintendent **accountabilities** that take account of the district's particular circumstances, needs, priorities, and plans.

The actual evaluation of superintendent performance should be conducted and examined in light of district-level **process** and **product** evaluation of school programs and services.

The board's main tasks in evaluating superintendent performance are delineating, obtaining, reporting, and applying both district-level and superintendent-level evaluation results.

Figure 1. MATRIX OF SUPERINTENDENT RESPONSIBILITIES

SUPERINTENDENT COMPETENCIES (AASA)

SUPERINTENDENT DUTIES (Texas)	1. Leadership and District Culture	2. Policy and Governance	3. Communications and Community Relations	4. Organizational Management	5. Curriculum Planning and Development	6. Instructional Management	7. Human Resource Management	8. Values and Ethics of Leadership
1. Foster Student Growth and Development	X	X	X	X			X	
2. Foster Equality of Opportunity	X	X	X	X	X	X	X	X
3. Foster a Positive School Climate	X		X	X			X	X
4. Lead School Improvement	X	X	X	X	X			
5. Foster Improvement of Classroom Instruction	X					X	X	
6. Lead and Manage Personnel		X		X			X	
7. Manage District Resources		X		X			X	X
8. Assure/Provide a Safe, Orderly Environment	X	X	X	X				X
9. Foster Effective School-Community Relations	X	X	X					X
10. Engage in Professional Development	X	X	X	X	X			X
11. Relate Effectively to the Board	X	X	X	X				X

Delineating the superintendent's annual accountabilities involves deciding on uses and authorized users of the evaluation, data sources, indicators, weights, and standards. It is important to determine these matters in advance of collecting data and issuing reports <u>and</u> to adhere to the advance agreement. The generic duties common to all superintendents and the previous year's superintendent accountabilities are considered in reviewing and updating the accountabilities, as are previous evaluations of the district's needs and problems, plans, performance, and accomplishments.

Information **obtained** to assess superintendent performance basically concerns implementation of duties and accomplishments. District-level information on the quality of programs and services and student accomplishments can help assess the superintendent's effectiveness and put it in the proper perspective, but must be checked for validity and used appropriately. It is reasonable for the board to expect the superintendent to maintain a portfolio of information on performance and accomplishments. Using that and other information, the board members can then periodically rate, both independently and collectively, the superintendent's effectiveness in fulfilling duties.

The obtained information and ratings support both **formative feedback** to the superintendent during the year and a later **summative report**. The board should interpret both formative and summative findings in light of the broader district context and use the findings in accordance with predetermined purposes.

Summative reports service **personnel decisions**, including continuation and salary determinations. **Professional development, district improvement,** and **accountability** functions are served by both formative feedback and summative reports.

Superintendent performance evaluations do not distinguish precisely between superintendent performance and district performance, nor between superintendent performance and board performance. While this can be problematic (if roles are not carefully delineated), it is also appropriate and desirable. For the board and superintendent to benefit maximally from superintendent performance evaluation, they need to evaluate needs, plans, processes, and outcomes--keyed not just to improving the superintendent's performance to duties, but more fundamentally to improving the collaborative work of the board and superintendent and school district functioning, especially student achievement. Since the superintendent serves as the district's chief administrator, it is reasonable to key judgments of her/his performance to judgments of the district's functioning and achievements. Of course, in evaluating the superintendent's performance, the board should take into account its own role and performance plus district constraints not under the superintendent's control. This requires, at a minimum, some self-evaluation by the board.

Implementing the Proposed Model

The board needs to integrate its evaluation of the superintendent into its regular work with the superintendent. The board can and should use its evaluation of superintendent performance as an added means to focusing on and addressing district needs and problems. The board should assess both the superintendent's performance and its own in the context of district priorities and constraints. They should review their evaluation plans and reports against *The Personnel Evaluation Standards*. They should maintain a clear appeal process for the superintendent to pursue if the validity of evaluation findings is at issue.

In order to implement sound superintendent performance evaluation, the board and superintendent must define, assign, and schedule evaluation tasks to fit the district's annual agenda. Given the great diversity of school districts, no one sequence and set of assignments will fit all situations. Some districts will need to start the evaluation cycle early in the fiscal year, others in April, September, or some other time.

Figure 2 provides a general guide to assign and sequence individual and joint responsibilities of the superintendent and board in evaluating superintendent performance. An underlying principle is differentiation of evaluation tasks in accordance with the board's governance and policy-making authority and the superintendent's responsibilities for implementing board directives. Also, the responsibilities are organized according to the quarter when they must be conducted, keeping in mind that different districts will employ different calendar starting points. Essentially, the superintendent provides data and advice to the board, and the board uses the input along with other relevant information to evaluate superintendent performance and take appropriate follow-up actions. In addition, the board and superintendent jointly use the evaluative information to engage in collaborative strategic planning and constructive assessment of their working relationship.

Conclusions

School districts need to improve their superintendent performance evaluation systems. While present practice and extant models are inadequate guides to the needed improvements, AASA and NSBA along with other education organizations have produced definitive, prescriptive, professionally defined standards for school district personnel evaluation systems. But the vast majority of districts have not implemented the Standards. It is time for boards and superintendents to lead their districts to adopt and implement *The Personnel Evaluation Standards*. The Evaluation Center stands ready to assist interested districts in developing and installing superintendent performance evaluation systems that satisfy the Joint Committee Standards; focus on key superintendent duties and competencies; encourage and support board and superintendent collaboration; take into account the district's context, including the board's performance of its duties; and above all promote improved teaching and learning.

Figure 2. EVALUATION-RELATED RESPONSIBILITIES OF SUPERINTENDENT AND BOARD IN EACH QUARTER

	QUARTER #1	QUARTER #2	QUARTER #3	QUARTER #4
Superintendent and Board	1. Review Context Evaluation data 5. Discuss superintendent evaluation plan for the year	2. Discuss campus plans	3. Review progress in implementing plans (Process Evaluation)	3. Gather data from community, students, schools 6. Develop P.I.P. 8. Recycle strategic plan
Superintendent	3. Update strategic plan	1. Evaluate campus plans (Input Evaluation) 3. Adjust strategic plan	1. Maintain portfolio of key activities 2. Provide progress reports	1. Maintain portfolio of accomplishments (Product Evaluation) 2. Provide accountability report to Board
Board	2. Set general priorities 4. Approve strategic plan 6. Update superintendent duties	4. Approve revised strategic plan 5. Establish superintendent evaluation design	4. Formative evaluation of superintendent performance	4. Summative evaluation of superintendent performance 5. Personnel decisions 7. Report to community

Epilogue

Improving superintendent evaluation practice will not be easy, and evaluation improvement projects must consider and effectively address a great diversity of contextual influences within and among districts. We hope that interested superintendents and board members, in small, medium, and large districts, will become involved with the authors in examining and improving the proposed new standards-based superintendent performance evaluation model. The book that forms the basis for this summary provides extensive background information on superintendent evaluation and introduces a new, carefully designed model for superintendent evaluation.

Superintendents, boards, and other parties might find CREATE's draft model and supporting information useful for several purposes:

- As a conceptual organizer for discussing the characteristics of sound superintendent performance evaluation systems
- As an experimental model to be adapted, operationalized, and tested
- As an overlay for developing a superintendent performance portfolio
- As a set of checklists for examining the completeness of an existing superintendent performance evaluation system
- As a guide to defining school district policy on superintendent performance evaluation
- As a template for school district committees to use in designing a new superintendent performance evaluation system
- As an illustration of how to apply the Joint Committee's *The Personnel Evaluation Standards*

The authors need feedback on the draft superintendent performance evaluation model in order to improve it and prepare it for field testing. We would welcome and use reactions and recommendations for improving the model. We would also like to hear from any groups with interest in participating in collaborative adaptations and field tests of the model. Both the districts' and authors' developmental work can only benefit from such collaboration.

References

American Association of School Administrators. (1993). *Professional standards for the superintendency.* Arlington, VA: Author.

Candoli, I.C., Cullen, K., & Stufflebeam, D. L. (1994). *Superintendent performance evaluation: Current practice and directions for improvement.* Kalamazoo, MI: Center for Research on Educational Accountability and Teacher Evaluation, Western Michigan University Evaluation Center.

The Joint Committee on Standards for Educational Evaluation. (1988). *The personnel evaluation standards.* Newbury Park, CA: Sage.

Contributors

Authors   Carl Candoli (Austin, Texas)
                    Karen Cullen (Cornell University)
                    Daniel Stufflebeam (Western Michigan University)

Project Director   Daniel Stufflebeam

Project Monitors   Sherrin Marshall (U.S. Department of Education)
                        Hunter Moorman (U.S. Department of Education)

Advisory Panel   Edwin Bridges (Stanford University)
                        Patricia First (Western Michigan University)
                        Jason Millman (Cornell University)
                        Gary Wegenke (Des Moines, Iowa, Public Schools)

Consultants   Barbara Kreuzer (Kalamazoo, MI)
                        Craig Nicholls (Cornell University)

Reviewers   Joyce Annunziata (Miami/Dade County Public Schools)
                        Luvern Cunningham (The Ohio State University)
                        James Davis (Battle Creek, MI)
                        Howard Farris (Western Michigan University)
                        Thomas Glass (University of Northern Illinois)
                        Jay Goldman (American Assn. of School Administrators)
                        John Kingsnorth (Otsego, Michigan, Public Schools)
                        Donald Leu (Seattle, WA)
                        Jack Mawdsley (W.K. Kellogg Foundation)
                        David Nevo (Tel Aviv University)
                        Darrell Root (University of Dayton)
                        Ellen Rowe (Plainwell, MI)
                        Michael Scriven (Pt. Reyes, CA)
                        Sam Sniderman (Lansing, MI)

Project Evaluator   Stanley Nyirenda (Western Michigan University)

Editor   Sally Veeder (Western Michigan University)

Word Processor   Patricia Negrevski (Western Michigan University)

Preface

The school district superintendent, as the chief executive officer of the board of education, plays a crucial role in the education of America's school children. Concern about standards of educational performance and the recent accountability movement have spurred interest in the evaluation of school system personnel. While the evaluation of teachers has a substantial body of research literature associated with it to guide and inform practice, there is a lack of literature relating to the evaluation of administrators and, in particular, school district superintendents. The purpose of this book is to provide a detailed synthesis of current thinking, research, and practice in superintendent performance evaluation as a basis for promoting improved practice and further research in this important area of educational evaluation.

Evaluation may be carried out at several points in the career of a school district superintendent, namely, to establish whether or not an applicant has the *aptitude* to succeed in a superintendent preparation program; once graduated from such a program, to determine if the candidate has developed sufficient competence to be *certified (licensed)* for service as a superintendent; thereafter, to establish whether or not a certified superintendent has the *special qualifications* to succeed in a particular position; once employed, to gauge how well the superintendent is fulfilling job *performance* requirements; and lastly, to identify *highly meritorious service* that deserves special recognition.

This book focuses on the on-the-job *performance* of school district superintendents as they implement school board policy. The decision to focus on performance evaluation reflects the importance of this kind of evaluation in the move to raise educational standards and improve educational accountability.

There are approximately 15,449 school districts nationwide. Each of these is governed by a school board, empowered by state law to levy taxes for the support of education, to set policy, and to employ a superintendent (unless state law stipulates that the superintendent is to be elected). However, in some small districts it would not be cost-effective to appoint a superintendent, and a combination principal/superintendent is employed instead.

Members of the board of education are drawn from the local citizenry. Generally, they are elected, although in some areas they are appointed, usually by the mayor or city council. Board members are essentially state officials elected (or appointed) at the local level to implement state education law. They have the power to establish policy, based on state law, for governing the local school district, monitoring progress, and evaluating results for a wide range of administrative duties.

The role of the superintendent is subject to controversy. Most educators and researchers favor a model of the superintendent as the chief executive officer of the school board within the local district. The administrative functions legally assigned to the board are delegated to the superintendent, who is responsible for carrying out policies formulated by the board.

The definition of a "model" for evaluating superintendent performance that guided this research work is a distinctive and coherent conception, approach, system, or method for producing data and judgments on the performance of the superintendent. A model is characterized by the following elements which, depending on the level of development of the model, are defined in more or less detail: a range of possible purposes or uses of the evaluation; defined criteria for judging the superintendent's performance; a specified method or methods of data collection, analysis, and reporting; an approximate schedule for conducting the evaluation; and intended participants in the evaluation process. Further, a model has as its foundation a supportive theory or set of assumptions regarding the nature of educational administration, in addition to standards and procedures for monitoring, judging, and improving the evaluation process.

This book is the product of one of several research projects conducted at the Center for Research on Educational Accountability and Teacher Evaluation (CREATE). This center was established in 1990 with funding from the U.S. Department of Education's Office of Educational Research and Improvement (OERI) and served as the focal point for efforts to improve the evaluation of educational personnel in America's school systems.

The process of identifying and analyzing models of superintendent evaluation involved a broad search for evaluation systems; the filing and organization of all materials pertaining to these systems; conceptual analysis of the evaluation systems represented in these materials to arrive at a useful characterization of them; synthesis to show the major superintendent evaluation models available to school districts; and, finally, a systematic evaluation of these major models, identifying strengths and weaknesses, in terms of the 21 personnel evaluation standards established by the Joint Committee on Standards for Educational Evaluation in 1988. The concluding section of the book outlines a new model designed to overcome the weaknesses of existing models while building on their strengths.

The search for relevant materials included an examination of the extensive files held at The Evaluation Center, library searches using the Educational Resources Information Center (ERIC) database, and written requests for information to professional associations, state education departments, district education offices, university departments, and individuals known to be active in this area. In addition, more informal requests for information were made to colleagues and other individuals with expert knowledge in the field; and, finally, a general call was made at the second National Evaluation Institute held in Kalamazoo, Michigan.

As with all other CREATE projects, the products of this research were subjected to the CREATE product review and approval process, which involved both internal and external reviewers. The product review and approval process drew on *The Personnel Evaluation Standards*, so that all 21 standards of Propriety, Utility, Feasibility, and Accuracy were reflected in the instrument for soliciting comments from reviewers. This review process involved a nationwide network of evaluation experts and was designed to enable CREATE to fulfill its commitment to provide high quality products aimed at promoting sound evaluation theory and practice.

This work will be of interest to those directly involved in the development and implementation of systems for evaluating superintendents, including school district superintendents themselves, school board members, those responsible for educating and training superintendents, and officers of professional associations of educational administrators, as well academics and researchers working in the field of educational evaluation.

We encourage readers to respond to the findings, analyses, and ideas presented in this book, and to use this document as a foundation for promoting improved practice and further research on the evaluation of school administrators.

Acknowledgements

Support for the development of this work was provided by the U.S. Department of Education, Office of Educational Research and Improvement (OERI) through its grant to Western Michigan University for the work of the national research and development center called Center for Research on Educational Accountability and Teacher Evaluation (CREATE), Grant No. R117Q00047. The views expressed in this work are those of the authors, and no official support by the U.S. Department of Education is intended or should be inferred.

1 INTRODUCTION

The school district superintendent, as the chief executive officer of the board of education, plays a crucial role in the education of America's schoolchildren. Concern about standards of educational performance has led practitioners and researchers to seek ways to improve the performance not only of students but also of educational personnel, including teachers, principals, and school district superintendents. This concern, coupled with the recent accountability movement, has spurred interest in the evaluation of school system personnel. While the evaluation of teachers has a substantial body of research literature associated with it to guide and inform practice, there is a lack of literature relating to administrator evaluation. This is particularly marked in the case of the evaluation of school district superintendents. Nevertheless, reflecting the growing interest in the performance of school district superintendents, there has been an increase over the past decade in the number of districts using formal superintendent evaluations (Robinson & Bickers, 1990). The purpose of this book is to provide a detailed synthesis of current thinking, research, and practice in superintendent performance evaluation as a basis for promoting improved practice and further research in this important area of educational evaluation.

Evaluation may be carried out at several points in the career of a school district superintendent, namely, to establish whether or not an applicant has the *aptitude* to succeed in a superintendent education program; once graduated from such a program, to determine if the candidate has developed sufficient competence to be *certified*[1] for service as a superintendent; thereafter, to establish whether or not a certified superintendent has the *special qualifications* to succeed in a particular position; once employed, to gauge how well the superintendent is fulfilling job *performance* requirements; and, lastly, to identify *highly meritorious service* that deserves special recognition. This book focuses on the evaluation of the on-the-job *performance* of school district superintendents as they implement school board policy. The decision to focus on this particular aspect of superintendent evaluation is due in part to the lack of materials related to either research or practice in the remaining four areas of superintendent evaluation identified above. Clearly, this focus in turn may be seen as a reflection of the relative priority accorded performance evaluation by researchers and practitioners. More fundamentally, then, the decision to focus on performance evaluation is due to the relative importance of

---

[1] Technically, "licensed" is the more correct term, but we shall follow the traditional practice of referring to these state awards as certification.

this kind of evaluation in the move to raise educational standards and improve educational accountability.

It is hoped that practitioners will be able to draw on the findings presented in this book to develop improved systems for evaluating the performance of school district superintendents. Primary audiences, then, for this work are those directly involved in the development and implementation of systems for evaluating superintendents, including school district superintendents themselves, school board members, those responsible for the education and training of superintendents, and officers of professional associations of educational administrators. In addition, by synthesizing current knowledge and identifying key research questions, we hope that this work will stimulate further study of superintendent performance evaluation. Additional primary audiences, therefore, are academics and researchers working in the field of educational evaluation.

This book will also be of interest to a number of educators who may be more tangentially involved in the evaluation of school district superintendents, or who simply share a professional interest in this area of work. Thus, secondary audiences for this book include school personnel evaluation officers, state education department officials, school principals, and teachers.

Context and Definitions

To set the evaluation of school district superintendents in context, brief descriptions of school districts, school boards, and school district superintendents in the contemporary American school system are provided on the following pages. Also included is the definition of a model for evaluating superintendent performance that guided this research work.

School districts are the local unit of government empowered by state law to administer a public school system, or in some cases a single public school. Legally then, school board members are state officials elected and acting at the local level. Currently, there are estimated to be approximately 15,449 districts nationwide (Glass, 1992). The school district is controlled by a governing body, usually referred to as the school board, which has the power to generate tax dollars from local citizens and to appoint a superintendent, although in some districts the superintendent is elected. Not all boards choose to appoint a superintendent; this is often the case for rural school districts with a single, 1-room school. For example, a number of small districts, with pupil enrollments of less than 300, employ a combination principal/superintendent (Glass, 1992).

School districts were first established in New England in the late 18th century and quickly spread to other parts of the country except the South where the county unit prevailed and still exists (Campbell, Cunningham, Nystrand, & Usdan, 1990). The dominance of the Church of England in southern counties ensured the continuation of church authority over education through the county unit, which was a pattern that was transferred directly from England. The school district is the unit through which education is managed at the local level, and it is both subject to the jurisdiction of the state and answerable to the local community.

The school board is made up of local citizens and, according to Robinson and Bickers (1990), typically has 5 or 7 members but can vary from 4 to 10 or more members; this number appears to be related to the enrollment size of the school district. The board members are usually elected: Robinson and Bickers found that 96.5 percent of school boards in their survey were elected, and Glass (1992) noted a figure of 94.3 percent. However, in a number of areas, most commonly in the South and, according to Glass, in some large districts such as Chicago and Boston, board members are appointed, typically by the mayor or city council. The school board member's term of office is usually 3 or 4 years and most board members serve several terms in office (Robinson & Bickers, 1990).

This body is not always referred to as the school board and may be known variously as the school committee, the school trustees, the board of school directors, the board of school commissioners, and the board of school inspectors. However it is known, the school board must ensure the fulfillment of the mandates of the state and must also reflect the will and safeguard the interests of the public it serves. Although the precise role of the school board is debatable, generally speaking, the board is responsible for establishing policy, monitoring progress, and evaluating the results for a wide range of administrative duties.

Similarly, the role of the superintendent is subject to controversy. Most researchers and educators, however, favor a model of the superintendent as chief executive of the school board within the local district. The administrative functions legally assigned to the board are delegated to the school district superintendent, who is responsible for carrying out policies formulated by the members of the board. The history of this position and the nature of the role of the superintendent are described more fully in Section 4 of this book. The important point to note here is that the term "superintendent" is sometimes applied to the chief school officer at the state level or at an intermediate district level. However, in the present context, superintendent refers specifically to the chief executive officer of a board of education in an operating school district.

The definition of a "model" for evaluating superintendent performance that guided this research work is a distinctive and coherent conception, approach, system, or method for producing data and judgments on the performance of the superintendent. A model is characterized by the following elements which, depending on the level of development of the model, are defined in more or less detail: a range of possible purposes or uses of the evaluation; defined criteria for judging the superintendent's performance; a specified method or methods of data collection, analysis, and reporting; an approximate schedule for conducting the evaluation; and intended participants in the evaluation process. Further, a model has as its foundation a supportive theory or set of assumptions regarding the nature of educational administration in addition to standards and procedures for monitoring, judging, and improving the evaluation process. However, not all elements of a model are, or can be, described in full for each of the evaluation alternatives presented in Section 6 of this book.

Book Overview

Brief summaries of the main sections of this book are given below. In addition, the key research questions addressed in the study are identified in the section summaries to which they relate, so that readers with specific concerns or interests in mind may turn immediately to the relevant section of the book.

Following this introductory section, **Section 2** of the book describes the research methodology used in the study. This section includes descriptions of the composition of the research team and advisory panel, the method of working, the approach used to identify relevant materials and literature, the internal review process developed at CREATE for evaluating research products, and how the research findings are to be published and disseminated.

Section 3 provides a detailed description of the conceptual framework that guided this research. It begins with a discussion of the need for evaluation researchers to begin to move toward a consensus position with regard to evaluation practice. Next, the *AASA Professional Standards for the Superintendency* are presented; these represent agreement on the knowledge and skills required for the preparation, certification, and professional development of superintendents. Following the argument that the performance evaluation of the superintendent should be based on the duties of the position, we present a draft list of generic administrator duties, which is intended to stimulate further discussion and research among interested readers. Lastly, there is a detailed description of *The Personnel Evaluation Standards*, developed by the Joint Committee on Standards for Educational Evaluation, and the role these standards played in guiding the research presented in this book.

Section 4 is concerned with the nature of the superintendency in the contemporary American school system. This is an important issue since any evaluation system has as its starting point an assumption of the need for the job and a particular conception of the nature of the role to be evaluated. Section 4 provides a useful framework for superintendents and boards to develop and articulate a common view of the superintendency within the school system. Key research questions addressed in this section include the following. What is the history and evolution of the school district superintendency in the U.S.? What are the duties of the school district superintendent, and what is the generic role? What does a typical superintendent job description look like? In order to answer these questions, this section includes an overview of the history of the superintendency; a discussion of the entry requirements and board expectations for the superintendency; a detailed discussion of the duties and skills required of the superintendent; a description of the functions of the office of the superintendent; and, finally, a brief analysis of superintendent contract and tenure.

Section 5 presents the findings of the research literature on superintendent evaluation. This section describes the current status of superintendent performance evaluation as reflected in the research literature and, in particular, attempts to identify the most important issues and problems that need to be addressed in order to improve superintendent evaluations. Key questions discussed in this section include the following. How widespread is the practice of superintendent performance evaluation in the U.S. at the present time? How frequently do such evaluations take place? What are the purposes of superintendent performance evaluation? What are the criteria or behaviors by which superintendents are evaluated? What methods or procedures are typically used in the performance evaluation of superintendents? Who are the evaluators of school district superintendents, and how well qualified are these individuals to carry out this duty? What other stakeholder groups are involved in the evaluation process? Finally, to what extent do such evaluations contribute to the effectiveness of the superintendency and/or the school system? This section closes with a summary of the main findings relating to each of the above research questions.

Section 6 addresses the following key research questions. What alternative models are used to evaluate school district superintendents? What are the distinguishing features of these models, and what are their main strengths and weaknesses? This section begins with a list of the 12 evaluation models identified in the study and brief definitions of the descriptors used to characterize them. The models are categorized according to how evaluation judgments are made; namely, whether evaluation conclusions are based mainly on global judgment, judgment driven by specified criteria, or judgment driven by data. The following information is presented for each of the alternative models: a description of the model in terms of its distinctive features, common variations, main purposes/uses, performance criteria, performance standards, data collection methods, data sources, method of reporting, general timetable, evaluator/participant groups, its guiding concept of administration, and the mechanism for overseeing the evaluation process and the provision for appeals; a summary, overall evaluation of the model; a listing of the model's most important strengths and weaknesses; and recommendations for improving the model with respect to *The Personnel Evaluation Standards*. Included at the end of the section is a table giving summary descriptions and assessments for all 12 models. The descriptions and summary evaluations included in this section are based on an extensive analysis of each model according to the details of the 21 personnel evaluation standards and are intended to assist readers to select among and improve upon existing superintendent evaluation systems.

The question of what new model can be developed to improve existing models is addressed in **Section 7**. In this section a new generic model is developed and presented as a first step in the attempt to improve current systems of superintendent evaluation. This model builds on the analysis of the strengths and weaknesses of existing evaluation approaches in terms of the 21 personnel evaluation standards presented in Section 6 and is intended to provide an improved alternative for evaluating administrator performance. Thus, the draft CREATE Administrator Performance Evaluation Model has been designed to meet the full range of personnel evaluation standards and, it is hoped, will stimulate further discussion and research among interested readers.

In addition, materials relating to existing evaluation models, which were collected as part of the research project, are included in **Appendices A, B, C,** and **D.** These documents include board policy statements, a compensation plan tied to evaluation, job descriptions, statements of performance objectives, rating scales, questionnaires, evaluation forms, descriptions of professional activities, a performance contract, a professional development plan, a goal accountability plan, and employment contracts. These materials serve to illustrate the various evaluation models as they have been developed and are currently used in American school systems. The examples presented here were selected to give an indication of the full range of materials presently used in the evaluation of school district superintendents, and no comment is intended on their merit or worth as evaluation tools. Where relevant, to illustrate particular instances of current evaluation practice, the appropriate appendix or appendices are cross-referenced in the text of this book.

References

Campbell, R. E., Cunningham, L. L., Nystrand, R. O., & Usdan, M. D. (1990). *The organization and control of American schools.* New York: Merrill, an imprint of Macmillan.

Glass, T. E. (1992). *The study of the American school superintendency.* Arlington, VA: American Association of School Administrators.

Robinson, G. E., & Bickers, P. M. (1990). *Evaluation of superintendents and school boards.* Arlington, VA: Educational Research Service.

2 METHODOLOGY

This book is the product of one of several research projects conducted at the Center for Research on Educational Accountability and Teacher Evaluation (CREATE). This center was established in 1990 with funding from the U.S. Department of Education's Office of Educational Research and Improvement (OERI) and was the focal point for efforts to improve the evaluation of educational personnel in America's school systems. The project that gave rise to this book aimed to improve the evaluation of school administrators, both superintendents and principals, through study of current practice and research and, in the longer term, through the development of new models for administrator evaluation. This book represents the work of the first phase of the project, which focused on superintendent evaluation, and provides the foundation for the future development of improved models for evaluating school district superintendents.

The research team involved in the project included Dr. Carl Candoli, who has himself been a superintendent of schools in a number of districts and has served as professor of educational administration at Ohio State University and at the University of Kansas. He is a well-known authority on school effectiveness, site-based decision making, and school finance. He also was the Deputy Commissioner of Education for the state of Texas. The graduate research assistant working on the project was Karen Cullen, a student in the Educational Research Methodology program at Cornell University. She has a bachelors degree in Experimental Psychology and formerly worked in educational publishing in Great Britain. The project team leader was Dr. Daniel Stufflebeam, director of both CREATE and The Evaluation Center at Western Michigan University, where CREATE was based. He is the past chair of the Joint Committee on Standards for Educational Evaluation, which produced professional standards for both program evaluation and personnel evaluation.

In addition, the project was guided by 4 expert advisers. This team included Dr. Edwin Bridges, Professor of Educational Administration at Stanford University. He has written extensively on evaluation and the incompetent teacher and was a member of CREATE's National Advisory Panel. Also serving as an expert adviser was Dr. Patricia First, Chair of the Department of Educational Leadership at Western Michigan University. She has written widely on school leadership and is a member of the Board of Directors of the National Organization on Legal Problems in Education. The third advisor was Dr. Jason Millman, Professor of Educational Research Methodology at Cornell University. He was past president of the National Council on Measurement in Education, has published widely in the areas of educational measurement and evaluation, has edited 2 handbooks of teacher evaluation, and was a member of CREATE's National Advisory Panel. Finally, the advisory team included Dr. Gary Wegenke, Superintendent of Schools in Des Moines, Iowa. He chaired the CREATE National Advisory Panel.

The 3 project team members met regularly for working sessions during which information was shared and discussed; some of these meetings were also attended by the advisory team members. Each of these individuals reviewed the various drafts of this book, providing comments and suggestions, which were incorporated in subsequent drafts. Dr. Millman contributed substantially to the development of the new superintendent evaluation model presented in Section 7.

The process of identifying and analyzing systems of superintendent evaluation involved the following stages: a broad search for evaluation systems; the filing and organization of all materials pertaining to these systems; conceptual analysis of the evaluation systems represented in these materials to arrive at a useful characterization of them; synthesis to show the major superintendent evaluation models available to school districts; and, finally, a systematic evaluation of these major models, identifying strengths and weaknesses in terms of the full range of the 21 personnel evaluation standards. Dr. Barbara Kreuzer, visiting scholar at The Evaluation Center, assisted with this analysis of the models.

The search for relevant materials included an examination of the extensive files held at The Evaluation Center; library searches using the Educational Resources Information Center (ERIC) database; and written requests for information to professional associations, state education departments, district education offices, university departments, and individuals known to be active in this area. In addition, more informal requests for information were made to colleagues and other individuals with expert knowledge in the field and, finally, a general call for assistance was made at the second National Evaluation Institute held in Kalamazoo, Michigan. Further details of the search for relevant research literature are given in Section 5.

As with all other CREATE projects, the products of this particular research were subjected to the CREATE product review and approval process, which involved both internal and external reviewers. The external reviewers were persons not associated with the product or the project, including potential users of the product, such as curriculum subject area specialists, instructional specialists, administrators, teachers, and special support personnel, in addition to experts familiar with school costs and the adoption and installation of school products. Their role was to ensure the integrity and validity of the product. The internal review board comprised CREATE's Director, Associate Director, Director of Information and Product Development, and Assistant Director. This board was responsible for the final approval of products for dissemination. The board was assisted by the Internal Evaluator who coordinated the process and ensured that the projects' directors and staff took into account the recommendations of both the external and internal reviewers before the Director finally signed the product off to the Office of Educational Research and Improvement of the U.S. Department of Education.

The product review and approval process drew on *The Personnel Evaluation Standards* developed by the Joint Committee. All 21 standards of Propriety, Utility,

Feasibility, and Accuracy were reflected in the instrument for soliciting comments from reviewers. This was a stringent and rigorous review process involving a nationwide network of evaluation experts, and was designed to enable CREATE to fulfill its commitment to providing high quality products aimed at promoting sound evaluation theory and practice.

References

Stufflebeam, D., & Nevo, D. (1993). Principal evaluation: New directions for improvement. *Peabody Journal of Education, 68*(2), 24-46.

3 CONCEPTUAL FRAMEWORK

The Need for Consensus

It is our view that evaluation researchers need to inventory their past work in developing and applying evaluation systems and move toward a consensus position. Such a consensus should be carefully and rigorously developed so that it can be defended in terms of sound logic; consideration and use of what research has revealed about both effective and ineffective evaluation models; and what school professionals would find feasible, useful, and worth the investment. Ultimately, researchers should hammer out their agreements--for example, on a common evaluation model--to cut across evaluations of teachers, administrators, support personnel, programs, curricula, and schools. In order to move in the direction of developing a common model, researchers and practitioners first need to review extant systems in terms of features and criteria that are important in applying an evaluation model in school settings.

Such a move toward a consensus position on evaluation now seems within reach for the following reasons:

1. There is widespread dissatisfaction, especially on the part of the public but among school professionals as well, concerning evaluations of school professionals, schools, and programs. Clearly, the time is right for evaluation researchers to speak authoritatively, usefully, and with a common voice concerning the models, evaluation procedures, and involvement processes that schools can use to improve their evaluations and strengthen their communications with the public and their public credibility.

2. The field of educational evaluation has reached wide agreement, through the work of the Joint Committee on Standards for Educational Evaluation (1981, 1988, 1994), on the basic requirements for sound evaluation of educational personnel and educational programs, projects, and materials. Moreover, the Joint Committee is a standing body; works under the oversight of the American National Standards Institute; and, in an ongoing manner, assesses the adequacy of the standards and periodically conducts projects aimed at improving them.

3. There is growing agreement that educational evaluations must be grounded in assessments of student progress. Some researchers, accepting the public demand for educational accountability based on student achievement measures, have been working to develop defensible methods for doing so.

Millman and Sykes (1992); Sanders and Horn (1994); Webster and Edwards (1993); and Webster, Mendro, and Almaguer (1993) have been making substantial contributions to the theory and practice for considering student performance data in evaluations of school districts, schools, and teachers. This line of inquiry needs to be carefully examined and incorporated into the development of a consensus model for administrator performance evaluation.

4. As one looks through the writing of "model developers," there seems to be considerable commonality on the generic tasks in evaluations of personnel, institutions, and programs. For example, the model by Stronge and Helm (1991) draws from the work of Scriven (formative and summative evaluation), the Joint Committee standards, and the CIPP Model in developing a 6-step model. It is important to note that Stronge and Helm bind together the 6 steps in their model through an emphasis on ongoing, rich communication.

5. The American Association of School Administrators (AASA) has reached agreement on and published a set of competencies for the superintendency (1993). The AASA professional standards draw on earlier AASA publications (AASA, 1982; Hoyle, English, & Steffy, 1985; Hoyle, English, & Steffy, 1990) and were developed with input from multiple stakeholders, including education governors, business executives, national and state education officials, superintendents, principals, classroom teachers, and members from a number of national organizations. The professional standards consolidate the knowledge base of educational administration with recent research on performance goals, competencies, and skills needed by effective superintendents. Their purpose is to define the knowledge and skills that should form the basis of superintendent **preparation, certification**, and **professional development**. It is important to distinguish such knowledge and skills from the specific tasks, functions, or "duties" that make up the work of the superintendent and that we argue below should form the basis of the superintendent's performance evaluation. However, the AASA competencies may be useful in the evaluation process, specifically in providing for and assessing the ongoing professional development of the superintendent.

6. Carter, Glass, and Hord (1993) describe research work at the University of Texas aimed at mapping out the competency requirements of superintendents as a basis for superintendent preparation, selection, and professional development. In particular, researchers have been developing the Diagnostic Executive Competency Assessment System (DECAS), which is a system for diagnosing professional needs and formulating self-directed personal growth plans based on assessment center methods (Carter & Harris, 1991; Carter, Estes, Loredo, & Harris, 1991). DECAS has as its foundation a hierarchy of fundamental leadership domains, tasks, and competencies. The leadership domains form the top layer of the hierarchy; these are divided into task areas, which are themselves specified behaviorally in terms of tasks and subtasks;

and, finally, the subtasks are analyzed into their underlying competencies. Despite these efforts (and those of AASA, mentioned above) to define the professional requirements of the superintendency, Carter, Glass, and Hord note research findings that indicate the importance of personality and political factors in board decisions to hire and fire school district superintendents. The failure to give primacy to professional factors in such decisions is, in our view, misguided and may be harmful to the school district, since decisions made in this way are not oriented to meeting the educational needs of students and the school system. Boards should be given assistance, therefore, in establishing criteria for evaluating superintendents--whether the evaluation is for selection purposes or for assessing job performance--that are based on the **professional competencies and duties** of the position as defined by the profession.

7. Scriven has made a strong case in the literature (1994) for grounding evaluations in the generic duties of particular professional groups. A definition of "duty" that seems applicable here is "obligatory tasks, conduct, service, or functions enjoined by order, ethical code, or usage according to rank, occupation, or profession." In accordance with Scriven's position, we have drawn information from a systematic effort by the Texas Education Agency to define what might be labeled the duties of school district and school administrators in Texas in order to develop an initial working list of administrative duties that are appropriate for consideration in evaluating the competence and performance of school district superintendents. This list is presented below.

8. Webster (1993) and Glass and Martinez (1993) have pointed out that there must be significant and ongoing communication and involvement by consumers as well as school professionals in defining the evaluative criteria that will be used in particular evaluations. The use of a standing accountability commission, as described by Webster, provides one concrete mechanism for assuring regular input from consumers and exchange between them and school professionals. Particular Joint Committee standards (especially Defined Role, Work Environment, Formal Evaluation Guidelines, Political Viability, and Evaluator Credibility) speak to this issue and provide some concrete advice on which we can build. At the same time, there are many knotty issues to be examined relative to administrator evaluations in school situations. Especially, how can school professionals defensibly use and combine an approach that weights different indicators of performance and yet takes account of acceptability thresholds for each indicator? Our list of duties mainly provides a starting point for the evaluation design efforts of school groups.

In consideration of the above, this book draws on the latest research and current practice to develop a draft model for guiding the evaluation of educational administrators. This model is designed to meet the Joint Committee standards, to integrate the strong features of other evaluation systems, and to address the special needs of administrator evaluation. The model is focused on the list of generic administrator duties presented below and builds on the analysis of alternative evaluation systems that forms part of the work of this study. A detailed description of the proposed CREATE Administrator Performance Model is provided in Section 7.

Administrator Competencies

The AASA competencies for the superintendency referred to in point 5 above are reproduced on the following pages. The *Professional Standards for the Superintendency* draw on earlier AASA publications, in particular *Guidelines for the Preparation of School Administrators* (AASA, 1982) and the first and second editions of *Skills for Successful School Leaders* (Hoyle, English, & Steffy, 1985; 1990). The competencies were developed through a consultation process involving a national "Jury of 100" comprising "Education Governors," business executives, corporation training officers, national and state education officials, superintendents, professors, principals, and classroom teachers. Comment was also sought from the National Council of Professors of Educational Administration, the University Council for Educational Administration, and the AASA Executive Committee. However, the National Association of State Boards of Education, the National School Boards Association, and education consumers were not included in the consultations, so this cannot be claimed to represent a consensus position.

The AASA professional standards define the specific knowledge and skills that those consulted agree should form the basis of superintendent **preparation, certification,** and **professional development**. That a superintendent has demonstrated such competencies does not mean that the context of a particular position calls for the exercise of such competencies or that the superintendent necessarily utilizes them in carrying out the office of the superintendency. It is important to distinguish such knowledge and skills from the specific tasks or functions that form the superintendent's day-to-day work. The latter are the "duties" of the position which, in line with Scriven (1993), we argue should provide the basis for the performance evaluation of the superintendent. These duties are discussed in detail below.

By presenting the AASA professional standards in this book we hope to stimulate discussion and ultimately triangulation on the broad areas of performance that pertain to the superintendency and, more generally, to educational administration. Boards and superintendents may find the AASA professional standards useful in providing for and assessing the ongoing professional development of the superintendent as part of the performance evaluation process. In addition, the professional standards may provide useful source material for boards and superintendents to refer to in developing a superintendent job description and a duties list tailored to district needs. The *AASA Professional Standards for the Superintendency* are listed below:

Standard 1: Leadership and District Culture - demonstrate executive leadership by developing a collective district vision; shape school culture and climate; provide purpose and direction for individuals and groups; demonstrate an understanding of international issues affecting education; formulate strategic plans, goals, and change efforts with staff and community; set priorities in the context of community, student and staff needs; serve as an articulate spokesperson for the welfare of all students in a multicultural context.

Indicators - a superintendent should know and be able to:

- Formulate a written vision statement of future direction for the district.
- Demonstrate an awareness of international issues affecting schools and students.
- Promote academic rigor and excellence for staff and students.
- Maintain personal, physical, and emotional wellness.
- Empower others to reach high levels of performance.
- Build self-esteem in staff and students.
- Exhibit creative problem solving.
- Promote and model risk taking.
- Respect and encourage diversity among people and programs.
- Manage time effectively.
- Facilitate comparative planning between constituencies.
- Conduct district school climate assessments.
- Exhibit multicultural and ethnic understanding.
- Promote the value of understanding and celebrating school/community cultures.

Standard 2: Policy and Governance - develop procedures for working with the board of education that define mutual expectations, working relationships, and strategies for formulating district policy for external and internal programs; adjust local policy to state and federal requirements and constitutional provisions, standards, and regulatory applications; recognize and apply standards involving civil and criminal liabilities.

Indicators - a superintendent should know and be able to:

- Describe the system of public school governance in our democracy.
- Describe procedures for superintendent/board of education interpersonal and working relationships.
- Formulate a district policy for external and internal programs.
- Relate local policy to state and federal regulations and requirements.
- Describe procedures to avoid civil and criminal liabilities.

Standard 3: Communications and Community Relations - articulate district purpose and priorities to the community and mass media; request and respond to community feedback; and demonstrate consensus building and conflict mediation. Identify, track, and deal with issues. Formulate and carry out plans for internal and external communications. Exhibit an understanding of school districts as political systems by applying communication skills to strengthen community support; align constituencies in support of district priorities; build coalitions to gain financial and programmatic support; formulate democratic strategies for referenda; relate political initiatives to the welfare of children.

Indicators - a superintendent should know and be able to:

- Articulate district vision, mission, and priorities to the community and mass media.
- Demonstrate an understanding of political theory and skills needed to build community support for district priorities.
- Understand and be able to communicate with all cultural groups in the community.
- Demonstrate that good judgment and actions communicate as well as words.
- Develop formal and informal techniques to gain external perception of a district by means of surveys, advisory groups, and personal contact.
- Communicate and project an articulate position for education.
- Write and speak clearly and forcefully.
- Demonstrate formal and informal listening skills.
- Demonstrate group membership and leadership skills.
- Identify the political forces in a community.
- Identify the political context of the community environment.
- Formulate strategies for passing referenda.
- Persuade the community to adopt an initiative for the welfare of students.
- Demonstrate conflict mediation.
- Demonstrate consensus building.
- Demonstrate school/community relations, school business partnerships, and related public service activities.
- Identify, track, and deal with issues.
- Develop and carry out internal and external communication plans.

Standard 4: Organizational Management - exhibit an understanding of the school district as a system by defining processes for gathering, analyzing, and using data for decision making; manage the data flow; frame and solve problems; frame and develop priorities and formulate solutions; assist others to form reasoned opinions; reach logical conclusions and make quality decisions to meet internal and external customer expectations; plan and schedule personal and organization work; establish procedures to regulate activities and projects; delegate and empower at appropriate organizational levels; secure and allocate human and material resources; develop and manage the district budget; maintain accurate fiscal records.

Indicators - a superintendent should know and be able to:

- Define processes for gathering, analyzing, and using data for informed decision making.
- Demonstrate a problem framing process.
- Define the major components of quality management.
- Develop, implement, and monitor change processes to build capacities and to serve clients.
- Discuss legal concepts, regulations, and codes for school operations.
- Describe the process of delegating responsibility for decision making.
- Develop a process for maintaining accurate fiscal reporting.
- Acquire, allocate, and manage human, material, and financial resources to effectively and accountably ensure successful student learning.
- Use technological applications to enhance administration of business and support systems.
- Demonstrate financial forecasting, planning, and cash flow management.
- Perform budget planning, management, account auditing, and monitoring.
- Demonstrate a grasp of practices in administering auxiliary programs, such as maintenance, facilities, food services, etc.
- Demonstrate planning and scheduling of personal time and organization work.

Standard 5: Curriculum Planning and Development - design curriculum and a strategic plan that enhance teaching and learning in multiple contexts; provide planning and future methods to anticipate occupational trends and their educational implications; identify taxonomies of instructional objectives and validation procedures for curricular units, using theories of cognitive development; align and sequence curriculum; use valid and reliable performance indicators and testing procedures to measure performance outcomes; and describe the proper use of computers and other learning and information technologies.

Indicators - a superintendent should know and be able to:

- Develop core curriculum design and delivery systems for diverse school communities.
- Describe curriculum planning/futures methods to anticipate occupational trends and their educational implication for lifelong learners.
- Demonstrate an understanding of instructional taxonomies, goals, objectives, and processes.
- Describe cognitive development and learning theories and their importance to the sequencing of instruction.
- Demonstrate an understanding of child and adolescent growth and development.

- Describe a process to create developmentally appropriate curriculum and instructional practices for all children and adolescents.
- Demonstrate the use of computers and other technologies in educational programming.
- Conduct assessments of present and future student learning needs.
- Develop a process for faculty input in continued and systematic renewal of the curriculum to ensure appropriate scope, sequence, and content.
- Demonstrate an understanding of curricular alignment to ensure improved student performance and higher order thinking.

Standard 6: Instructional Management - exhibit knowledge of instructional management by implementing a system that includes research findings on learning and instructional strategies, instructional time, advanced electronic technologies, and resources to maximize student outcomes; describe and apply research and best practice on integrating curriculum and resources for multicultural sensitivity and assessment strategies to help students achieve at high levels.

Indicators - a superintendent should know and be able to:

- Develop, implement, and monitor change processes to improve student learning, adult development, and climates for learning.
- Demonstrate an understanding of motivation in the instructional process.
- Describe classroom management theories and techniques.
- Demonstrate an understanding of the development of the total student, including the physical, social, emotional, cognitive, and linguistic needs.
- Formulate a plan to assess appropriate teaching methods and strategies for all learners.
- Analyze available instructional resources and assign them in the most cost-effective and equitable manner to enhance student outcomes.
- Describe instructional strategies that include the role of multicultural sensitivity and learning styles.
- Exhibit applications of computer technology connected to instructional programs.
- Describe alternative methods of monitoring and evaluating student achievement based on objectives and learning outcomes.
- Describe how to interpret and use testing/assessment results to improve education.
- Demonstrate knowledge of research findings on the use of a variety of instructional strategies.
- Describe a student achievement monitoring and reporting system.

Standard 7: Human Resources Management - develop a staff evaluation and development system to improve the performance of all staff members; select appropriate models for supervision based on adult motivation research; identify alternative employee benefits packages; and describe and apply the legal requirements for personnel selection, development, retention, and dismissal.

Indicators - a superintendent should know and be able to:

- Develop a plan to assess system and staff needs to identify areas for concentrated staff development.
- Demonstrate knowledge of adult learning theory and motivation.
- Evaluate the effectiveness of comprehensive staff development programming to determine its effect on professional performance.
- Demonstrate use of system and staff evaluation data for personnel policy and decision making.
- Diagnose and improve organizational health/morale.
- Demonstrate personnel management strategies.
- Understand alternative benefit packages.
- Assess individual and institutional sources of stress and develop methods for reducing stress (e.g., counseling, exercise programs, and diet).
- Demonstrate knowledge of pupil personnel services and categorical programs.

Standard 8: Values and Ethics of Leadership - understand and model appropriate value systems, ethics, and moral leadership; know the role of education in a democratic society; exhibit multicultural and ethnic understanding and related behavior; adapt educational programming to the needs of diverse constituencies; balance complex community demands in the best interest of the student; scan and monitor the environment for opportunities for staff and students; respond in an ethical and skillful way to the electronic and printed news media; and coordinate social agencies and human services to help each student grow and develop as a caring, informed citizen.

Indicators - a superintendent should know and be able to:

- Exhibit multicultural and ethnic understanding and sensitivity.
- Describe the role of schooling in a democratic society.
- Demonstrate ethical and personal integrity.
- Model accepted moral and ethical standards in all interactions.
- Describe a strategy to promote the value that moral and ethical practices are established and practiced in each classroom and school.
- Describe how education undergirds a free and democratic society.
- Describe a strategy to ensure that diversity of religion, ethnicity, and way of life in the district are not violated.
- Formulate a plan to coordinate social, health, and other community agencies to support each child in the district.

Generic Administrator Duties

The administrator duties referred to in point 6 above are illustrated by the administrator duties listed below. These duties are not proposed as a consensus response to the need for widespread agreement on generic duties against which administrator performance can be evaluated. Instead, they are offered as a working draft of the needed duties list. The duties are derived from the work that Stufflebeam conducted in the 1990s with the Texas Education Agency to develop a list of generic duties for school administrators. We invite readers of this book to critique and improve our duties list and to send us their criticisms, adaptations, and suggestions. We plan to use such input to improve the validity and usability of the generic duties list.

1. **Promote and support student growth and development** - activities include:

   - Diagnose student needs.
   - Examine and improve school/district offerings.
   - Monitor student achievement and attendance.
   - Help students develop a sense of self-worth.
   - Foster educational efforts among parents and teachers.

2. **Honor diversity and promote equality of opportunity** - activities include:

   - Recruit qualified minority and majority staff.
   - Examine and address gaps in achievement for different groups of students.
   - Work toward integrating schools and programs.

3. **Foster a positive school climate** - activities include:

   - Assess and plan improvement of the school/district/community environment.
   - Reinforce excellence.
   - Promote a positive, caring climate for learning.
   - Employ effective communication skills.

4. **Provide leadership in school improvement efforts** - activities include:

   - Collaborate in the development and articulate a common vision of improvement.
   - Encourage appropriate risk taking.
   - Ensure continuous renewal of curriculum, policies, and methods.

5. **Stimulate, focus, and support improvement of instruction** - activities include:

   - Assist teachers in designing learning experiences for students.

- Use evidence to evaluate and suggest areas for improvement in the design, materials, and implementation of educational programs.
- Encourage the development and piloting of innovative instructional programs.
- Facilitate the planning and application of emerging technologies in the classroom.

6. **Lead and manage personnel effectively** - activities include:

- Delegate appropriately.
- Recognize exemplary performance of subordinates.
- Encourage personal and professional growth and leadership among staff.
- Comply with applicable personnel policies and rules.
- Secure the necessary personnel resources to meet objectives.
- Evaluate the job performance of subordinates.

7. **Manage administrative, fiscal, and facilities functions effectively** - activities include:

- Obtain broad-based input for fiscal/financial analysis.
- Compile reasonable budgets and cost estimates.
- Ensure that facilities are maintained and upgraded as necessary.
- Manage a broad range of operations (e.g., attendance, accounting, payroll, transportation, etc.).

8. **Assure a safe, orderly environment** - activities include:

- Develop and communicate guidelines for student conduct.
- Ensure that rules are uniformly observed.
- Discipline students for misconduct in an effective and fair manner.
- Promote collaboration by working with faculty.
- Encourage student/parent participation.

9. **Foster effective school-community relations** - activities include:

- Articulate the school/district mission and student needs to the community.
- Seek support for school and district programs.
- Involve students, parents, and others from the community in serving school programs.
- Involve oneself in community activities that foster rapport between the school/district and the larger community.

10. **Embody and promote professionalism** - activities include:

- Participate actively in professional organizations.

- Conduct oneself in an ethical and professional manner.
- Stay abreast of professional issues and developments in education.
- Disseminate ideas and information to other professionals.
- Seek and use evaluative information for improvement of performance.

11. **Relate effectively to the school board/council** - activities include:

- Meet the board's information needs.
- Interact with board members in an ethical, sensitive, and professional manner.
- Demonstrate competence in written and verbal communications to the board.
- Educate the board about education.
- Recommend policies to enhance teaching and learning.

The above list will help school boards and superintendents to ensure that the criteria used to evaluate superintendent performance are sufficiently broad and cover all the important areas of the superintendent's work. Of course, the specific criteria, weights, and performance standards will vary across superintendents as a function of local issues and priorities and will need to be tailored accordingly (sample superintendent job descriptions currently in use are provided in Appendix B).

The Personnel Evaluation Standards

The Personnel Evaluation Standards were developed by the Joint Committee on Standards for Educational Evaluation, which included representatives from 14 major professional associations concerned with education. The Joint Committee studied personnel evaluation practices and obtained input from hundreds of teachers, administrators, board members, and other interested groups to develop a set of draft standards. This and subsequent drafts were reviewed by knowledgeable professionals and field tested in various institutional settings throughout the U.S. to produce *The Personnel Evaluation Standards*, published in 1988. Through a standing Joint Committee, the standards are subject to an ongoing process of review by users, who are invited to submit their comments and recommendations for developing and refining *The Personnel Evaluation Standards*.

The Standards are intended primarily to assist professional educators in developing, assessing, adapting, and improving systems for evaluating educational personnel. Essentially, they provide criteria for judging evaluation systems, procedures, and reports in the U.S. context. The assessment of the alternative evaluation models presented in Section 6 of this book is based on an extensive analysis of each model according to the full range of the 21 personnel evaluation standards summarized below in the 4 categories to which they relate.

Propriety Standards require that evaluations be conducted legally, ethically, and with due consideration for the welfare of evaluatees and of the clients of the evaluation. The 5 Propriety standards are listed below:

P1 Service Orientation. Evaluations of educators should promote sound education principles, fulfillment of institutional missions, and effective performance of job responsibilities, so that the educational needs of students, community, and society are met.

P2 Formal Evaluation Guidelines. Guidelines for personnel evaluations should be recorded in statements of policy, negotiated agreements, and/or personnel evaluation manuals, so that evaluations are consistent, equitable, and in accordance with pertinent laws and ethical codes.

P3 Conflict of Interest. Conflicts of interest should be identified and dealt with openly and honestly, so that they do not compromise the evaluation process and results.

P4 Access to Personnel Evaluation Reports. Access to reports of personnel evaluations should be limited to those individuals with a legitimate need to review and use the reports, so that appropriate use of the information is assured.

P5 Interactions with Evaluatees. The evaluation should address evaluatees in a professional, considerate and courteous manner, so that their self-esteem, motivation, professional reputations, performance, and attitude toward personnel evaluation are enhanced, or at least, not needlessly damaged.

Utility standards are intended to guide evaluations so that they will be informative, timely, and influential. There are 5 Utility standards, as follows:

U1 Constructive Orientation. Evaluations should be constructive, so that they help institutions to develop human resources and encourage and assist those evaluated to provide excellent service.

U2 Defined Uses. The users and the intended uses of personnel evaluation should be identified so that the evaluation can address appropriate questions.

U3 Evaluator Credibility. The evaluation system should be managed and executed by persons with the necessary qualifications, skills, and authority, and the evaluators should conduct themselves professionally, so that evaluation reports are respected and used.

U4 Functional Reporting. Reports should be clear, timely, accurate, and germane, so that they are of practical value to the evaluatee and other appropriate audiences.

U5 Follow up and Impact. Evaluations should be followed up, so that users and evaluatees are aided to understand the results and take appropriate actions.

Feasibility standards call for evaluation systems that are as easy to implement as possible, efficient in their use of time and resources, adequately funded, and viable from a number of other standpoints. There are 3 Feasibility standards:

F1 Practical Procedures. Personnel evaluation procedures should be planned and conducted so that they produce needed information while minimizing disruption and cost.

F2 Political Viability. The personnel evaluation system should be developed and monitored collaboratively, so that all concerned parties are constructively involved in making the system work.

F3 Fiscal Viability. Adequate time and resources should be provided for personnel evaluation activities, so that evaluation plans can be effectively and efficiently implemented.

Accuracy standards require that the obtained information be technically accurate and that conclusions be linked logically to the data. The 8 Accuracy standards are as follows:

A1 Defined Role. The role, responsibilities, performance objectives, and needed qualifications of the evaluatee should be clearly defined, so that the evaluator can determine valid assessment data.

A2 Work Environment. The context in which the evaluatee works should be identified, described, and recorded, so that environmental influences and constraints on performance can be considered in the evaluation.

A3 Documentation of Procedures. The evaluation procedures actually followed should be documented, so that the evaluatees and other users can assess the actual, in relation to intended, procedures.

A4 Valid Measurement. The measurement procedures should be chosen or developed and implemented on the basis of the described role and the intended use, so that the inferences concerning the evaluatee are valid and accurate.

A5 Reliable Measurement.   Measurement procedures should be chosen or developed to assure reliability, so that the information obtained will provide consistent indications of the performance of the evaluatee.

A6 Systematic Data Control. The information used in the evaluation should be kept secure and should be carefully processed and maintained, so as to ensure that the data maintained and analyzed are the same as the data collected.

A7 Bias Control. The evaluation process should provide safeguards against bias, so that the evaluatee's qualifications or performance are assessed fairly.

A8 Monitoring Evaluation Systems. The personnel evaluation system should be reviewed periodically and systematically, so that appropriate revisions can be made.

Generally, although all of the standards will be relevant to all personnel evaluation systems, some standards may warrant more or less emphasis for certain evaluation purposes. *The Personnel Evaluation Standards* stress that the relative importance of the 21 standards will vary according to the intended use of the evaluation. Thus, in many situations it is unlikely to be possible to give full weight to all 21 standards, so there is likely to be a trade-off between them; users must exercise judgment in deciding on the relative emphasis to give each one.

However, crucial to the fairness of all personnel evaluation is the recognition and systematic consideration of those standards relating to formal guidelines (P2), access to reports (P4), defined uses (U2), and bias control (A7).   Adherence to these standards will assure the protection of employee rights as well as mitigate potentially adverse legal actions.

The Evaluation Process

The evaluation process involves 4 main task areas: **delineating** the information to be obtained and processed; **obtaining** the information; **providing** the information to the appropriate audiences; and **applying** the information to personnel decisions and improvement efforts. The broad task areas, in turn, can be operationalized in terms of specific tasks, which provide the basic procedures for conducting the evaluation. These tasks are explicated in relation to a proposed new model for superintendent evaluation, presented in Section 7 of this book.

Categories of Evaluation Information

The information required in the evaluation process may be categorized as context, input, process, and product information. These are the categories of the CIPP Model introduced by Stufflebeam in 1966 (Stufflebeam, 1966; 1983; Stufflebeam et al., 1971). Evaluations of district contexts, inputs, processes, and products should be an essential part of and feed into the evaluation of educational personnel. How this information can be used in the evaluation of the superintendent is discussed in Section 7.

Context evaluation concerns the context or setting within which the evaluatee works. It assesses needs, opportunities, problems, and goals. Needs are the elements necessary or useful for fulfilling some defensible purpose, such as the education of students. There are two kinds of needs: consequential needs concern the levels of attainment on indicators related to the purpose of the organization, such as student achievement scores; and instrumental needs relate to the elements of the delivery system required to fulfill the consequential needs, such as a sound curriculum and competent superintendents. Opportunities are unused ideas and resources that are potentially available to the organization. Problems are the barriers to meeting student or system needs or to using potentially available ideas and untapped resources, such as inadequate funds to hire well-qualified teachers. Goals are the intended outcomes that the organization works to achieve, such as an increase in student graduation rates or a broadening of curriculum offerings.

The key point is that educational organizations and roles exist to serve the educational needs of society and young people. An evaluation would therefore be faulty if it determined that a school or superintendent had achieved stated goals, but didn't also confirm that these goals adequately addressed identified student and system needs. Context evaluations of needs, opportunities, problems, and goals help the board and superintendent to set targets and priorities for the superintendent's leadership during a given time period.

Input evaluation assesses the relative strengths, weaknesses, and costs of alternative courses of action for meeting identified needs and fulfilling professional duties. The aim of input evaluation is to find more effective strategies for carrying out district functions and to ensure that the district's resources are being used to best advantage. Input evaluations assess district strategic plans as well as the work plans of individual professionals. They assess both written plans and the planning process. Examples of key criteria employed in input evaluation include involvement of an appropriate scope of stakeholders in the planning process; extent to which each alternative intervention is keyed to meeting identified student and district needs; clarity and appropriateness of procedures; sufficient staff to carry out work; and cost-efficiency of the work plan.

Process evaluation documents and assesses the implementation of district plans and operations. Process evaluation is conducted both to help guide an effort (formative evaluation) and to document and assess the quality of implementation (summative evaluation). Formative process evaluation is intended to check on the implementation of plans and to influence needed corrections either in the plans or in their execution. Summative process evaluation sums up and assesses the appropriateness and quality of activities carried out in the attempt to implement plans and to fulfill assigned duties.

Product evaluation focuses on accomplishments, in particular the fulfillment of student needs in such areas as academic achievement, health, racial integration, and graduation. In addition, product evaluation looks for improvements in the delivery system; for example, in teaching, curriculum, facilities, and district policy. Product evaluation is broad in scope and seeks both unanticipated and anticipated and negative as well as positive effects. Essentially, it aims to assess the effectiveness of the school system in meeting identified needs.

Evaluation of superintendent performance is complex. This section has presented the essential elements of a sound evaluation system. These elements include the rationale for a consensus approach, administrator competencies and duties, standards of sound evaluation, the tasks in the evaluation process, and the generic categories of information involved in evaluations.

References

American Association of School Administrators. (1982). *Guidelines for the preparation of school administrators.* Arlington, VA: Author.

American Association of School Administrators. (1993). *Professional standards for the superintendency.* Arlington, VA: Author.

Carter, D. S. G., Estes, N., Loredo, J., & Harris, B. (1991). Evolving a diagnostic system for formative use by senior school system executives in the USA. *School Organization, 11*(1), pp. 53-63.

Carter, D. S. G., Glass, T. E., & Hord, S. M. (1993). *Selecting, preparing and developing the school district superintendent.* Washington, DC: Falmer Press.

Carter, D. S. G., & Harris, B. M. (1991). Assessing executive performance for continuing professional growth. *Journal of Personnel Evaluation in Education, 4*(1), pp 7-19.

Glass, G. V., & Martinez, B. A. (1993, June). Politics of teacher evaluation. *Proceedings of the CREATE Cross-Cutting Evaluation Theory Planning Seminar.* Kalamazoo, MI: Center for Research on Educational Accountability and Teacher Evaluation.

Hoyle, J. R., English, F. W., & Steffy, B. (1985). *Skills for successful school leaders.* Arlington, VA: American Association of School Administrators.

Hoyle, J. R., English, F. W., & Steffy, B. (1990). *Skills for successful school leaders* (2nd ed.). Arlington, VA: American Association of School Administrators.

Joint Committee on Standards for Educational Evaluation. (1981). *Standards for evaluations of educational programs, projects, and materials.* New York: McGraw-Hill.

Joint Committee on Standards for Educational Evaluation. (1988). *The personnel evaluation standards.* Newbury Park, CA: Sage.

Joint Committee on Standards for Educational Evaluation. (1994). *The program evaluation standards, second edition.* Thousand Oaks, CA: Sage.

Millman, J., & Sykes, G. (1992). *The assessment of teaching based on evidence of student learning.* (Research Monograph No. 2). National Board for Professional Teaching Standards.

Sanders, W. L., & Horn, S.P. (1994, October). The Tennessee value-added assessment system: Mixed methodology in educational assessment. *Journal of Personnel Evaluation in Education, 8*(3), 299-312.

Scriven, M. (1993, June). *Using the duties-based approach to teacher evaluation.* Paper presented at the annual meeting of the Center for Research on Educational Accountability and Teacher Evaluation/Phi Delta Kappa National Evaluation Institute, Kalamazoo, MI.

Scriven, M. (1994, July). Duties of the teacher. *Journal of Personnel Evaluation in Education, 8*(2), pp. 151-184.

Stronge, J. H., & Helm, V. M. (1991). *Evaluating professional support personnel in education.* Newbury Park, CA: Sage.

Stufflebeam, D. L. (1966). A depth study of the evaluation requirement. *Theory Into Practice, 5*(3), pp. 121-133.

Stufflebeam, D. L., Foley, W. J., Gephart, W. J., Guba, E. G., Hammond, R. L., Merriman, H.O., & Provus, M. (1971). *Educational evaluation and decision making.* Itasca, IL: Peacock.

Stufflebeam, D. L. (1983). The CIPP Model for program evaluation. Chapter 7 in G. F. Madaus, M. Scriven, & D. L. Stufflebeam, *Evaluation models.* Boston: Kluwer-Nijhoff Publishing.

Texas Education Agency, Division of Management Assistance and Personnel Development. (1990). *Superintendent appraisal: System development - A training module.* Austin, TX: Author.

Webster, W. J. (1993, June). Summary of seminar. *Proceedings,* CREATE Cross-Cutting Theory Planning Seminar. Kalamazoo, MI: Radisson Hotel.

Webster, W. J., & Edwards, M. E. (1993, April). *An accountability system for school improvement.* Paper presented at the annual meeting of the American Educational Research Association, Atlanta, GA.

Webster, W. J., Mendro, R. L., & Almaguer, T. O. (1993, April). *Effectiveness indices: The major components of an equitable accountability system.* Paper presented at the American Educational Research Association, Atlanta, GA.

4   THE SUPERINTENDENCY

This section discusses the nature of the superintendency as it has evolved and as it currently exists in the American public school system. The section begins with an overview of the history of the school district superintendency in the U.S. and presents an analysis of the duties and skills required of the superintendent. This section is intended to provide a useful framework for superintendents and members of the board to develop and articulate a common view of the superintendency within the contemporary American school system.

It is important to note that, of the 15,500 or so school districts in the country, many are small, inefficient units where the office of superintendent is not cost-effective and is of questionable value. Also, with recent organizational changes, such as site-based management, site councils, educational vouchers, decentralization, charter schools, privatization, etc., a redefinition of the role of the superintendent may be in order. Such redefinition could dramatically alter the duties on which superintendent evaluations are based. Thus, systems for evaluating the district's chief executive officer should consider the important issue of the need for the role in the first place and its distinctive requirements in different settings.

History

As the various states began to develop a commercial and industrial base, the cities of the country started to grow and the school systems serving those cities also grew. With growth, they recognized the need for more direction and supervision than the lay board of education could provide. By the early 1800s, several of the major cities had explored the addition of an educator as the head of the entire school system of the particular city. Finally, the Buffalo, New York, common council appointed a superintendent of common schools on June 9, 1837, while on July 31, 1837, the first superintendent of public schools was chosen in Louisville, Kentucky (Reller, 1935). As time went on, boards of education in some states were given statutory authority to appoint superintendents; in other states, the boards proceeded to make such appointments without specific legislative authorization. By 1860, 27 city school districts had established the office of superintendent (Reller, 1935).

Establishment of the superintendency in noncity areas did not occur until the 20th century. For years, noncity schools were rural schools and, as had been the case in the cities earlier, each school district had tended to have a 1-room, 8-grade school. Moreover, a structural plan for giving minimum supervision to those schools had been resolved with the creation of the county superintendency (Reller, 1935).

In time, however, the movement to combine rural districts into larger administrative units took hold. Utah was one of the early states to move toward large consolidated school systems. In 1915, the Utah legislature mandated the so-called county unit plan of school district organization (Reller, 1935).

Two major events were instrumental in the development of the superintendency in the United States. The first was the famous Michigan Supreme Court decision in 1874 on the Kalamazoo case, which established the right of local school boards to tax property owners for support of secondary education (high schools) as well as for elementary education. This decision gave a tremendous boost to the establishment of public high schools across the country and assisted in creating a need for a single head of the consolidated school system.

The Kalamazoo decision also led to the consolidation of many of the rural elementary school districts into comprehensive 1-12 districts that provided for the total educational needs of the students living in the district. As the number of high school districts grew, the need for systemic leadership grew and the position of superintendent expanded. This was not a quick change but a long, sometimes painful, transition from 1-room schools to multicampus districts serving the total educational needs of an area.

The other major event that led to the expansion of multicampus school systems and, ultimately, to the need for a superintendent was the invention and development of the motor vehicle as a means for moving people from one place to another. This permitted the massing of students into student bodies of sufficient size to make it effective and efficient to offer programs to serve diverse needs. This also gave rise to various vocational programs to train workers needed in an industrial society. The evolution of the school bus fleet was an important element in the creation of the massive consolidated school systems seen today. The growth in the position of superintendent paralleled the growth of the public schools in the United States. The position is also inextricably linked to the evolution of school boards.

Many early superintendents faced serious challenges, including the survival of the common school movement itself. Those men (mostly men--then and now) taking up the call of the superintendency and the common school were true school reformers. They traveled from large cities to villages preaching the gospel of a free public education. In some respects, many early superintendents were like secular clergy. They served as moral role models and spreaders of the democratic ethic.

The American public school superintendency has changed a great deal since its inception in the first half of the 19th century. The original role was that of schoolmaster, with the board of education making almost all decisions of any importance. By the end of the 19th century, most superintendents in cities had shed this role of supervisor of students and teachers to become managing administrators.

Superintendents became responsible for operations in the district, and these day-to-day decisions were usually not subject to examination by the board of education (Callahan, 1966). Schools reflected the transition in the late 19th and early 20th centuries from an economy and culture dominated by rural farm concerns to one in which heavy industry would play an increasingly large role.

Transition to an Industrial Society

Gaining operational authority separate from the board did not occur overnight. Ellwood Cubberley, a former superintendent who conducted most of the early research on the superintendency and wrote many books and articles on school administration in the early 1900s, called this transition the struggle to become "true professionals" (Cubberley, 1920).

The position of superintendent as we know it today evolved from the struggle of superintendents to become professionals during the first part of the 20th century. The "grand old men" of the superintendency--Cubberley, George Strayer, and Frank Spaulding--championed the cause of the common school and advocated an executive type of leadership. They wrestled with boards of education in large cities such as Chicago, where political spoils systems determined which teachers would be hired, what textbooks would be purchased, and which vendors would be patronized (Callahan, 1966).

In addition to their efforts to reform schools and school boards, the early educational leaders also worked to prepare future school executives who would be able to provide civic leadership, scientific management, and established business values in the schools.

Early superintendents were also aware of the need for those in their field to be up-to-date in their knowledge of curriculum and instruction, teacher preparation, and staff training.

The Era of Scientific Management

There have been 3 major trends in the study of organizational and management theory. The first of these began with the industrial revolution and is referred to as the scientific or classical theory of management. Frederick Taylor, the father of scientific management, wrote the book *Principles of Scientific Management* in 1911 and identified the following 5 principles of scientific management: (1) large daily task, (2) standard conditions, (3) high pay for success, (4) loss in case of failure, and (5) expertise in large organizations.

Other theorists followed Taylor with corollaries to and explications of the notion of scientific management.

Commenting on the era of scientific management in his 1966 book, *The School Superintendent*, Daniel Griffiths discusses the first phase in the development of the role of the superintendency. He describes the "quasi-businessman" attempting to form school districts into industrial models through principles of scientific management. During this period, a significant degree of control over decision making was moved from boards of education into the hands of the superintendent. The tenets of scientific management, and the resulting bureaucracy, still guide the practices of some local school boards today, despite the fact that many researchers and reformers believe that highly centralized, hierarchical structures are a chief obstacle to school reform.

The Human Relations Approach

In the late 1920s and early 1930s, the human relations theory of management was developed through the writings and research of people like Mary Parker Follett, Elton Mayo, and Fritz Roethlisberger. Mayo and Roethlisberger conducted the famous Hawthorne studies at the Western Electric Company's Hawthorne plant near Chicago, which resulted in the following conclusions, typical of the tenets of the human relations theorists:

1. The economic factor is not the only significant motivator. In fact, noneconomic social sanctions limit the effectiveness of economic incentives.
2. Workers respond to management as members of an informal group, not as individuals.
3. Production levels are limited more by the social norms of the informal organization than by physiological capacities.
4. Specialization does not necessarily create the most efficient organization of the work group.
5. Workers use informal organization to protect themselves against arbitrary decisions of management.
6. Informal social organizations will interact with management.
7. A narrow span of control is not a prerequisite to effective supervision.
8. Informal leaders are often as important as formal leaders.
9. Individuals are active human beings, not passive cogs in a machine.

The human relations or social systems theory provided a balance for the scientific or classical theory of administration during the first half of the 20th century. The effect of this school of thought upon the superintendency was to establish a defensible base for valuing the human relations skills of the superintendent. The human relations approach was dominant in organizational theory in the late 1940s and early 1950s.

The Behavioral School of Management

During the 1950s, the behavioral approach began making inroads on thinking about administration and by the 1960s the behavioral theory of management was in the forefront of contemporary thought. Among the leading theorists and model builders of the behavioral school of management are Egon Guba, Jacob Getzels, Charles Bidwell, and Joseph Letterer. The behavioral school itself was developed by such organizational theorists as Chester Barnard, Herbert Simon, Douglas McGregor, James March, and others. This approach led to a shift from democratic prescription to analytic formulation, from a field orientation to a discipline orientation, and from a narrow conception to one encompassing multidisciplinary research and theory in the field of administration.

With the realization that the classical (scientific) theory and the social system (human relations) theory were not appropriate and did not accommodate the real world, model building became an increasingly productive activity by management theorists. Model building is integral to the scientific study of a phenomenon and is useful for increasing the knowledge of the phenomenon. Examples of model building abound; the concept of the school as a social system is prevalent among models in the field of education. By studying the models created, for example through the analysis of established facts and the projection of possible actions to be taken, the theorist can resolve issues that might otherwise cripple the organization.

Evolution of the Position

Because the American superintendency has experienced much turmoil and has undergone many dramatic changes over the years of its existence, it is appropriate to review the various phases of the position to see if there is any unifying thread from which a model for the evaluation of the position can be constructed.

It is possible to trace the evolution of the position, starting with the notion of the superintendent as the master teacher and the leader of the students and teachers of a school system. In the next phase, the superintendent acts as the manager of the school system, held accountable by the board for all of the activities of the system. The progression then moves further toward the concept of the superintendent as the chief executive officer of the school organization and as the expert manager of the organization. Finally, we arrive at the current notion of the superintendent as responsible for developing and implementing a variety of different models to respond to the many publics that make up the modern school system.

An examination of the social changes since the 1950s reveals that today's superintendent must perform vastly different tasks than did the position incumbent before that time. Beginning in the 1960s and 1970s when dramatic civil upheaval and immense social tension brought tremendous and significant changes to the American public school systems that has continued through to today, the position of superintendent of schools has become a vastly different kind of leadership post.

Issues such as equal educational opportunity for minority students, community control of schools, intergovernmental and interagency cooperation, compensatory programs, and desegregation resulted in a greater focus on performance by the makers of policy on the training and selection of superintendents.

In the latest study of the superintendency entitled *The Study of the School Superintendency*, published in 1992, Thomas E. Glass writes, "Perhaps the greatest challenge to the superintendency during the civil rights era was the encroachment into the authority of the superintendency by a more involved citizenry and school board. At the same time, a wide array of legislative mandates also were lessening school system autonomy. The superintendent's traditional role of "expert" was challenged by many parents and board members because the schools were not meeting community expectations . . . . The disenchantment with American schools was especially pronounced in large urban centers, where increasing numbers of disadvantaged students dropped out or were chronic underachievers. In such school systems, superintendent firings often were front page news."

Glass implies in his document that during the 1980s and 1990s the policy-making pendulum has been swinging between the superintendent and the board, reflecting the fact that education leaders and theoreticians disagree about what constitutes policy-making and what constitutes management. Most researchers on the superintendency favor a model of the superintendent as chief executive officer, a concept partially borrowed from corporate America. In many cases, what has been viewed as policy development in the world of public education is seen as management prerogative in the private sector. At this point in time, the argument continues with strong feelings on both sides of the debate.

Entry Requirements: Evaluation by Credential

Because progress in evaluation efforts and the development of evaluation instruments has been slow, the main mechanism for evaluating superintendents has been through the credentialing process. What this means, then, is that the certification requirements of the state have become the method by which the superintendent is evaluated. This permits the board of education to note that the superintendent was legally certified by the state because he or she fulfilled the minimum requirements for state certification.

Typically, certification for the superintendency requires at least a masters degree in educational administration. However, states are increasingly requiring candidates for the superintendent's certificate to meet additional requirements. Texas, for example, requires candidates to take and pass an examination before being admitted to full certification as a superintendent. Other states are increasing admission requirements as well. For example, some states require the masters degree as a prerequisite for taking the course work required for certification as a superintendent. This mandated course work usually requires at least 30 hours beyond the M.A., and often includes specified courses to be taken by candidates. In addition, several states are moving toward the requirement of an internship with a practicing superintendent before certification is awarded. In a few cases, typical certification requirements have been waived so that noneducators, such as attorneys, could be appointed to the superintendency.

These expanding requirements are in addition to the customary experience required in the certification codes of most states. These requirements range from a certain number of years of teaching experience (3 is most common) to experience in other administrative positions in the system.

California, for example, requires every potential educator to have completed the B.A. degree before starting any certification program for entry into the field of education. The sequence of course work to be completed virtually guarantees that every teacher and educator has, as a minimum, a masters degree before entering the education profession. Administrative certification requirements add to the number of hours of graduate course work taken so that an individual who opts to enter administration in California will have at least 45 hours beyond the M.A. before being granted certification.

While the standards for certification vary from state to state, and sometimes within states and districts, the various states seem to be approaching a consensus that the persons being certified as superintendents must be well qualified in terms of preparation and education.

Reflecting this growing consensus on the requirements of the superintendency, the AASA recently published *Professional Standards for the Superintendency* (AASA, 1993). The AASA professional standards specify the skills and knowledge that those consulted agree should form the basis of superintendent **preparation, certification**, and **professional development**. These competencies were developed from earlier AASA publications, namely, *Guidelines for the Preparation of School Administrators* (AASA, 1982) and the first and second editions of *Skills for Successful School Leaders* (Hoyle, English, & Steffy, 1985; 1990). They were subject to an extensive consultation process involving a national "Jury of 100" and members of the National Council of Professors of Educational Administration, the University Council for Educational Administration, and the AASA Executive Committee. However, a major group not included in the consultation process was the National School Boards Association, which represents the employing body for superintendents and whose members conduct superintendent selection and evaluation procedures. Nevertheless, it is likely that an increasing number of organizations involved in the preparation and certification of superintendents will adopt these AASA *Professional Standards for the Superintendency*.

The general performance areas of the AASA professional standards, as presented in Section 3 of this book, are consistent with the broad areas of the generic duties also listed in Section 3, as well as the sample job description presented later in this section. By presenting these lists in this book, we hope to stimulate discussion among practitioners and researchers with the ultimate hope of reaching consensus on the broad areas of performance that pertain to the office of the superintendency.

Other work aimed at delineating the requirements of the superintendency is reported by Carter, Glass, and Hord (1993) in their book *Selecting, Preparing, and Developing the School District Superintendent*. These researchers reviewed all the available literature on the superintendency, including unpublished doctoral dissertations concerned with the domains, tasks, concepts, and skills involved in the work of the superintendent. In particular, the book refers to research under way at the University of Texas, funded by a grant from the Meadows Foundation, that seeks to identify 6 performance domains of the superintendency. These domains are divided into task areas, which are themselves subdivided into behaviorally specified tasks. Finally, the tasks are analyzed into the underlying competencies, or skills and knowledge, required for their execution. This is a difficult and work-intensive project, and limited progress has been realized to date.

Carter, Glass, and Hord are to be commended for their exhaustive work and commitment in researching the available literature on the superintendency. They focus primarily on the preparation and selection of the superintendent, but also suggest some interesting alternatives for the evaluation of practicing superintendents. The book gives support to the superintendent in conducting formative evaluations, particularly formative self-evaluation. However, in our view there is an overemphasis on this kind of evaluation. Effective evaluation should include summative evaluation of superintendent leadership and service on behalf of students and the school system.

An important finding discussed in the book is that the performance of the superintendent is judged mainly by the personality of the incumbent and the state of board/superintendent relations. This finding is echoed by the comments of Dr. Joyce Annunziata, Director of Evaluation for the Dade County (Florida) Public Schools. As part of her critique of this manuscript, Dr. Annunziata stated, "During the first year, the honeymoon period, the Board and the Superintendent perform a ritual dance where give and take and conciliatory politeness reign. By year two, the Superintendent has recognized problems and set programs in motion and put people in place to address these identified needs. Programs and/or personnel can be politically damaging to the Board. Hence, by year three (or earlier), the marriage between the Board and the Superintendent becomes shaky." Dr. Annunziata also made the point that careful selection criteria are essential during the recruitment process.

The apparent importance of personality and political factors in board decisions to hire, judge, and fire superintendents underscores the need for efforts to define the competencies and duties of the superintendency and to adopt these as evaluation criteria. A carefully crafted evaluation design could help deemphasize political factors and extend average superintendent tenure by assisting and encouraging the board and superintendent to focus strictly on performance. The provision of meaningful leadership to the organization, the improvement of student performance, the management of what is commonly the largest budget in the community, the development of educational programs to meet student needs, and the communication of the school message to the community are all important elements of what the superintendent does and should be included in superintendent evaluations.

In addition, the book is useful in showing that the competency needs of the superintendent will vary according to the size, locality, and type of school district. Typically, the local employing agency, namely the local board of education, has certain specific job expectations and requirements that are usually expressed through the job description and during the job interview. These vary from district to district but usually include some specific requirements related to the circumstances of the particular school system. It is not unusual for such local needs and expectations, which may be quite different from the state certification and legal requirements, to determine the success and/or failure of candidates for the superintendency.

It is crucial for the prospective superintendent to understand that the board of education will determine the extent to which the evaluation process shall be an open and objective process or a closed and subjective process. This important aspect of the superintendent's job should be discussed during the selection process; in particular, the potential evaluation design should be outlined in brief.

Duties of the Superintendent

A typical job description of the superintendent, taken from the Lansing, Michigan, and Fort Worth, Texas, board policy documents, is as follows. The superintendent of schools is the chief executive officer of the school system appointed by and directly responsible to the board of education for the discharge of his or her responsibilities. The superintendent acts in accordance with the policies, rules, and regulations established by the board and the laws and regulations of the state and the federal government. Lastly, the administration of the entire school system is delegated to the superintendent.

The superintendent has the following general duties:

1. To lead the public school system and the community and to develop the present and long-term plans for the program of public education in the school district.
2. To advise the board on the formulation of policies for the governance of the school system and to execute the policies subsequently adopted by the board.
3. To be responsible for the comprehensive planning effort for the school district. The superintendent shall prepare, not later than June of each year, a comprehensive report describing the status, plans, and predictions regarding the various operational components of the school system for periods of 1 year and 5 years.
4. To serve as "clerk" of the board of education and prepare complete and accurate records of board activities. To notify board members of all regular, adjourned and special meetings, and to attend all meetings of the board of education. Except at the request of the board, the superintendent is not generally present at any board meeting convened to discuss the superintendent's own salary or tenure. The chief school executive officer has the right to speak at board meetings on all matters.
5. To interpret board policy and develop administrative regulations for policy implementation.
6. To establish and maintain an organizational system with clearly defined lines of authority and responsibility for all school staff.
7. To recruit, select, and assign the employees of the school district.
8. To develop and implement regulations that will prohibit discriminatory actions by employees or other persons acting in the name of the school district. Such discriminatory actions may be defined as those that would cause any student or employee to be excluded from participation in, or denied the benefits of,

any educational program, activity, employment opportunity, or assignment on the basis of race, creed, sex, color, national origin, or because of a handicap that is unrelated to the individual's ability to perform.

9. To carry out the following specific, but not exhaustive duties:

   a. Supervise instruction, control and manage pupils, formulate the curricula and develop courses that shall be subject to the approval of the board.

   b. Prepare the annual budget and submit it to the board of education for approval.

   c. Supervise school buildings, grounds, and equipment.

   d. Recommend and execute plans for repairs and renovations of all school property and for new construction.

   e. Represent the board of education as principal negotiator in collective bargaining with any bargaining group that has been recognized or certified. The superintendent shall select the bargaining team and assign duties to the members of the team. The superintendent shall negotiate on behalf of the board of education. No agreement is valid or binding unless adopted by the board.

   f. Receive, hear, and adjudicate complaints against the schools in other matters of school controversy involving school employees and pupils, parents of students, or patrons.

   g. Receive reports from agencies like the auditor, the Fire Department, and the State Department of Education, and inform the board of the action taken pursuant to recommendations made in these reports.

   h. Enforce compulsory attendance laws.

   i. Assign and transfer employees of the district.

   j. Suspend school employees at any time, until the next meeting of the board.

   k. Recommend textbooks and other instructional materials, instructional supplies, and school equipment for adoption or approval by the board.

   l. Delegate to subordinates any of the powers and duties that the board has entrusted to the superintendent, but continue to be responsible and accountable to the board for the execution of the powers and duties thus delegated.

Comparison of these duties with the draft list of generic administrator duties presented in Section 3 reveals considerable overlap. However, 2 main duties referred to in the generic administrator duties list are absent from the above list, namely, promoting and supporting student growth and improvement and fostering professional development of school personnel. Any contemporary listing of duties should include these as vital components. Moreover, the duties list in Section 3 does not appear to include 9e, 9f, and 9g from the above list. We present these 2 lists without attempting to reconcile their differences in order to stimulate discussion about what duties should be included in any generic list of administrator duties and as a first step toward reaching consensus and triangulation on this important issue.

The accepted role of the superintendent is as the school district's leader and chief executive officer responsible for all that goes on in the school system and for ensuring that the system functions optimally. In performing the leadership function, the superintendent has the parallel responsibility of interpreting and implementing the policies of the board of education in such a way that these policies become the driving force behind the operation of the public school system. The board is recognized as the policy-developing body and the governance force for the school district. The board alone has the responsibility for setting policy; for interpreting the needs of the students, staff, and patrons of the district; and for establishing the governance mechanisms to be implemented within the school system. The superintendent must promote and support student achievement and the professional development of school personnel.

Considering the changes that have transpired during the past 3 or 4 decades in American society and in American schools, a modified role for the modern superintendent might be that of **consensus builder**, of **planner**, of **communicator**, and of **visionary** for the school system as well as that of **competent manager**. The chief executive officer must be aware of the societal changes that have taken place and those that are just emerging and must prepare the district to respond to these many changes with appropriate programs of education for its students.

The superintendent as leader is quite different from the superintendent as manager. Although all superintendents must be accomplished managers, the really effective superintendents are those who can provide transformational leadership to the organization they lead. Contemporary authors and researchers such as Sergiovanni, Cuban, Bridges, Peters, Miskel, and Hoy are committed to the theory that the modern leader must possess those visionary and messianic skills as well as the skills of being good managers of the organization. They point out that the modern, complex, multifaceted school organization cannot function as before and hope to meet the educational needs and aspirations of its diverse constituents. These writers agree that the modern superintendent must be a master at blending the various components of the organization into a smooth functioning whole.

Most states provide for the position of superintendent of schools and delegate the authority for selecting the position holder to the local school board. Texas, for example, in its Education Code, Subchapter F, Superintendents and Principals states: "(a) The superintendent is the educational leader and the administrative manager of the school district." Many states have similar provisions for the position of superintendent, but some have much more stringent and demanding criteria for this important position.

Administrative Skills Defined

Considerable effort and time has been invested in defining the administrative skills for which the superintendent has responsibility. These skills have been developed as a basis for selection and in-service training. As such, they should provide the basis for any developmental effort and could identify those specific tasks against which the performance of the superintendent is measured.

The Texas LEAD Center, under a grant from the Texas Education Agency in 1988, convened a group of experts representing the major educational leadership organizations, the universities of the state, and the private sector to develop a Guide for Developing Management and Leadership Skills. This work identified 4 basic or core areas of administrative responsibility and related subareas. The group of experts also devised a scheme for providing assistance in gaining these core skills. The basic core skills and related subareas are shown in the following table.

In addition to these basic and required skills, the group recommended that each district develop a "Job Specific" performance category in which the specifics of the superintendent's job in the particular district are identified. Moreover, it was recommended that these specific job responsibilities be measured in the evaluation process. In this way, individual district circumstances and expectations are taken into account in the superintendent's job description. Further, the Texas advisory group is developing specific job descriptions for the many administrative positions found in the modern school system.

Table 1 Administrative Skills as Defined by the Texas LEAD Center

Administrative Skills	Conceptual Skills
Planning	Strategic thinking
Needs identification	Creative planning
Problem solving	Quality control
Decision making	Strategies
Organization	Observations
Culture/climate	Perceptions
Philosophies	Standards
Role identification/functions	Tests
Implementation	Problem Analysis
Programs	Data Analysis
Process	Alternatives
Assessment/evaluation	Conclusions
Delegation	Creative thinking
Monitoring/coaching	Basic research
Time organization	Assumptions
Change management	Analysis
Styles	Format
Research adaption	Risk assignment
Innovation/entrepreneurship	Entrepreneurship
Characteristics	Non-traditional
	Modification
	Evaluation
	Models/design
	Ongoing

Table 1   Administrative Skills as Defined by the Texas LEAD Center (continued)

Interpersonal Skills	Resource Skills
Human relations (individuals)	Fiscal
Culture	Accounting
Trust	Budgeting
Respect	Data management
Authority relationships	Process management
Collegiality	Purchasing
Human relations (groups)	Resource management
Group dynamics	Personnel
Persuasive techniques	Human relations grievances
Power	Legal issues
Collaborative techniques	Data management
Receptive communications	Personnel management
Listening skills	Facilities
Open	Needs
Humanistic	Building maintenance
Verbal/nonverbal	Safety
Expressive communications	Data technology
Public relations	Systems (long/short term)
Speaking skills	Data analysis
Reinforcement	Data utilization
Motivation	Evaluation
Feedback skills	Evaluation design
Conflict resolution	Support systems
Mutuality	Pupil personnel
Negotiations	Legal services
Mediation	Community
Arbitration	Special school services
Reflective practice skills	
Multiple goals	
Situational sensitivity	
Pattern rationality	
Value consensus	
Motivation	
Extrinsic	
Intrinsic	

Functions of the Office of Superintendent

Because the concept of the superintendent as the chief executive officer of the school district organization has become accepted throughout the United States, the idea that the superintendent is responsible for the provision of the major functions that are called for in any school system to meet the needs of its students has also become accepted. There are many descriptions of the essential functions of the school system. Candoli (1991) identified a set of 7 functions that are considered by most theorists as the basic functions of the school organization. The superintendent is charged with ensuring that these functions are provided for in the organization that he or she heads. These organizational functions are listed below:

1. **The Planning Function** - all activities and programs of the organization should be carefully planned, giving specific attention to the goals and objectives of the organization. The programs of the organization must be mutually supportive and aimed at producing the best possible educational benefits for the students.
2. **The Delivery Function** - once planned, the programs and activities must be delivered to the appropriate audience. This is usually the largest and most expensive function in the organization because it encompasses all direct instruction and the staff who provide students with academic programs.
3. **The Evaluation Function** - once programs are planned and delivered, they must be evaluated to determine whether or not they served the purpose for which they were intended. This function is often slighted by many educational organizations until too late in the delivery of the program. Ongoing and careful evaluation helps to ensure that the programs meet their goals and objectives and can be useful in identifying possible changes and adjustments necessary to make such programs more effective.
4. **The Business Management Function** - all programs and activities must be adequately financed and managed in order to provide the maximum effort and opportunity for the students of the school organization. The garnering and allocation of resources is an important and crucial function for all school organizations.
5. **The Communications Function** - as decisions are made and as plans are readied for implementation, communication becomes more and more important to the educational organization. Citizens, community, participants, and staff are all important components of the school organization and must be allowed to participate in the decision-making process through effective communication channels.
6. **The Instructional Support Function** - this function includes all the direct and indirect instructional support activities that are so important to the school organization. Direct support includes such activities as counseling and library services, while indirect support includes such activities as curriculum development and pupil personnel activities. These services are important and necessary to the health of the organization.

7. **The Noninstructional Support Function** - this includes the myriad activities without which the district could not operate but which, nevertheless, are not direct student support functions. These activities include maintenance and operations, transportation, food services, security and other important yet indirect service activities.

Many superintendent evaluation instruments are predicated on the quality of the provision of the above functions to the district. The superintendent, as chief executive of the school system, is responsible for all of the above activities, and the board charges the superintendent with the provision of these functions in a manner that permits the students of the district to profit from the educational programs offered. Thus, the superintendent's performance is judged, in part, according to how well these functions are provided to the system.

Superintendent Contract and Tenure

Most superintendents are not in tenure accruing positions. They serve at the pleasure of the school board and are usually employed under terms of a negotiated contract. Some states set limits for the length of the superintendent's contract ranging from a single year to a term of 5 years. Many states provide the opportunity for a "roll over" or renewal of the contract whereby the superintendent's contract is extended at the time of the annual evaluation date. This extension is usually for 1 year so that the superintendent always has a period of from 2 to 3 years remaining on his or her contract. Some school systems are departments of city or county government organizations and, as such, are considered to be dependent school districts because they cannot levy school taxes independently of another governing body. Examples of this type of school system include the New York City school system as well as the Nashville public schools.

Many states require, and most individual superintendent contracts provide, that the annual summative performance evaluation be completed by the end of February in order to accommodate existing state professional employment laws. These laws usually specify that if notice is not given by the end of February regarding continued employment on a contract that expires at the end of the current year, the superintendent's contract is automatically extended for another year. This is intended to protect the superintendent as well as the board of education--the superintendent because it provides ample time for notice of deficiencies in performance, and the board because it meets legal requirements for notification of intent to terminate the superintendent's contract. Thus, the process permits 3 options: the first is termination for cause, the second is an assigned professional improvement plan with corrective actions to be met by a certain time, and the third option is a contract extension or continuation of employment as superintendent.

Because the performance evaluation of the superintendent is such a complex, demanding, rigorous activity, we strongly suggest a quarterly sequencing of evaluation tasks as part of the board calendar and that these tasks should be initiated according to legal parameters as established by state law or by the negotiated contract in force. A suggested evaluation calendar is presented in Section 7 of this document as a guide for the conduct of the performance evaluation of the superintendent.

References

American Association of School Administrators. (1982). *Guidelines for the preparation of school administrators.* Arlington, VA: Author.

American Association of School Administrators. (1993). *Professional standards for the superintendency.* Arlington, VA: Author.

Callahan, R. E. (1966). *The superintendent of schools: A historical analysis.* Eugene, OR: ERIC.

Candoli, I. C. (1991). *School system administration: A strategic plan for site-based management.* Lancaster, PA: Technomic Publishing.

Carter, D. S. G., Glass, T. E., & Hord, S. M. (1993). *Selecting, preparing and developing the school district superintendent.* Washington, DC: Falmer Press.

Cubberley, E. P. (1920). *The history of education.* Boston: Houghton Mifflin.

Glass, T. E. (1992). *The study of the American school superintendency.* Arlington, VA: American Association of School Administrators.

Hoyle, J. R., English, F. W., & Steffy, B. (1985). *Skills for successful school leaders.* Arlington, VA: American Association of School Administrators.

Hoyle, J. R., English, F. W., & Steffy, B. (1990). *Skills for successful school leaders* (2nd ed.). Arlington, VA: American Association of School Administrators.

Reller, T. L. (1935). The development of the city superintendency of schools in the United States. Philadelphia: Author.

5 LITERATURE REVIEW FINDINGS

The purpose of this section is to describe the current status of superintendent performance evaluation as reflected in the research literature and, in particular, to attempt to identify the most important issues and problems that need to be addressed in order to improve the evaluation of school district superintendents. Questions relating to the following issues are addressed in turn:

o What is the extent and frequency of superintendent performance evaluation?
o What are the purposes of superintendent performance evaluation?
o What criteria are used to evaluate superintendents and who establishes these criteria?
o What methods are used to evaluate superintendent performance?
o Who conducts superintendent evaluations and how well qualified are they to perform this function?
o What other stakeholder groups provide input into the evaluation process?
o What is the importance of superintendent performance evaluation for the effectiveness of the superintendency and/or the school system?

The literature search involved an examination of the archives held at The Evaluation Center and a detailed search of the ERIC database using various combinations of the following search terms: administrator evaluation, administrator effectiveness, administrators, superintendents, evaluation methods, evaluation criteria, personnel evaluation, performance, job performance, and boards of education. Relevant research literature was also acquired through formal requests to professional associations and individuals known to be active in the field; at meetings of various organizations concerned with education; and through informal contacts with others working in this area. In particular, the following organizations were contacted: American Association of School Administrators, Leadership in Educational Administration and Development, National Association of State Boards of Education, National School Boards Association, North Central Regional Educational Laboratory, Southern Regional Education Board, and Southwest Educational Development Laboratory. Furthermore, various individuals, school districts, and local educational organizations were contacted in the states of Alabama, California, Connecticut, Florida, Illinois, Iowa, Kentucky, Michigan, Missouri, New York, North Carolina, Pennsylvania, Tennessee, Texas, and Wisconsin.

This section draws heavily on 5 surveys of school districts; 2 are nationwide surveys (Glass, 1992; Robinson & Bickers, 1990) and 3 were conducted at the state level (Anderson & Lavid, 1988; Dillon & Halliwell, 1991; Edington & Enger, 1992). To a large extent, there is considerable agreement in the findings of these surveys; however, there are instances of conflicting findings among the studies. These discrepancies may in part be attributed to differences in the composition of the samples surveyed and to differences in focus among the studies.

The surveys of Glass and Robinson and Bickers were conducted on randomly selected nationwide samples. Whereas Anderson and Lavid surveyed nearly all new-to-site superintendents in Kansas, Dillon and Halliwell randomly selected 250 out of the 750 school districts in New York State, and Edington and Enger surveyed half (161 out of 321) of the districts in Arkansas using questions taken from Robinson and Bickers' study. Certain aspects of these samples may affect the survey results. For example, the new incumbents to the superintendency in Kansas may have a particular perspective on superintendent evaluation; the state of New York includes an unusual mix of extremely large, urban districts and much smaller, rural school districts, with their own special sets of priorities and problems; Edington and Enger surveyed school board presidents only, whereas the other studies surveyed superintendents and, in the case of Dillon and Halliwell, school board presidents as well; and, to an extent, these more localized surveys are likely to reflect the policies and legal mandates of the state in which they were conducted.

Likewise, the two nationwide surveys were based on different sampling techniques. Glass drew a random sample of school districts, which was stratified according to 4 categories of pupil enrollment numbers. This method provided 1,724 usable returns representing a 68 percent return rate and 11 percent of all superintendents. The survey was mailed in the fall of 1990 and it included questions relating to superintendent evaluation, which were embedded in a multiple-choice survey instrument of 110 questions relating to various aspects of the superintendency.

Robinson and Bickers used a 2-tier sampling strategy to obtain 1,245 usable responses to their Fall 1989 survey, which represented a 48 percent return rate. The first stage of their sampling technique involved the selection of every 1 in 10 school districts from the total of all public school districts in the U.S. The remaining districts in the universe were then stratified by pupil enrollment, and additional districts were randomly selected from each of 4 enrollment groups. The result is that this particular survey draws on a larger proportion of very small districts (less than 300) and a smaller proportion of the larger categories of district enrollment, in particular 25,000 or more, than Glass' survey. Another difference is that Robinson and Bickers' survey was focused exclusively on superintendent and board evaluation, whereas Glass' study was concerned with the broader subject of the American school superintendency and is therefore wider in scope. These differences in the samples surveyed and in the nature of the questions posed may contribute in part to the discrepant findings between these 2 nationwide studies.

What is the Extent and Frequency of Superintendent Performance Evaluation?

In accordance with the recommendations of researchers and knowledgeable professionals in the field (for example, Bippus, 1985; Calzi & Heller, 1989;

Dickinson, 1980; Foldesey, 1989) and the advice given in many state school board association documents (see, for example, Lindgren, 1985, and New Jersey School Boards Association, 1987), the vast majority of school district superintendents currently undergo annual performance evaluations.   Nationwide surveys of superintendents reveal that close to 90 percent of superintendents are evaluated at least annually, and of these, approximately 80 percent are evaluated precisely once a year (Robinson & Bickers, 1990; Glass, 1992). In Arkansas, 68 percent of school board presidents reported that formal evaluations of the superintendent are conducted in their district (Edington & Enger, 1992), and this figure was found to be significantly lower than the national percentage figure calculated by Robinson and Bickers. Of the 68 percent of superintendents in Arkansas who are evaluated formally by their school boards, 95 percent are evaluated at least annually.

Figures for those evaluated more than once a year vary slightly from 7 percent (Robinson & Bickers, 1990) to nearly 10 percent who are evaluated semiannually (Glass, 1992). In Arkansas, the corresponding figure is found to be lower at close to 5 percent (Edington & Enger, 1992). Similarly, figures for superintendents who have never been evaluated in their current positions vary from 5 percent (Robinson & Bickers, 1990) to approximately 3 percent (Glass, 1992).   Although these percentage figures are relatively small, they nevertheless represent several hundred school districts throughout the nation that do not, as a matter of policy, evaluate their chief school administrative officers. Further, more than half (54 percent) of the superintendents who are not evaluated see no reason to formalize an evaluation process with their school boards (Glass, 1992).

What are the Purposes of Superintendent Performance Evaluation?

A number of possible purposes for superintendent performance evaluation are identified in the literature, as detailed below. Examples of statements of evaluation purposes included in existing board policy documents are presented in Appendix A.

To improve educational performance in the nation's schools. Robinson and Bickers (1990) in their review of the literature note that this is a basic reason for such evaluations and point to the effect the superintendent has, as chief executive officer in the school district, on principals and teachers and through them the instruction received by students in the classroom. Similarly, state school board policy documents make reference to this purpose. For example, the California School Boards Association (Lindgren, 1985) notes that "The underlying common goal is to work toward the improvement of education," and the New Jersey School Boards Association (1987) gives the following evaluation purpose: "improve the quality of the education received by the pupils served by the public schools." Moreover, professional education associations agree that the primary purpose of evaluation is to improve instruction in the nation's schools (Foldesey, 1989).

To improve communication between the board and the superintendent (American Association of School Administrators & the National School Boards Association, 1980). The establishment of a formal evaluation process that is undertaken regularly can be a useful mechanism for keeping channels of communication open (Robinson & Bickers, 1990). The need for good communication between boards of education and superintendents is underlined by Hord (1992), who in her interviews with experienced and trainee superintendents noted an emphasis on the importance of open communication with the board.

To clarify the roles of the superintendent and the board members in running the district school system (Dickinson, 1980; Robinson & Bickers, 1990). In establishing criteria that will form the basis of the evaluation of the superintendent, the board is compelled to define in some detail the role of the superintendent and to distinguish this from the role of the board. The board, therefore, is also forced to clarify its own role. The demarcation between these roles can be problematic and is often the source of tension between the board and the superintendent (Glass, 1992; Hord, 1992).

To improve board/superintendent relations (Bippus, 1985; Robinson & Bickers, 1990). As noted by the American Association of School Administrators and the National School Boards Association (1980), superintendent evaluation can be useful in fostering a high level of trust between the superintendent and the board. Clearly, such improved relations can be constructive in enabling the superintendent and the board to work better together in serving the interests of the district's school children. The importance of this is emphasized by Hord (1992) who, in her interviews with experienced superintendents and superintendents in preparation, found that relations between the board and the superintendent can be troubling and often result in the departure of the superintendent. Similarly, Hall and Difford (1992), in their naturalistic study of the "exiting phenomenon" in superintendents, noted that respondents referred to the importance of the relationship between the school board and the superintendent, and the part this plays in causing superintendents to want to leave their jobs.

To inform the superintendent of the board's expectations in terms of job performance (Bippus, 1985; Robinson & Bickers, 1990), and to **provide feedback to the superintendent** on how well these performance expectations are being met (Bippus, 1985; Lindgren, 1985). The American Association of School Administrators and the National School Boards Association (1980) include in their list of the purposes of superintendent evaluation the idea that such evaluation will "clarify board expectations of his (her) performance" and "enable the superintendent to know how he (she) stands with the board." Clearly, a thorough understanding of performance expectations and feedback on how well these are being met will enable superintendents to perform their jobs more effectively.

To improve planning. According to Robinson and Bickers (1990), the process of setting goals and establishing priorities for the superintendent is a useful planning tool. In addition, this process helps to focus the board on the important task of setting district goals and objectives, thus further promoting educational planning within the school district. In line with this, the California School Boards Association (Lindgren, 1985) recommends superintendent performance evaluation for the purpose of identifying priorities for both the superintendent and the school system. This, they argue, will ensure a better use of time and talent, and ultimately the more efficient management of the school district. In a related vein, school district goals and priorities may change from year to year, so that an annual evaluation of the superintendent provides a useful forum for the board and superintendent to establish new priorities and changes in the superintendent's responsibilities for the coming year (Robinson & Bickers, 1990).

To aid in the professional development of the superintendent. The California School Boards Association (Lindgren, 1985) refers to the use of superintendent evaluation to "identify strengths and weaknesses and to determine ways to improve performance and effectiveness." Similarly, the American Association of School Administrators and the National School Boards Association (1980) include in their list of the purposes of superintendent evaluation its use in identifying areas of strength and weakness. Clearly, the identification of such strengths and weaknesses enables the superintendent and members of the board to build on and make good use of the superintendent's existing strengths, on the one hand, and to establish professional development and training needs, on the other hand.

As a basis for personnel decisions (Robinson & Bickers, 1990). Documents of past and present evaluations can be used as evidence to assist in decisions regarding salary levels, merit awards, contract renewal, and contract termination. Candoli (1986), for example, refers to an early publication of the American Association of School Administrators, which recommends that the superintendent's contract include provision for evaluation as a mechanism for "roll over" of the contract. He cites the following as typical of the phrasing that currently appears in superintendent's contracts: " . . . the board will hold a personnel session . . . to evaluate the superintendent's performance. Following such evaluation, the board, in its sole discretion, may extend the term of this contract for one additional year." Similarly, the California School Boards Association (Lindgren, 1985) refers to the use of evaluation results as a basis for decisions regarding reemployment and salary increases.

As an accountability mechanism. The American Association of School Administrators and the National School Boards Association (1980) note that evaluation of the superintendent will enable the board to hold the superintendent accountable for carrying out its policies and responding to its priorities. Similarly, the California School Boards Association (Lindgren, 1985) refers to the use of evaluation in providing for accountability on the part of the superintendent in carrying out district policy. Taking a slightly different approach, Robinson and Bickers (1990) refer to the use of superintendent evaluation in demonstrating to district staff that administrators are being held accountable for the performance of the staff they supervise.

To fulfill legal requirements, such as those enshrined in many state education codes. In California, for example, the Stull Bill requires that "governing boards establish a uniform system of evaluation and assessment of performance of all certified personnel" (E.C. 44660; cited in Lindgren, 1985). Similarly, the New Jersey Administrative Code requires boards of education to annually evaluate the tenured Chief School Administrator (N.J.A.C. 6:3-1.22; cited in New Jersey School Boards Association, 1987). Finally, as a further example, the Texas Education Code stipulates that "The State Board of Education shall adopt an appraisal process and criteria on which to appraise the performance of school administrators" (T.E.C. 13.354; cited in Texas Education Agency, 1990).

It is possible to group the many purposes of superintendent performance evaluation. MacPhail-Wilcox and Forbes (1990), for example, refer to the 2 categories of formative and summative evaluation, drawing on a distinction originally made by Scriven in 1967. Thus, the term formative may be applied to an evaluation system that seeks to continue the development of or to improve the subject of the evaluation, in this case the school district superintendent. Summative evaluation, on the other hand, refers to an evaluation system that seeks to provide a statement or summation of the evaluatee's performance, usually as an aid to decision making but also possibly to fulfill legal or bureaucratic requirements.

As an illustration of the range of evaluation purposes often adopted by district boards of education, the following lists are drawn from the state education codes for New Jersey (cited in New Jersey School Boards Association, 1987) and Texas (cited in Texas Education Agency, 1990). Examples of the statements of the purposes of superintendent evaluation, published by individual school boards, are provided in Appendix A for the interested reader. Thus, according to the New Jersey Administrative Code, the purposes of the annual evaluation of the superintendent are to

1. Promote professional excellence and improve the skills of the administrator.
2. Improve the quality of the education received by the pupils served by the public schools.
3. Provide a basis for the review of the performance of the tenured chief school administrator.
4. Improve communication between the board and the superintendent.

The Texas Administrative Code is more straightforward in its approach: "The results of the appraisal of administrators shall be used for staff development (relating to Standards for Management and Leadership Development for Administrators) purposes and may be used for contract renewal considerations."

Surveys of superintendent and school board presidents' perceptions of the major purposes of formal superintendent performance evaluations are inconclusive in their results. For example, Robinson and Bickers (1990) in their nationwide survey and Edington and Enger (1992), who used questions from Robinson and Bickers to survey Arkansas school board presidents, posed questions related to only 1 specific purpose of superintendent evaluation, namely, the use of evaluation results to determine compensation. Unfortunately, therefore, these particular studies are limited in scope as far as the range of purposes of current practice in superintendent evaluation is concerned. Nevertheless, the results of Robinson and Bickers' survey suggest that for the majority of superintendents (approximately 72 percent), salary levels are unrelated to performance evaluation outcomes, and this is more likely to be true in very small districts with an enrollment of less than 300. However, for a minority of superintendents (nearly 25 percent), some part of their compensation is based on evaluation results, and this is more often the case for superintendents in suburban communities. By contrast, in Arkansas 37 percent of school districts with formal evaluation procedures in place use evaluation results to determine compensation, and statistical tests revealed that this figure is significantly higher than the national percentage figure calculated by Robinson and Bickers. See Appendix A for an example of a compensation plan for administrators that is tied to evaluation.

Related to the issue of compensation, in his nationwide survey Glass (1992) asked superintendents what they considered were the major reasons they are evaluated by school boards. He found that a smaller minority of superintendents (approximately 13 percent) gave the determination of salary levels as a major purpose. However, unlike Robinson and Bickers (1990), he found that the use of performance evaluations to determine salary levels is less likely to be true in large districts with enrollments of 25,000 or more pupils.

According to Glass, the major reasons superintendents gave for being evaluated by their boards are primarily to establish systematic accountability (54 percent of respondents chose this response) and to establish performance goals (selected by 32 percent of respondents). The next 2 most important reasons given by superintendents were to assess performance with standards (indicated by 29 percent of respondents) and to identify areas needing improvement (according to 25 percent of respondents).

Less than 2 percent of superintendents thought that the major reason they are evaluated by their boards is to provide evidence for dismissal, and a substantial number (18 percent) saw their performance evaluations primarily as intended to comply with board policy.

These findings, however, differ from those of Dillon and Halliwell (1991), who surveyed both superintendents and school board presidents in selected districts in New York State. When asked what they considered were the major purposes of superintendent evaluation, the most frequently cited response given by both superintendents (49 percent chose this option) and board presidents (58 percent selected this purpose) was to strengthen working relationships with the community and between the board of education and the superintendent.

In contrast to the results of the survey conducted by Glass, a small minority of both superintendents (7 percent) and board presidents (12 percent) thought the primary purpose of superintendent evaluation was to provide for superintendent accountability.

As far as compensation is concerned, even fewer respondents than in the Glass study viewed the primary purpose of superintendent evaluation as being to assist in making decisions related to salary and employment (9 percent of superintendents and 8 percent of board presidents selected this response).

As discussed in the introduction to this section, a number of differences in the way the surveys were conducted may have contributed to these discrepant findings, including the fact that a different set of questions was asked in each case.

Despite its restriction to selected districts in New York, the Dillon and Halliwell study is interesting for the differences of perception it reveals between superintendents and board presidents. For example, almost two-thirds of board presidents (65 percent) thought that a major purpose of superintendent evaluation was to improve the instructional leadership role of the superintendent. However, only slightly more than an eighth (13 percent) of superintendents chose this as a major purpose. Dillon and Halliwell view this as an important discrepancy and recommend that school board members share with their superintendent the ways in which they see superintendent evaluation as improving the instructional leadership role of the superintendent. Such divergent views between school district superintendents and members of the board regarding superintendent evaluation is an important aspect of the board/superintendent relationship, which deserves further study.

The importance of clarifying and specifying, preferably in writing, the purpose of superintendent evaluation is underlined by Foldesey (1989) who refers to the "hidden agenda" of evaluation. He cautions against the use of evaluation to justify "either the continuance or termination of employment with little or no consideration given to improvement." This may serve to create an atmosphere of fear and distrust, which can be damaging for board/superintendent relations. In particular, the superintendent may be pushed into a defensive position of hiding weaknesses or failures and is focused on staying in position rather than improving performance. Similarly, Redfern (1980) notes that evaluation is a sensitive process involving complex interpersonal relationships, and is therefore bound to be subject to problems. Related to this, Dillon and Halliwell found that a major weakness of formal superintendent evaluation procedures, ranked second by superintendents and first by school board presidents, was that such procedures represent a negative process that may deal with an issue or issues that are subjective and/or political in nature. The recommendation of the Joint Committee (1988) to clearly identify the intended uses and users of personnel evaluation is designed to help guard against such pitfalls.

What Criteria are Used to Evaluate Superintendents and Who Establishes These Criteria?

Superintendents should be evaluated only with respect to those things for which they have operational responsibility and can directly affect themselves (Robinson & Bickers, 1990). This being so, it is important for the board and the superintendent to clarify their respective responsibilities before the start of each evaluation period, particularly if, for example, the board has recently taken over a function previously held by the superintendent. Furthermore, this implies that the criteria for evaluation should draw heavily on the superintendent's job description, which should be reviewed periodically and kept up to date. Indeed, this is emphasized by the Joint Committee on Standards for Educational Evaluation (1988), which notes that fundamental requirements of fair and valid performance evaluations are to develop valid job descriptions, keep them up-to-date, and use them as a basis for evaluating job performance.

Glass (1992) investigated the extent to which superintendent job descriptions are used to establish the criteria for performance evaluation. He found that the vast majority of responding superintendents (approximately 88 percent) do in fact have written job descriptions, a moderate increase from 1982 when 76 percent of superintendents had job descriptions (Cunningham & Hentges, 1982). However, of those with job descriptions, only a little more than half (57 percent) are evaluated according to criteria specified in the job description, representing about the same level as the 1982 Cunningham and Hentges study when 59 percent of superintendents were evaluated on the basis of criteria contained in the job description. Glass views these findings as reinforcing "the notion that the quality of the interpersonal relationships between the superintendent and board members is really what counts." He also suggests that many job descriptions are taken from books or manuals with little thought as to whether or not the criteria fit with the needs and priorities of the school district. Examples of job descriptions currently in use may be found in Appendix B. Clearly, job descriptions represent an area of concern and warrant further attention from researchers on the one hand, and boards and superintendents on the other hand.

Other sources of evaluation criteria include state mandates, school board policies, the superintendent's job contract, the superintendent's own description of the job, and district goals (Dickinson, 1980; Robinson & Bickers, 1990). See Appendices A and B for examples of such documents.

Turning to the more specific question of the types of criteria that are used to evaluate superintendents, the literature is colored with a rich, sometimes ill-defined, terminology that includes duties, responsibilities, performance standards, traits, characteristics, skills, competencies, management objectives, and goals. A useful system for categorizing types of evaluation criteria is outlined by MacPhail-Wilcox and Forbes (1990). This system describes 3 main types of evaluation criteria: administrative traits, administrative processes and behaviors, and administrative outcomes. Similar types of criteria are identified in Candoli (1986) under the headings personal qualities, inputs, and outputs.

Thus, administrative traits (personal qualities) are defined as characteristics possessed by the individual that tell us something about what the person is capable or likely to do. Such traits may include personality variables, sometimes listed as polar adjectives; for example, energetic/lethargic and open-minded/closed-minded; attitudes; particular knowledge; job-related skills; professional training; and prior experiences. This type of criterion tended to be used in the early part of the 20th century but is used less nowadays largely because it has proved to be ineffectual in discriminating between effective and ineffective administrators (MacPhail-Wilcox & Forbes, 1990).

The use of personality traits in the evaluation of superintendents is questioned in the literature. Thus, Candoli (1986) argues that while personal qualities such as integrity, commitment, honesty, and creativity are important and deserve some consideration in the evaluation process, he notes that such traits are difficult to translate into measurable criteria. He goes on to caution that "an evaluation based solely upon personal characteristics is really an assessment of the charm and engaging personality of the evaluatee and is quite subjective in nature."

Related to this is Scriven's (1993) argument concerning the use of teaching "style" to evaluate teachers. A style of teaching is defined as a way of performing the duties of teaching, but is distinct from the duty itself. For example, conducting valid assessment of students and reporting the results is a duty, whereas setting multiple-choice tests is a style or way of performing the duty of assessing students. Scriven regards the use of style characteristics to evaluate teachers as illicit. Using such criteria, teachers are rated as good to the extent that their teaching style matches the style that empirical studies have shown to be characteristic of good teachers as compared with unsuccessful teachers. Scriven argues that individuals should never be judged on the basis of the group to which they belong. He makes the analogy that if whites are twice as likely to be guilty of domestic violence as blacks, the statistic of skin color cannot be weighted to any extent in a court trial. Similarly, in the case of teacher evaluation, weight cannot be given to style characteristics even if such characteristics have been shown to be correlated with effective teaching. It is more scientific, as well as more ethical, to judge each teacher, or in this case each superintendent, by the individual's track record on comparable or prerequisite tasks.

Administrative processes (inputs) are described as activities such as planning, organizing, coordinating, staffing, budgeting, and so on. Although, like administrative traits, these processes were defined in the early part of the 20th century and have endured as standard definitions of what administrators do, researchers have not yet been able to define exactly what these processes consist of, nor yet how best to measure them. Similarly, administrative behaviors, which are a more recent introduction in the evaluation field, have proved difficult to define clearly. As an example, consider the superintendent's role as instructional leader. Many different behaviors might be associated with this role, and it becomes problematic to select a group of behaviors appropriate to this particular function in all situations. As a result, many of the administrative behaviors referred to in relation to superintendent job performance are vaguely defined.

Finally, administrative outcomes (outputs), as the name implies, are essentially the results of administrative processes or behaviors. Again, this is a more recent category of evaluation criteria that was only introduced into the research literature during the latter half of the 1980s. Student test scores could be considered an example of an outcome evaluation criterion, as could specific budgetary targets or curriculum goals, such as the establishment of a new curriculum for mathematics at grade levels K-3. Given the wide span of control and scope of responsibilities assigned to school superintendents, the list of possible administrative outcomes is enormous. Therefore, in order to define a manageable set of outcome criteria, boards must prioritize outcomes for each administrative area, possibly according to the strengths and weaknesses of the superintendent or to the needs and goals of the school district. A further problem with outcome criteria, which demands caution in their use, is that situational variables--for example, district and state limitations on the allocation of resources or background community factors--may affect the achievement of such outcomes regardless of the efforts of the superintendent.

In recent years there has been much interest in the use of student test scores as a basis for evaluating school systems, individual schools, and educational professionals. The idea that the criteria for superintendent evaluation should be only those things for which the superintendent has operational responsibility and can directly affect raises questions about the use of student test scores to evaluate school district superintendents. Not only are students' test scores an insufficient index of school effectiveness, but superintendents affect such measures indirectly through a complex and diffuse network of relationships. Moreover, the school district superintendent is only one of many diverse contributors to student achievement.

Accepting similar shortcomings with respect to teacher evaluation, Millman and Sykes (1992) have nevertheless recommended the inclusion of a student learning component in the assessment system for the certification of accomplished classroom teachers, albeit with certain cautions regarding the use of such measures. Their argument is based on the public's insistent demand for student-derived data, such as test scores, numbers of students scoring below standard, and dropout rates, all of which are seen as "vital signs of school health."

Related work is under way in Dallas, Texas, where an accountability system for school improvement, which uses student outcome measures as indices of school effectiveness, is being developed and implemented (Webster & Edwards, 1993; Webster, Mendro, & Almaguer, 1993). This system involves the use of student outcome measures in combination with other information, such as class background information and teacher generated information, to aid the principal in evaluating classroom teachers. Similarly, the Tennessee Value-Added System uses student achievement data to assess the effectiveness of educational systems, schools, and teachers (Sanders & Horn, 1994). As part of this work, a system of teacher assessment is due to be implemented in 1995 that is based on a minimum of 3 years and a maximum of 5 years of data collected for each teacher from students who have been in the teacher's class at least 150 days in a year. Clearly, attention is being directed to the inclusion of student outcome measures in the evaluation of teachers. However, the use of student-derived data for the evaluation of school district superintendents is an issue that has not yet been fully explored.

The following are examples of the advice given to school boards by their state school boards associations regarding the criteria that should form the basis for the evaluation of the superintendent. The New Jersey School Boards Association (1987) suggests that "While the board's primary concern should be whether the superintendent is making progress toward district objectives, the board will also want to concern itself with the leadership style of the superintendent." This is referred to as the "executive skills" of the superintendent, and the Association offers guidelines on defining such executive skills, including be clear and reasonable; reflect the job description and district needs; be specific and complete; require examples whenever possible; and group skills into broad categories. The Association also emphasizes that the "executive skills document" should avoid addressing personal traits as executive skills.

The California School Boards Association (Lindgren, 1985) offers the following evaluation criteria for consideration by school boards: "Traits, characteristics, and skills come with each individual. They are an important part of superintendent selection, but probably won't change from year to year. Results [are] based on performance in carrying out responsibilities. These measure progress toward district goals." The authors are at pains to emphasize that the evaluation of the superintendent should discuss specific behaviors rather than personality or vague criticism. The important point is that evaluation criteria should focus on measurable behaviors or outcomes supported by specific examples rather than nebulous personality traits or management style variables, which are difficult to demonstrate, let alone measure. For examples of statements of performance objectives and indicators currently used as a basis for superintendent evaluation, see Appendix B.

Nationwide surveys of the criteria by which superintendents are most often evaluated show a high degree of consistency in their findings. Thus, Robinson and Bickers (1990) noted that the two criteria most frequently identified as having a "high" degree of importance in the evaluation of responding superintendents are "board/superintendent relationships" (identified by 75 percent of respondents) and "general effectiveness of performance" (indicated by 73 percent of superintendents). Likewise, Glass (1992) found that the 2 most important criteria for evaluating superintendents were "general effectiveness" (according to 88 percent of respondents) and "board/superintendent relationships" (selected by 75 percent of superintendents).

The next 2 most important criteria were identified by Robinson and Bickers as "budget development and implementation" (indicated as of "high" importance in 57 percent of districts) and "level of agreement between board/superintendent priorities" (chosen by 51 percent of respondents). Glass found the next 2 most important criteria to be "management functions" (according to 75 percent of superintendents) and "budget development/implementation" (in 66 percent of districts).

The findings of these nationwide surveys differ slightly from the state survey of Edington and Enger (1992) in Arkansas. In their survey of school board presidents, the 2 most important criteria in the evaluation of superintendents were found to be "general effectiveness" (rated high in importance by 86 percent of school board presidents), in accordance with nationwide surveys, and "leadership" (selected as of high importance by 84 percent of school board presidents). The next 2 most important criteria were "budget development and implementation" (indicated as high in importance by 75 percent of respondents) and "knowledge in the field of education" (rated as of high importance by 71 percent of respondents).

The use of student achievement outcomes as evaluation criteria was not investigated by Glass, but Robinson and Bickers found such criteria to be of "high" importance in approximately 19 percent of districts and of "moderate" importance in close to 45 percent of school districts.

Studies of the reasons why boards hire and fire superintendents shed light on the criteria boards use in practice to evaluate superintendents, for selection on the one hand and to evaluate job performance on the other hand.

As discussed in Section 3, recent work has attempted to define the competencies and skills required of entering superintendents. Examples of such work include the AASA professional standards for the superintendency (1993) and the hierarchy of leadership domains, tasks, and competencies developed as part of the Diagnostic Competency Assessment System (Carter & Harris, 1991; Carter, Estes, Loredo, & Harris, 1991). Nevertheless, despite such efforts to formalize the professional requirements of superintendents, research shows that the primary reasons superintendents are hired by their boards are for personal and political reasons rather than because of their professional qualifications. Glass (1993) points to research indicating the importance of the right "chemistry" between the superintendent and the board in selection decisions. In addition, Hord and Estes (1993) in their review of the research note that political factors such as the selection committee's attitudes and political orientation may affect hiring decisions. In addition, Hord and Estes highlight the importance of the old boys network--"the good ole boys"--which was seen as a positive factor contributing to the selection and advancement of superintendents. However, for women the old boys network was seen as an impediment to their entry into and progress in the superintendency.

Interview research (Hord & Estes, 1993) reveals that once hired and in position, the superintendent's success depends to a large extent on receiving a consistent majority vote from the board at each consecutive board meeting and on the superintendent fitting in with board preferences and expectations for the role of the position holder. One respondent labeled these roles as *maintainer, developer,* and *change agent.* Generally, problems arise not because of professional shortcomings but because of errors in political judgment. As one superintendent put it, "It's not usually that you really made some big, bad mistake; you just made some dumb political mistake."

These findings indicate the importance of personal and political factors in board decisions to hire and fire superintendents. Decisions made in this way are not oriented to meeting the *educational* needs of students and ultimately may be harmful to the school district. Clearly, to better serve students and the school system, it is important for boards to focus on the **professional** qualifications and performance of superintendents and to reduce as far as possible the influence of personality and political factors in superintendent evaluations. Boards can begin to move in this direction by using the lists of competencies and duties developed by the profession, and presented in this book and elsewhere, as a basis for establishing superintendent evaluation criteria.

The use of student achievement outcomes as evaluation criteria was not investigated by Glass (1992), but Robinson and Bickers (1990) found such criteria to be of "high" importance in approximately 19 percent of districts and of "moderate" importance in close to 45 percent of school districts.

Wherever the criteria are drawn from and whatever types of criteria are chosen to form the basis of the evaluation, it is preferable for the criteria to be defined and agreed upon by the superintendent working in conjunction with the members of the board (Redfern, 1980; Robinson & Bickers, 1990). This participation will be more motivating and will give ownership to the superintendent.

Involvement of the superintendent in selecting the evaluation criteria is reflected to a large extent in current practice, according to Robinson and Bickers (1990), who found that close to 66 percent of superintendents surveyed nationwide determine the criteria for their evaluations jointly with the board. Even so, for a substantial number (24 percent) of responding superintendents their evaluation criteria are established solely by the members of the school board. Interestingly, a very small minority of superintendents (2 percent) determine the criteria for evaluation themselves without assistance from the board. Once again, however, these figures conflict with those of Glass (1992) who, in his nationwide survey, found that only 18 percent of responding superintendents were evaluated according to criteria previously agreed upon with the board. He noted that fewer (nearly 5 percent) superintendents than in Robinson and Bickers' study were evaluated using criteria developed solely by the board.

An intermediate figure is indicated by Edington and Enger (1992) in their survey of Arkansas school board presidents, who found that in 46 percent of districts the evaluation criteria are established jointly by the board and the superintendent. They also found that the superintendent develops the criteria for evaluation alone, without input from the board, in close to 2 percent of Arkansas school districts and that no explicit criteria are used in nearly 16 percent of school districts.

What Methods are Used to Evaluate Superintendent Performance?

An extensive range of methods is available for the evaluation of superintendents; these methods are discussed in depth in Section 6 of this book, where a detailed discussion of the evaluation models identified in the present study is provided. The purpose of this section is to review the research findings in an attempt to identify the methods that are currently used most often in the evaluation of school district superintendents and to identify the most important issues and concerns that emerge in the literature.

The research findings relating to the methods used to evaluate superintendents have greater consistency than the findings concerning the purposes of such evaluations. Specifically, the research suggests that the majority of superintendents are evaluated using checklists or rating forms. Glass (1992) found that this applies to 48 percent of respondents; Robinson and Bickers (1990) noted a figure of nearly 80 percent of superintendents; Edington and Enger (1992) found that 76 percent of school board presidents in Arkansas use such instruments; and Anderson and Lavid (1988), in their study of new-to-site superintendents in Kansas, indicated that 74 percent are evaluated in this way. To illustrate the broad range of printed rating forms currently used in school districts across the U.S., a number of examples are reproduced in Appendix C.

Similarly, for most superintendents, their performance evaluation is discussed with them at a meeting of the superintendent and the board. Glass noted that this was true for 48 percent of respondents, and Anderson and Lavid found that this was the case for an average of 77 percent of superintendents over a 2-year period.

Another method of superintendent evaluation commonly used is discussion among board members. Robinson and Bickers found that this approach was used in 71 percent of districts; Edington and Enger noted that 89 percent of Arkansas school board presidents indicated using discussion among the board to evaluate the superintendent; and Anderson and Lavid calculated that an average of 50 percent of boards over 2 consecutive years in Kansas held such discussions, usually in executive session without the superintendent present.

There is less agreement in the literature about other methods commonly used to evaluate superintendents. For example, according to Robinson and Bickers, 61 percent of superintendents are evaluated using written comments or an essay format. Similarly, Edington and Enger calculated that 62 percent of school board presidents in Arkansas use this method to evaluate their superintendent. However, Glass noted a figure of 20 percent in his survey, and Anderson and Lavid gave figures of 31 percent and 12 percent for superintendents evaluated in this way over a 2-year period.

Direct observation of the superintendent by board members was identified as a common method of evaluation in the study by Anderson and Lavid; they found an average figure of 71 percent for superintendents evaluated in this way. However, Glass calculated that only 11 percent of superintendents were evaluated using "observation and association," and Robinson and Bickers estimated that less than 1 percent of respondents were evaluated on the basis of "observation by an outside party."

Concern is expressed in the literature about a lack of objectivity in some of the methods used to evaluate superintendents. Anderson and Lavid, for example, note that "Data collection, the methods employed, the format for collection . . . appear to rely less on objective data and more on feelings and opinions." These authors underline the need for boards and superintendents to ensure that data are collected in a systematic and objective way. Similarly, according to Glass, superintendents agree that the subjective opinions of board members often enter into informal evaluation processes.

Though the research shows that a majority of boards use a rating form or checklist to evaluate the superintendent, Anderson and Lavid found that almost half of the boards of education surveyed created their own instruments rather than using an established evaluation tool. In view of this, Anderson and Lavid raise the question of the availability or knowledge about the existence of established superintendent evaluation instruments. Furthermore, they express concern about the ability and competency of superintendents and boards to design their own instruments. State school board associations, on the other hand, recommend that boards review samples of established evaluation rating scales to identify an instrument that can be adapted to their own needs. Thus, the New Jersey School Boards Association (1987) gives the following advice: " . . . it is important for the board and superintendent to review samples and 'customize' a list that reflects their values and expectations." Likewise, the California School Boards Association (Lindgren, 1985) states that "The board and superintendent will want to review different evaluation processes and agree upon a system for their own district. Each district should personalize the system. Forms or checklists from other districts should be modified." Clearly, needs and priorities will vary from district to district, and it is important for boards to have the flexibility to employ evaluation instruments tailored to the particular circumstances of their school district. However, such instruments should provide reliable and valid information concerning the performance of the superintendent. Boards and superintendents, therefore, have a need for technically sound, widely available superintendent evaluation instruments that permit flexibility of use.

Who Conducts Superintendent Evaluations and How Well Qualified Are They to Perform This Function?

The overwhelming majority of school district superintendents are evaluated by their school boards, and often this is coupled with a self-evaluation by the superintendent. Robinson and Bickers (1990) found that in almost 98 percent of surveyed districts, the board has formal input into the evaluation process, and in 60 percent of cases the superintendent has input. These figures are similar to those of Edington and Enger (1992) in their survey of Arkansas school board presidents, who found that in districts with formal evaluation procedures, the board has formal input in all cases (100 percent) and the superintendent has input in 56 percent of districts.

The findings of Anderson and Lavid (1988), in their survey of new-to-site superintendents in Kansas, confirm that the data used in the evaluation process come predominantly from the boards of education themselves (in approximately 90 percent and 70 percent of districts in 2 consecutive years). However, they noted a lower incidence of self-evaluation by the superintendent (an average of 47 percent over 2 consecutive years). The issue of other groups who contribute information to the evaluation process is addressed on the following pages.

Self-evaluation encourages superintendents to reflect on their experiences, establish goals, and determine strategies for achieving such goals. It can be useful, therefore, in serving to promote the superintendent's professional development. However, self-evaluation results may be subject to the vested interests of the individual, so that the objectivity of such data is questionable. For this reason, a cautionary note should be sounded with respect to the use of self-evaluation data to evaluate the school district superintendent for summative purposes.

The Personnel Evaluation Standards emphasize the importance of evaluator credibility, referring to the necessity for evaluation procedures to be carried out by suitably qualified individuals who have the requisite skills, sensitivity, authority, and training to perform this function (Joint Committee, 1988). Despite the importance of this issue, it is an area that has not been addressed so far in the research literature. Although state board association policy documents generally offer fairly detailed guidelines for setting up and implementing evaluation systems, rarely do such publications refer to the prerequisite skills or training needed by evaluators. One exception to this is the state of Texas, which includes in its Administrative Code (cited in Texas Education Agency, 1990) the stipulation that "Prior to conducting appraisals, all appraisers shall provide evidence of training in appropriate personnel evaluation skills related to the locally established criteria and process." To support this mandate, the Texas Education Agency (1990) has published materials to train those involved in developing superintendent appraisal systems.

That school board members may not be adequately prepared to perform the job of evaluating the district superintendent is suggested by Dillon and Halliwell (1991). In their survey of school districts in New York State, they found that more than 43 percent of responding superintendents thought that a major weakness of formal evaluation procedures for superintendents was that they require evaluation skills most board members do not possess. Interestingly, this need was recognized by considerably fewer (16 percent) school board presidents. As MacPhail-Wilcox and Forbes (1990) note, "Lack of training--or what may be even more important, poor training--is a primary reason why personnel appraisal systems fail." Clearly, training is an issue that is crucial to the development of improved superintendent evaluation systems and therefore deserves further research.

What Other Stakeholder Groups Provide Input Into the Evaluation Process?

A number of other stakeholder groups, apart from the members of the board and the superintendent, could potentially have input into the evaluation process. These groups include peers, for example, chief executive officers from other sectors; subordinates, such as administrative personnel, principals, and teachers; constituents on whose behalf the administrator acts, namely, parents and the surrounding community; and, finally, students, in whose service the organization exists.

Evidence from surveys of superintendents suggests that such stakeholder groups provide input into the evaluation process in very few districts. Glass (1992) found that the board consults others during the evaluation process in less than 3 percent of districts. Similarly, Robinson and Bickers (1990) estimated that no other individual or group has input in more than about 10 percent of districts.

As far as specific stakeholder groups are concerned, Robinson and Bickers noted that central office staff have formal input into the evaluation process in 7 percent of districts; principals and assistant principals have input in close to 11 percent of cases; and teachers have a formal role in 12 percent of instances. In Arkansas school districts with formal evaluations in place, Edington and Enger (1992) found that central office staff have input in 8 percent of such districts; principals and assistant principals provide input in 11 percent of cases; and teachers contribute to the evaluation in 13 percent of districts. Anderson and Lavid (1988) in their survey of new-to-site superintendents in Kansas, found that data generated from staff/administrators/noncertified personnel were used by 33 percent of districts in the first year and 21 percent of districts in the second year.

Input from parents is used in 6 percent of districts, and information from other community members is used in 4 percent of districts, according to Robinson and Bickers. Edington and Enger note that the corresponding figure for parents in the state of Arkansas is 11 percent. In Kansas, Anderson and Lavid reported that information provided by patrons of the community was used in 28 percent and close to 12 percent of districts in two consecutive years.

Input from the remaining stakeholder group, namely, students, was utilized in approximately 2 percent of responding districts in Robinson and Bickers' nationwide survey. In Arkansas, Edington and Enger reported that students have input in close to 5 percent of school districts with a formal evaluation process in place, whereas in Kansas, according to Anderson and Lavid, students provided information that was used to evaluate superintendents in close to 8 percent of districts in the first year and in no districts whatsoever in the second consecutive year.

These figures may reflect a lack of interest in the use of information provided by other stakeholder groups in the evaluation of school district superintendents. Anderson and Lavid, on the basis of the trend data obtained in their study, suggest that such figures reflect ". . . decreasing interest in surveying the people most affected by the educational system." Interestingly, Robinson and Bickers found that input from teachers and parents tends to be included in the evaluation process more often in smaller, rural, and small-town school districts than in large, urban, and suburban districts. Similarly, Edington and Enger found this to be true for districts with smaller enrollments in Arkansas. Therefore, factors related to the size and complexity of the school district organization and the nature of the links it has with the community may make it more or less practicable to involve other stakeholder groups in the evaluation of the superintendent. The issue then may be less one of interest and more one of feasibility and know-how. What may be needed, therefore, are practical guidelines on methods for obtaining and using input from such groups in the evaluation of district superintendents.

What is the Importance of Superintendent Performance Evaluation for the Effectiveness of the Superintendency and/or the School System?

The extent to which the evaluation of superintendent performance contributes to the effectiveness of the superintendency and the school system is clearly fundamental to the existence of such evaluations in the first place. According to *The Personnel Evaluation Standards* (Joint Committee, 1988), "Evaluations of educators should promote sound education principles, fulfillment of institutional missions, and effective performance of job responsibilities, so that the educational needs of students, community, and society are met." Research on the extent of support for this important consequence is scant and is mostly limited to the perceptions of superintendents, to the neglect of other stakeholder groups.

The views of superintendents regarding superintendent performance evaluation are, on the whole, fairly positive. Robinson and Bickers (1990), for example, found that half of the superintendents responding to their nationwide survey indicated that their boards' suggestions for improvement were "somewhat helpful," and a further 18 percent characterized such suggestions as "very helpful."

In Anderson and Lavid's (1988) survey of superintendents in Kansas, an average of 72 percent of respondents over 2 consecutive years said that their evaluation process was meaningful, and an average of only 16 percent felt that it was meaningless. However, fewer than an average of 15 percent of boards over the 2-year period gave specific directions for improvement to the superintendent. In the case of a professional superintendent, it is questionable whether or not a lay board can or should say how a problem ought to be solved. Of course, they might consult with an external professional. Evaluation can be useful even if it only identifies strengths and weaknesses.

In contrast, the picture painted by Dillon and Halliwell in their survey of New York State superintendents is less encouraging. When asked about the major strengths of formal evaluation procedures, only 10 percent of superintendents and close to 15 percent of board presidents thought that such procedures assisted in improving the performance of the superintendent and the district.

To some extent, it would seem, the results of such investigations depend on the precise nature of the questions asked and possibly also the locality where the study is conducted. Nevertheless, at present it cannot be said that a majority of board members and superintendents perceive performance evaluations as contributing to the overall effectiveness of the superintendency and the school system. This is an important concern that highlights the importance of CREATE's efforts.

A related issue is delineation of the possible mechanism by which performance evaluations contribute to the effectiveness of the superintendent and the school system. Although not directly addressed to this specific question, a potentially useful line of work is suggested by Crowson and Morris (1992) in an exploratory study of a small group of suburban superintendents near Chicago. These authors have identified 4 main ways or "dimensions of effect" in which superintendents exert an influence at the school site. Thus, the dimension of "relationships with the community" relates to the district's normative reputation in the surrounding community and the fostering of community involvement and support in the school district. The "dynamics of governing board/superintendent relationships" dimension is concerned with the maintenance of good relations with the board which, the authors argue, has implications for the school site. "Risk-taking" or risk management is deemed to be an important part of the job, since risk influences many executive behaviors and drives some of its rewards. Finally, the fourth dimension is that of "relationships with building principals," which tend to be characterized both by a certain distancing and by the encouragement of school building principals to keep the superintendent fully informed. Clearly, this work needs to be developed further, but a possible next step for evaluation researchers would be an analysis of the impact performance evaluation has on these 4 dimensions of effect.

Summary of the Literature Review Findings

The following is a summary list of the main findings of the review of the literature on superintendent performance evaluation.

The extent and frequency of superintendent evaluations

1. The vast majority of superintendents (nearly 80 percent) are evaluated annually, a small number (around 7 percent) are evaluated semiannually, and in a few districts (several hundred) the superintendent is never evaluated.

The purposes of superintendent evaluation

2. A broad range of purposes are identified in the literature:

      To improve educational performance
      To improve superintendent/board communication
      To clarify the roles of the superintendent and the board
      To improve board/superintendent relations
      To inform the superintendent of the board's expectations
      To improve planning
      To aid in the professional development of the superintendent
      As a basis for personnel decisions
      As an accountability mechanism
      To fulfill legal requirements

3. Nationwide surveys reveal that superintendent perceptions of the major purposes of evaluation are, in order of priority:

      As an accountability mechanism
      To establish performance goals

To assess performance with standards
To identify areas needing improvement

However, these findings differ from more localized statewide surveys.

4. One study found that superintendents and boards may differ substantially in their perceptions of the use of evaluation to improve the instructional leadership role of the superintendent.

The criteria used to evaluate superintendents and the persons who establish these criteria

5. The vast majority of superintendents (nearly 88 percent) have job descriptions, although only little more than half are evaluated according to the criteria specified in the job description.

6. Three main types of evaluation criteria are traits, processes, and outcomes.

7. In the light of public demand for student outcome measures to be included in the evaluation of educational professionals, researchers are working to develop techniques for validly including such data. This criterion is important to some degree in more than half of superintendent evaluations.

8. There is a high degree of agreement on the most important criteria by which superintendents are evaluated: board/superintendent relationships, general effectiveness, and budget development and implementation.

9. However, research indicates the primacy of personal and political factors in board decisions to hire and fire superintendents.

10. There is conflicting evidence about the number of superintendents who agree upon their evaluation criteria with the members of the board; estimates range from 18 to 66 percent.

The methods used to evaluate superintendents

11. The most commonly used methods are printed forms, in particular, rating scales and checklists, and discussion among board members without the superintendent present. Written comments or essays and observation are also frequently used, although there is less agreement in the literature on how widespread these particular methods are.

12. For nearly half of superintendents, their evaluation is discussed with them at a meeting of the board and superintendent.

13. There is concern about a lack of objectivity in some of the methods used to evaluate superintendents.

14. There is a need for technically sound, widely available, evaluation instruments that may be adapted to the particular circumstances of the school district.

The persons who conduct superintendent evaluations and their preparation for doing so

15. The overwhelming majority of superintendents (more than 90 percent) are evaluated by the members of the board, often with input from the superintendent.

16. Evidence suggests that school board members may not be adequately prepared for evaluating superintendents.

The involvement of other stakeholder groups

17. Input from other stakeholder groups, such as peers, subordinates, constituents, teachers, and students is solicited in no more than 10 percent of school districts.

The importance of superintendent performance evaluation

18. Empirical evidence bearing on this question is minimal and conflicting. But at present it cannot be said that a majority of board members and superintendents perceive performance evaluations as contributing to the overall effectiveness of the superintendency and the school system.

References

American Association of School Administrators. (1990). *A sample contract.* Arlington, VA: Author.

American Association of School Administrators & the National School Boards Association. (1980). *Evaluating the superintendent.* Arlington, VA: American Association of School Administrators.

Anderson, R. E., & Lavid, J. S. (1988). Evaluation of new-to-site superintendents. *ERS Spectrum, 6*(1), 29-32.

Bippus, S. L. (1985). A full, fair, and formal evaluation will enable your superintendent to excel. *The American School Board Journal, 172*(4), 42-43.

Calzi, F., & Heller, R. W. (1989). Make evaluation the key to your superintendent's success. *The American School Board Journal, 176*(4), 33-34.

Candoli, I. C. (1986, February). *Superintendent's evaluation process.* Paper presented at the annual meeting of the American Association of School Administrators, San Francisco.

Carter, D. S. G., Estes, N., Loredo, J., & Harris, B. (1991). Evolving a diagnostic system for formative use by senior school system executives in the USA. *School Organization, 11*(1), pp. 53-63.

Carter, D. S. G., & Harris, B. M. (1991). Assessing executive performance for continuing professional growth. *Journal of Personnel Evaluation in Education, 4*(1), pp 7-19.

Crowson, R. L., & Morris, V. C. (1992). The superintendency and school effectiveness: An organizational hierarchy perspective. *Journal of School Effectiveness and School Improvement, 3*(1), 69-88.

Cunningham, L. L., & Hentges, J. T. (1982). *The American school superintendency: A full report.* Arlington, VA: American Association of School Administrators.

Dickinson, D. P. (1980). Superintendent evaluation requires a sophisticated step-by-step approach like the one you'll find right here. *The American School Board Journal, 167*(6), 37-38.

Dillon, R. R., & Halliwell, J. W. (1991). Superintendents' and school board presidents' perceptions of the purposes, strengths and weaknesses of formal superintendent evaluations. *Journal of School Leadership, 1,* 328-337.

Edington, J. M., III, & Enger, J. M. (1992, November). *An analysis of the evaluation processes used by Arkansas school boards to evaluate superintendents.* Paper presented at the annual meeting of the Mid-South Educational Research Association, Knoxville, TN.

Foldesey, G. (1989, August). *Developing policy on evaluation and assessment of school board and superintendent performance.* Paper presented at the annual meeting of the National Council of Professors of Educational Administration, Tuscaloosa, AL.

Glass, T. E. (1992). *The study of the American school superintendency.* Arlington, VA: American Association of School Administrators.

Glass, G. V., & Martinez, B. A. (1993, June). Politics of teacher evaluation. *Proceedings of the CREATE Cross-Cutting Evaluation Theory Planning Seminar.* Kalamazoo, MI: Center for Research on Educational Accountability and Teacher Evaluation.

Hall, G. E., & Difford, G. A. (1992, April). *State administrators association director's perceptions of the exiting phenomenon.* Paper presented at the annual meeting of the American Educational Research Association, San Francisco.

Hord, S. M. (1992, April). *Entering and exiting the superintendency: Preparation, promises, problems.* Paper presented at the annual meeting of the American Educational Research Association, San Francisco.

Hord, S. M., & Estes, N. (1993). Superintendent selection and success. Chapter 5 in Carter, D. S. G., Glass, T. E., & Hord, S. M., *Preparing and developing the school district superintendent.* Washington, DC: The Falmer Press.

Joint Committee on Standards for Educational Evaluation. (1988). *The personnel evaluation standards.* Newbury Park, CA: Sage.

Lindgren, J. (Compiler). (1985). *Evaluating your superintendent.* Sacramento, CA: California School Boards Association.

MacPhail-Wilcox, B., & Forbes, R. (1990). *Administrator evaluation handbook.* Bloomington, IN: Phi Delta Kappa.

Millman, J., & Sykes, G. (1992). *The assessment of teaching based on evidence of student learning.* (Research Monograph No. 2). National Board for Professional Teaching Standards.

New Jersey School Boards Association. (1987, May). *Evaluating the chief school administrator: Fulfilling the board's governance responsibility.* Paper presented at the Action Lab of the New Jersey School Boards Association, West Windsor, NJ.

Redfern, G. B. (1980, January). *Personnel evaluation: Promises, problems, and prospects.* Paper presented at the annual meeting of the National Association of Secondary School Principals, Miami Beach, FL.

Robinson, G. E., & Bickers, P. M. (1990). *Evaluation of superintendents and school boards.* Arlington, VA: Educational Research Service.

Sanders, W. L., & Horn, S.P. (1994, October). The Tennessee value-added assessment system: Mixed methodology in educational assessment. *Journal of Personnel Evaluation in Education, 8*(3), 299-312.

Scriven, M. (1993, June). *Using the duties-based approach to teacher evaluation.* Paper presented at the annual meeting of the Center for Research on Educational Accountability and Teacher Evaluation/Phi Delta Kappa National Evaluation Institute, Kalamazoo, MI.

Texas Education Agency, Division of Management Assistance and Personnel Development. (1990). *Superintendent appraisal: System development - A training module.* Austin, TX: Author.

Webster, W. J., & Edwards, M. E. (1993, April). *An accountability system for school improvement.* Paper presented at the annual meeting of the American Educational Research Association, Atlanta, GA.

Webster, W. J., Mendro, R. L., & Almaguer, T. O. (1993, April). *Effectiveness indices: The major components of an equitable accountability system.* Paper presented at the American Educational Research Association, Atlanta, GA.

6 DESCRIPTION AND ASSESSMENT OF SUPERINTENDENT EVALUATION MODELS

This section presents a summary of the main models currently used to evaluate the performance of school district superintendents. Twelve distinct models have been identified, and they are categorized according to the basis by which evaluation judgments are made, namely, whether evaluation conclusions are based mainly on global judgment, judgment driven by specified criteria, or judgment driven by data. The labels assigned to each of the 12 evaluation models, and their categorizations, are as follows:

Global Judgment

> Board Judgment
> Descriptive Narrative Reports
> Formative Exchanges About Performance
> Stakeholder Evaluation

Judgment Driven by Specified Criteria

> Printed Rating Forms
> Report Cards
> Management by Objectives
> Performance Contracting
> Duties-Based Evaluation

Judgment Driven by Data

> Superintendent Portfolio
> Student Outcome Measures
> School and District Accreditation

The descriptions and assessments of the 12 models, contained in this section, are based on a thorough evaluation of each alternative by the project team and an outside consultant, with input from the team of expert advisers (see Section 2 for further information about the various team members). A summary of these in-depth analyses forms this section of the book.

The in-depth analysis for each evaluation alternative began with a description or characterization of the system under a series of headings, outlined below, incorporating the main elements of an evaluation model. These descriptions drew on the research literature and the evaluation materials acquired during the literature search, as well as the various team members' combined knowledge of and experiences with superintendent evaluation systems. Next, each model was evaluated using 21 separate checklists, each of which comprised a series of questions relating to one of the 21 personnel evaluation standards established by the Joint Committee (1988). The information obtained using these checklists was then synthesized to produce an extensive list of strengths and weaknesses for each of the 21 standards, and recommendations were made for improving the model in terms of the 4 main categories of *The Personnel Evaluation Standards*: Propriety, Utility, Feasibility, and Accuracy.

The summary of this work, presented in this section, is divided into 12 parts, 1 for each evaluation model. Each part includes first a description and then an evaluation of the model.

The description of each model is structured under the series of headings that was used for the in-depth analyses, as mentioned above. These headings incorporate the various elements of an evaluation model, as the term has been used throughout this book. However, not all elements are, or can be, described in full for each of the alternatives. The following are brief definitions of the description headings.

Distinctive Features: the various aspects of the model that best characterize and distinguish it as it is currently used in U.S. school districts.

Common Variations: aspects of the model that often vary from one school district to another.

Purposes/Uses: a listing of the main ways in which the evaluation model is typically utilized; these may be formative, summative, or both.

Performance Criteria: the dimensions by which superintendent performance is judged, e.g., traits, processes, or outcomes.

Performance Standards: the formally specified level of expected achievement for performance of the job function.

Data Collection Methods: the techniques, instruments, or systems used to gather information about the superintendent's performance.

Data Sources: the origins of the information that is gathered about the superintendent's performance, e.g., written or oral reports and school district records.

Reporting: the method of, and audiences for, formally communicating evaluation results

General Timetable: how often the evaluation is held.

Evaluator/Participants: the individuals who conduct the evaluation and make judgments about the superintendent's performance and also the stakeholders who have input in the evaluation process.

Concept of Administration: the underlying notion of school district administration.

Oversight of the Evaluation/Provision for Appeals: the procedures for monitoring and reviewing the evaluation system to ensure that it is implemented according to policy and to make changes as appropriate. Also, the procedures for handling disputes about the conduct of the evaluation and its results.

The assessment of each model includes a summary, overall evaluation of the model; a listing of its most important strengths and weaknesses; and recommendations for improving the model with respect to the personnel evaluation standards. Finally, included at the end of Section 6 is a table giving summary descriptions and assessments, in terms of strengths and weaknesses, for all 12 evaluation models.

Where relevant, cross-reference is made to illustrative materials included in the appendices. These materials were collected as part of the research project and serve to illustrate the various evaluation models as they have been developed and are currently used in American school systems. No comment is intended on their merit or worth as evaluation tools.

The information presented in this section is intended to assist readers to select among and improve upon existing superintendent evaluation models. In particular, the list of strengths and weaknesses for each alternative can be used to guide such work. Readers requiring a more exhaustive analysis of a particular evaluation model in terms of each of the 21 personnel evaluation standards should refer to the technical supplement mentioned above.

Global Judgment

MODEL LABEL
BOARD JUDGMENT/TRADITIONAL APPROACH

DISTINCTIVE FEATURES
Each board member provides a judgment of the superintendent's performance. The board then arrives at and conveys a composite judgment to the superintendent.

COMMON VARIATIONS
Judgments may be verbal or written. Evaluation reporting may be a scheduled annual event, more frequent, or ongoing.

PURPOSES/USES
Variable and often unspecified. May include feedback on strengths and weaknesses, setting priorities and planning, direction for improving performance, frank discussion on how the board and superintendent might improve their working relationship, and explanation of a salary decision.

PERFORMANCE CRITERIA
Typically unspecified and not constant from year to year. May assess 1 or a combination of traits, processes, and outcomes. May or may not consider student or system performance and needs.

PERFORMANCE STANDARDS
Unspecified

DATA COLLECTION METHODS
Board members as participant observers, usually nothing else.

DATA SOURCES
Superintendent oral and written reports, school district data, input from the community and school district stakeholders--used opportunistically and at the discretion of each board member.

REPORTING
Often in executive session; may be oral and/or written.

GENERAL TIMETABLE
Usually once a year, but may be more often or ongoing.

EVALUATOR/PARTICIPANTS
Board members

CONCEPT OF ADMINISTRATION
Sees the superintendent as the chief executive agent who serves at the pleasure of the board.

OVERSIGHT OF THE EVALUATION/PROVISIONS FOR APPEALS
None, other than legal channels and elections of board members and, in rare cases, recalls.

Evaluation of the Model

The well-entrenched Board Judgment/Traditional Approach to evaluating superintendent performance is highly flawed but has some decided strengths. Its main strengths lie in the Feasibility category: It is easy to apply, adopted by the district's top decision makers, and inexpensive. However, this model is seriously flawed in the Accuracy domain: The criteria and data are unclear, it is prone to bias, and there is no provision for regular independent review. Because of poor claims to Accuracy, the model is also limited in the Utility and Propriety domains. Basing judgments on faulty criteria and inadequate information hardly provides a fair and dependable guide to improving administrative performance or making defensible decisions about the superintendent. What the model has going for it is its grounding in direct exchange between the superintendent and board plus acceptance and support of the model by the board. Boards that desire to use this model should expand it so that it comprehensively addresses the full range of professional standards for sound personnel evaluation.

Most Important Strengths

- Provides for regular evaluations of the superintendent by the district's top policy group.
- This model involves the collection of multiple judgments as a basis for making the summary evaluation.
- There is a clear authority base for acting on the evaluation results.
- The evaluation motivates exchange between the board and superintendent focused on questions about quality of leadership and service in the district and how to improve superintendent performance.
- The superintendent evaluation system is directly approved by the district's policy board.
- The superintendent and board communicate directly and formally about the adequacy of the superintendent's performance and about their work together as a district leadership team.
- It is likely that the evaluation will provide the superintendent with the board's perspective on job areas needing reinforcement or improvement.
- Since this model tends to be data free, it encourages the superintendent to define his or her role and to assess and be accountable for effective performance.
- This model is easy to use.
- Evaluations are integrated in the regular process of board/superintendent exchange.
- Evaluations are politically viable.
- The model is inexpensive to implement.
- Grounding of the evaluation process in board/superintendent interactions facilitates role clarification and consideration of the superintendent's work environment.
- Flexibility in this model allows for considering a wide range of criteria and information.
- Multiple board member involvement helps to consider multiple perspectives and to identify and address discrepant views of the superintendent's performance.

Most Important Weaknesses

- There is a lack of prespecified criteria and procedures.
- This model does not provide for basing the evaluation on an up-to-date job description.
- The work environment may or may not be considered.
- Data used to reach judgments are unclear.
- There is a lack of auditable data.
- The evaluation is prone to bias and conflict of interest.
- This model lacks provision for or feasible prospect of auditing the evaluation or appeals.
- Procedures for resolving disputes among board members are lacking.
- Constructive involvement and input from principals, teachers, parents, students, and others are lacking.
- The evaluation is not clear about serving the information needs of any parties other than the superintendent and board.
- Board members may lack the expertise and training needed to conduct sound personnel evaluations.
- Ongoing feedback and assistance for improvement may or may not occur.
- There is little involvement of stakeholders in designing the evaluation system and understanding its results.
- Efforts to examine and improve criteria, data sources, data collection and review, the consensus process, and reporting are minimal.
- Too few resources may be expended to achieve a defensible evaluation.
- This model lacks provision and criteria for evaluating and improving the superintendent evaluation system.

Recommendations for Improving the Model

This model has some Utility advantages, especially through integration of the evaluation process into the ongoing exchanges between superintendent and board, and it is easy to apply. However, it has serious deficiencies in the Propriety and Accuracy areas. The model's lack of clear criteria and guidelines invites conflict of interest and bias in evaluations. In order to make effective use of the model, the board should expand and explicate it to correct its looseness and basic ambiguity. It is critical that the board and superintendent agree on job performance criteria and weights and key the evaluation to these. Boards should expand the model to include formal, public criteria based on the superintendent's up-to-date job description, plus a relevant, auditable data base. Stakeholders should be formally involved in designing, reviewing, and understanding the results of superintendent performance evaluation. Their input should be used to improve the clarity and defensibility of criteria, data, judgments, and follow-up actions involved in the evaluations. The board should then set a schedule of data collection that assures that their judgments at different points during the year can be informed by relevant evaluative information from multiple sources. The model's utility and defensibility could be greatly strengthened if the board adopts and subscribes to the full set of Joint Committee personnel evaluation standards.

Global Judgment

MODEL LABEL
DESCRIPTIVE NARRATIVE REPORTS

DISTINCTIVE FEATURES
The board prepares a written narrative report for presentation to the superintendent, which is then discussed at a meeting of the board and the superintendent.

COMMON VARIATIONS
The report may be structured under a series of headings, which guide the writing of the report, or the report may be open-ended. The superintendent may write a response or may develop a narrative report for comparison with that of the board. Any discrepancies form the basis of subsequent discussion.

PURPOSES/USES
Variable and often unspecified. May include superintendent growth and/or improvement, improvement of relations between the board and the superintendent, managerial control, personnel decisions, and legal mandate.

PERFORMANCE CRITERIA
May be unspecified or briefly sketched out, and unlikely to be constant from year to year. One or a combination of traits, processes, and outcomes may be assessed. May or may not consider student or system performance and needs.

PERFORMANCE STANDARDS
Unspecified

DATA COLLECTION METHODS
Board members as participant observers

DATA SOURCES
Board members' experiences of working with the superintendent during the evaluation period in question, and in a common variation of the model, superintendent oral and written reports.

REPORTING
A written report that is presented to the superintendent; discussion in executive session.

GENERAL TIMETABLE
Usually once a year

EVALUATOR/PARTICIPANTS
Board members and the superintendent when the latter produces a self-evaluation.

CONCEPT OF ADMINISTRATION
The superintendent as chief executive officer serving at the board's pleasure.

OVERSIGHT OF THE EVALUATION/PROVISIONS FOR APPEALS
None

Evaluation of the Model

The Descriptive Narrative Reports model for evaluating the superintendent has many flaws as well as a number of strengths. In particular, the model's strengths lie in the Feasibility domain; namely, it is easy to use, it is adopted by the school district's top policy board, and it is inexpensive to implement. The main weaknesses lie in the Accuracy category, since the model is usually associated with unclear criteria and data, it is prone to bias, and it is not periodically subjected to a process of review. These weaknesses, in turn, undermine the model's Utility and Propriety because judgments based on faulty criteria and inadequate information do not provide a fair and defensible guide for making decisions about the superintendent's performance. Use of the Descriptive Narrative Reports model can encourage boards to provide a thoughtful and considered evaluation of the superintendent's performance. This model can be strengthened if it is expanded to address the full range of 21 personnel evaluation standards established by the Joint Committee.

Most Important Strengths

- Regular evaluations of the superintendent by the district's top policy group.
- Encourages board reflection and a carefully considered evaluation of the superintendent.
- Motivates exchange between the board and the superintendent that is focused on questions about quality of leadership and service in the district.
- The board and superintendent interact formally, at least annually, and directly about the adequacy of the superintendent's performance.
- This model responds directly to the board's responsibility to oversee and assure that the superintendent is providing effective leadership.
- The board is duly authorized to evaluate the superintendent's performance and to act on the evaluation.
- The model is simple and easy to use.
- The evaluation is flexible and responsive to district needs and priorities.
- This model is politically viable.
- Evaluating the superintendent is inexpensive.

- The evaluation facilitates clarification of the roles of the superintendent and the board and considers the work environment in the superintendent's evaluation.
- The model is flexible and allows for consideration of a wide range of criteria and information.
- Multiple board member involvement helps to assure inclusion of multiple perspectives and to identify and address discrepant views of the superintendent's performance.
- Joint board and superintendent review of the evaluation report facilitates discussion of issues relating to the objectivity and soundness of the evaluation.

Most Important Weaknesses

- There is a lack of prespecified criteria and procedures.
- Criteria may be inadequately keyed to the full range of job requirements.
- There is a lack of auditable data.
- The evaluation is prone to bias and conflict of interest.
- This model does not include provision for auditing the evaluation or for an appeals process.
- There is no assurance of constructive involvement and input from principals, teachers, parents, students, and others in designing the evaluation system and in understanding its results.
- This model is not clear about serving the information needs of any parties other than the superintendent and the board.
- Board members may lack the expertise and training needed to conduct sound personnel evaluations.
- The scope and weights of the criteria covered in the evaluation are unclear and are left to the discretion of the board.
- This model does not assure ongoing feedback and assistance for improvement of the superintendent's performance.
- Little effort is made to examine and improve criteria, data sources, data collection and review, the consensus process, and reporting.
- Too few resources are expended on achieving a defensible evaluation of the superintendent's performance.
- There is no explicit provision for basing the evaluation on an up-to-date job description.
- There is no assurance that the evaluation will consider the work environment.
- The data used to make judgments about the superintendent's performance are unclear.
- The evaluation may not adequately reflect the many aspects of the superintendent's work.
- There are no provisions and no criteria for evaluating and improving the superintendent evaluation system.

Recommendations for Improving the Model

If this model is used, it should be based on formal evaluation procedures established in policy documents, including provisions for identifying and addressing conflicts of interest, a process of appeals, and for establishing who should have access to evaluation reports. (Examples of policy documents currently used by school boards may be found in Appendix A.) Boards should also set a schedule of data collection that assures that board members' judgments at different points during the year are informed by relevant evaluation information from multiple sources. In addition, evaluators may benefit from adequate training to enable them to carry out the evaluation of the superintendent as effectively as possible.

Boards wishing to use this model are also advised to formally involve stakeholders in designing, reviewing, and understanding the superintendent performance appraisal system. Their input should be used to improve the clarity and defensibility of procedures, criteria, data, judgments, and the follow-up actions of the evaluation.

The model can be improved considerably if the board and superintendent work together to agree on formal, public performance criteria and weights based on district needs and priorities, and if the evaluation is keyed to these. (See Appendix B for examples of job descriptions and performance objectives currently used in the evaluation of school district superintendents.) These criteria should be drawn from an up-to-date job description, and boards should establish a relevant and auditable base of data or information relating to the superintendent's performance. In short, to assure a defensible and effective evaluation, boards are advised to adopt and attempt to meet the full range of personnel evaluation standards published by the Joint Committee.

Global Judgment

MODEL LABEL
FORMATIVE EXCHANGES ABOUT PERFORMANCE

DISTINCTIVE FEATURES
This model involves regular, periodic exchanges about performance between the board and the superintendent, usually in executive session without the public present. The evaluation may be implicit in a discussion explicitly concerned with particular issues or specific incidents and therefore often involves a collaborative, formative process of problem-solving.

COMMON VARIATIONS
Variations occur in the scheduling of board/superintendent exchanges about performance. These may be periodic, occurring at set intervals, or they may be scheduled as needs arise.

PURPOSES/USES
Variable. Most likely includes organizational growth and/or improvement, superintendent growth and/or improvement, improvement of relations between the board and the superintendent, managerial control, and public accountability.

PERFORMANCE CRITERIA
Typically unspecified and unlikely to be constant from evaluation to evaluation. May include one or a combination of traits, processes, and outcomes, and may or may not consider student or system needs.

PERFORMANCE STANDARDS
Unspecified

DATA COLLECTION METHODS
Board members as participant observers

DATA SOURCES
Board members' experiences of working with the superintendent during the evaluation period, superintendent oral and written reports, school district data, stakeholder input.

REPORTING
Usually through discussion at executive meetings held during the year.

GENERAL TIMETABLE
Variable. May be periodic or as needs arise.

EVALUATOR/PARTICIPANTS
Board members and, in some cases, superintendent self-evaluation.

CONCEPT OF ADMINISTRATION
The superintendent as chief executive officer serving at the board's pleasure.

OVERSIGHT OF THE EVALUATION/PROVISIONS FOR APPEALS
None

Evaluation of the Model

Our analysis indicates that the Formative Exchanges About Performance model for evaluating the superintendent is considerably flawed, but that it also has a number of strengths. The main strengths of the model lie in the Feasibility category of *The Personnel Evaluation Standards*, in particular, its ease of use, its adoption by the school district's top policy board, and the fact that it is an inexpensive system to implement. However, the model has serious weaknesses with regard to the Accuracy standards, because the criteria and data for the evaluation are unclear, the model is open to bias, and there is no built-in mechanism for periodically reviewing the evaluation system. These deficiencies also weaken the model's Utility and Propriety because basing judgments on faulty criteria and inadequate information does not provide a reliable foundation for improving administrative performance and for making defensible decisions about the superintendent's job performance. Nevertheless, this model provides a useful means for an ongoing and continuous process of formative evaluation, and it is highly responsive to changing district needs and circumstances.

Most Important Strengths

- Regular and frequent evaluations of the superintendent by the district's top policy group.
- Highly flexible in enabling locally relevant criteria to be employed and in being responsive to local needs and problems, including unexpected or emergency situations.
- There is a clear authority base for acting on the evaluation results.
- This model motivates exchange between the board and the superintendent that is focused on questions about the quality of leadership and service provided in the school district.
- The board and superintendent interact formally, frequently, and directly about the adequacy of the superintendent's performance.
- The evaluation responds directly to the board's responsibility to oversee and assure that the superintendent is providing effective leadership.
- This model fits well with the regular structure for interactions between the board and the superintendent and can provide continuous feedback for improving performance.
- The evaluation is simple and easy to implement.
- The evaluation is politically viable.
- Evaluation using Formative Exchanges About Performance is inexpensive to implement.
- The evaluation encourages clarification of the roles of the superintendent and the board and considers the work environment in the evaluation of the superintendent.
- The model is flexible in allowing for consideration of a wide range of criteria and information.
- The involvement of all members of the board in the evaluation helps to assure inclusion of multiple perspectives and to identify and address discrepant views of the superintendent's performance.

Most Important Weaknesses

- There is a lack of prespecified criteria and procedures.
- Where criteria are specified, they may be inadequately keyed to the full range of job requirements.

- There is a lack of auditable data.
- This model is prone to bias and conflict of interest.
- The evaluation lacks provision for auditing the evaluation or for appeals.
- This model is not clear about serving the information needs of any parties other than the superintendent and the board.
- The members of the board may lack the expertise and training needed to conduct sound personnel evaluations.
- There is little involvement of stakeholders in designing the evaluation system and in understanding its results.
- There is little effort to examine and improve criteria, data sources, data collection and review, the consensus process, and reporting.
- Expenditure of resources to achieve a defensible evaluation of the superintendent is minimal.
- There is no explicit provision for basing the evaluation on an up-to-date description of the superintendent's job.
- There is no explicit assurance that the evaluation will consider the work environment.
- The data used to make judgments are unclear.
- There is a lack of provision and criteria for assessing and improving the superintendent evaluation system.

Recommendations for Improving the Model

Boards intending to use this model should extend it so that it addresses all 21 personnel evaluation standards. In particular, this model can be improved by establishing formal evaluation procedures in policy documents. These should include provisions for identifying and addressing conflicts of interest, identifying who should have access to evaluation reports, an appeals process, and periodic review of the evaluation system itself. Boards wishing to use this model should formally involve stakeholders in designing, reviewing, and understanding the superintendent performance appraisal system. In particular, this input should be used to improve the clarity and defensibility of procedures, criteria, data, judgments, and the follow-up actions of the evaluation.

The model can be improved if the board, superintendent, and other stakeholder groups work jointly to develop formal, public evaluation criteria and weights based on an up-to-date job description (refer to Appendix B for examples of superintendent job descriptions, performance indicators, and weights that have been developed and are currently used in U.S. school districts). These criteria and the weighting of them should take into account district priorities and needs and should consider the working environment of the superintendent. Furthermore, evaluators should establish a schedule for collecting, during the course of the year, auditable data regarding the superintendent's performance on which to base evaluation judgments. Finally, procedures should be developed for joint board/superintendent review of evaluation reports to facilitate discussion of the objectivity and soundness of the evaluation.

Global Judgment

MODEL LABEL
STAKEHOLDER EVALUATION

DISTINCTIVE FEATURES
Stakeholder evaluation is characterized by the involvement of the various school system participants in judging the performance of the superintendent. The stakeholder groups may be peers, subordinates, constituents, and students. This model assumes that the evaluation of the superintendent should involve the various groups in society that are affected by the work of the superintendent. This model also recognizes the democratic values that underlie the governance structure of the American public school system. Each of the stakeholders performs a separate evaluation of the superintendent, and these are then collated into a composite evaluation and used to determine the performance of the superintendent.

COMMON VARIATIONS
Variations occur in a variety of ways: the degree to which evaluation criteria are specified (e.g., unstructured, open-ended or forced-choice methods of data collection), the methods used to obtain stakeholder input (structured surveys, requests for letters, public meetings, private interviews), and the basis for sampling stakeholders (randomly, by self-selection, and by criteria such as ease of access or familiarity with the superintendent's work).

PURPOSES/USES
Involvement of many segments of the community in the governance of schools through participation in the evaluation process; and the stimulation of interest in, knowledge about, and involvement with the schools by constituent groups. Stakeholder input may facilitate review of board performance in addition to evaluation of the superintendent's performance. Local control may be enhanced because the stakeholder evaluation is responsive to the needs and priorities of the various stakeholder groups. The public relations function of the school district may be enhanced. The purpose of the evaluation is not focused directly on improving the superintendent's performance.

PERFORMANCE CRITERIA
Even if specified, the criteria are subject to interpretation by diverse groups operating from diverse value systems and knowledge bases. Judgments can be based on hearsay and isolated incidents and the predilections of individual stakeholders. This could lead to biased evaluations.

PERFORMANCE STANDARDS
May be specified; the degree of specificity varies.

DATA COLLECTION METHODS

Varied; may be used alone or in combination; may include requests for letters, structured surveys, private interviews, focus groups, public meetings, etc.

DATA SOURCES

This model is characterized by the gathering of a broad range of perspectives, including those of peers, subordinates, constituents, and students. Indeed, Stakeholder Evaluation is the only model that specifically encourages student input.

REPORTING

May initially be conveyed to the superintendent in executive session, orally or in writing, but the nature of stakeholder involvement demands some form of public sharing of the results. This kind of evaluation can be stressful for the superintendent and divisive for the school district.

GENERAL TIMETABLE

Administered at most once a year due to the administrative time needed to obtain the desired breadth of input. Could be used less often, alternating with other less time-consuming models for evaluating the superintendent.

EVALUATOR/PARTICIPANTS

Could be coordinated by a board member, but is perhaps best conducted by an evaluation consultant who is independent of the district or the superintendent. Participants include representatives of the district's immediate constituency and the community at large.

CONCEPT OF ADMINISTRATION

Sees the superintendent as a community leader charged with facilitating fusion of the school's mission with other segments of community governance and with the wishes and needs of community members themselves.

OVERSIGHT OF THE EVALUATION/PROVISIONS FOR APPEALS

None, formally; however, the public sharing of the process and the results provides for "appeal" via public opinion.

Evaluation of the Model

The Stakeholder Evaluation model meets many of the standards and could meet more of them if certain safeguards are undertaken by those involved in developing the evaluation design.

Most Important Strengths

- There are provisions for periodically reviewing and updating performance criteria and job descriptions.
- Encourages participation of the broader community in the evaluation of the superintendent.
- Includes provision for a continuing and representative stakeholder panel to periodically develop, revise, and propose evaluation policy.
- There are provisions for determining whether or not students, staff, and community receive fair treatment from the superintendent.
- There are provisions for considering and recording availability to the superintendent of professional, paraprofessional, and secretarial support services.
- There are provisions for considering and recording student, staff, and community characteristics as they affect the performance of the superintendent.
- There are provisions for the use of the district governing board-approved evaluation procedure and also of a governing board-approved evaluation instrument.
- There are provisions for collecting evaluation data from a variety of sources.
- There are provisions for secure and safe storage of evaluation reports and data.
- There are provisions for reporting relevant information even if it conflicts with general conclusions or recommendations.
- There are provisions for reviewing policies and procedures of evaluation that are no longer appropriate.

Most Important Weaknesses

- There is no explicit provision for including student learning as part of the evaluation of the superintendent.
- There is no provision for including the overall needs of the community as part of the evaluation process.
- There is no explicit provision for the superintendent to respond in writing to evaluation reports.
- This model does not include provision for assisting the superintendent to develop improvement plans consistent with the findings of the evaluation.
- The evaluation is time-consuming and difficult to implement.
- There are no procedures for monitoring the efficiency and effectiveness of the evaluation system.
- There are no provisions for the board and the superintendent to mutually agree on evaluation policy and procedures.
- There are no provisions for internal notification and external communication of both performance criteria and the level of performance acceptable in the school district.

- There are no procedures for investigating and resolving conflicting or inaccurate provisions with the position description of the superintendent.
- There are no provisions for keeping written records of conferences with the superintendent that are associated with performance evaluation.
- There are no provisions for evaluating performance against clear descriptions of performance criteria.
- There are no provisions for limiting the evaluation to assessing agreed-upon performance criteria.
- There are no provisions for training evaluators to apply criteria consistently and objectively.

Recommendations for Improving the Model

The Stakeholder Evaluation model for appraising the performance of the superintendent has much to recommend it, including the use of a variety of stakeholders in the evaluation process; the focusing of a variety of viewpoints on the evaluation process; several Accuracy, Feasibility, Utility, and Propriety standards as strong points in the model; and the potential for becoming even more strongly congruent with the personnel evaluation standards by careful application of them in the development of a new Stakeholder Evaluation design. Specific recommendations include the development of procedures for monitoring the efficiency and effectiveness of the evaluation system, provision for the board and superintendent to mutually agree on evaluation policy and procedures, and the development of clear performance criteria on which to base the evaluation.

By carefully merging this model with other models that are more duties/responsibilities focused, a hybrid version of a superintendent evaluation design can be developed that will objectively and effectively serve both the superintendent and stakeholder groups.

Judgment Driven by Specified Criteria

MODEL LABEL
PRINTED RATING FORMS

DISTINCTIVE FEATURES
Printed forms such as rating scales, checklists, and questionnaires are used to obtain numerical and/or descriptive assessments of superintendent performance. See Appendix C for examples of such forms.

COMMON VARIATIONS
May employ different types of evaluation forms and quantitative or narrative information. Usually only the board completes the form, but other groups might also complete it. The superintendent may complete the same form as the board in order to identify discrepancies between the board's and the superintendent's

ratings, which may form the basis for subsequent discussion. Also, subordinates or students may be requested to complete a form evaluating the superintendent's performance. Reporting of the results may be in executive session only, or a summary of the results may be made available to the public and media.

PURPOSES/USES

Mainly provides assessments of performance related to prespecified performance criteria, which may be either one or a combination of traits, processes, and outcomes. Results basically are used to provide feedback to the superintendent but may also factor into pay and other personnel decisions.

PERFORMANCE CRITERIA

Whatever the original source of the evaluation instrument, the board typically adapts it to include locally relevant performance criteria. May assess one or a combination of traits, processes, and outcomes. May or may not consider student or system performance and needs.

PERFORMANCE STANDARDS

Often unspecified. However, the categories for rating performance on each criterion (and all of them as a set) might include inherent standards such as "unsatisfactory," "marginally satisfactory," "satisfactory," and "exemplary."

DATA COLLECTION METHODS

Rating scales, checklists, and questionnaires can be used. Rating scales elicit judgments about aspects of administrator performance on a graduated scale. Typically, the scale has from 3 to 9 points. Checklists, on the other hand, consist of a series of statements, which the evaluator marks to indicate the presence or absence of specific indicators of performance. Questionnaires are more open-ended and usually comprise a series of queries or statements that are designed to produce short or extended answers about the superintendent's performance. A range of evaluation forms illustrating current practice is presented in Appendix C. The forms may be commercially published materials, state-developed instruments, or research tools. But they are often adapted to local needs and priorities.

DATA SOURCES

Typically, each board member completes a separate form before meeting to discuss and agree on a consensual evaluation of the superintendent's performance. As noted above, other stakeholders may also complete and submit the same form. It may be unclear what information, other than their own perceptions, board members and other respondents use to complete the evaluation form.

REPORTING

The superintendent may be given a table of mean ratings for each quantitative criterion and, less often, the range of ratings. Narrative information might be summarized in writing, showing illustrative specific narrative assessments from individual respondents. The report might be delivered in executive session and/or made public.

GENERAL TIMETABLE
Usually once a year.

EVALUATOR/PARTICIPANTS
Board members and possibly other stakeholders.

CONCEPT OF ADMINISTRATION
Sees the superintendent as the chief executive agent who serves at the pleasure of the board and who is responsible for performing well on set criteria as reflected in the evaluation form.

OVERSIGHT OF THE EVALUATION/PROVISIONS FOR APPEALS
Very little independent evaluation of this model. Legal channels available to the superintendent and elections of board members and, in rare cases, recalls--the public's main recourse--are a possible, although drastic, means of assessing this model. Quantitative forms provide the possibility of examining the adequacy of criteria and the reliability of ratings obtained. Such analysis is not often done.

Evaluation of the Model

The Printed Rating Forms model is appealing for a number of reasons. It is simple; it represents a straightforward procedure for defining and assessing performance criteria; use of data-collection forms serves well as a reporting device; it is amenable to checks for reliability, validity, and bias; and it is cost-efficient. However, the model is susceptible to some serious weaknesses. These include not keeping an up-to-date focus on the superintendent's evolving job, concentrating on narrow or superficial criteria, providing only end-of-year feedback, and not being grounded in sound information about the superintendent's performance. This model does not carry explicit requirements in key areas, such as validating the form and periodically updating it. Fortunately, these weaknesses can be overcome if the Printed Rating Forms model is made the centerpiece of a broader data-based model providing both interim and end-of-year feedback and if it is subject to regular review and revision against appropriate professional standards.

Most Important Strengths

- Helps to clarify and inform the public of the board's expectations of the superintendent.
- Use of a printed form helps to keep the respondents focused on the same performance criteria.
- A well-developed evaluation form may help to ensure that the evaluation is comprehensive.

- Offers the possibility of assessing the superintendent's effectiveness in terms of both overall performance and specific responsibilities.
- The use of questionnaires and the inclusion of open-ended and structured-response questions can provide qualitative as well as quantitative data.
- Multiple responses to a printed form help to consider multiple perspectives, to identify and address discrepant views of the superintendent's performance, and to check consistency of ratings from year to year.
- A printed form facilitates the gathering of focused feedback and the summarizing and reporting of findings.
- Summarizing and recording the information provided on standard printed evaluation forms is mainly a clerical task requiring no special training.
- The board has an opportunity to detect and address conflicts of interest by discussing each board member's ratings and possible discrepancies before finalizing a composite judgment.
- Printed forms offer a clear and straightforward agenda for the board and superintendent to follow in discussing performance strengths and weaknesses.
- The evaluation can uncover problems that might require professional development, remediation, or dismissal.
- This model, combined with the board's authority, is conducive to giving notices to remedy, constructive advice, or reemployment decisions along with the findings.
- Printed Rating Forms offer a systematic approach to superintendent evaluation.
- This model doesn't impose any heavy data collection burden.
- The evaluation is inexpensive to implement.
- Use of a printed evaluation form makes for easy review and analysis of the adequacy of the criteria employed.
- Completed forms provide an audit trail of what questions were asked, what criteria were considered, and what responses were received.
- Analysis of the results from use of a printed form provides clear feedback that is useful in detecting bias and assessing and improving the form.
- This model is conducive to evaluation against the *AERA, APA,* and *NCME Standards for Educational and Psychological Measurement* (1985).

Most Important Weaknesses

- There is little involvement of stakeholders in designing the evaluation system and understanding its results.
- Typically, there is no provision for validating the superintendent's job description.
- Criteria may be out-of-date and inadequately keyed to job requirements.
- The requirements of an easy-to-use form may result in evaluation criteria that are simplistic, superficial, or narrow.
- The printed form may emphasize general responsibilities to the exclusion of specific ones.

- This model might or might not assess the critical professional duties of the superintendent, e.g., promoting student development, honoring diversity, fostering equal educational opportunity, leading improvement efforts, maintaining educational accountability, evaluating and managing personnel, maintaining fiscal accountability, maintaining effective public relations, and keeping up-to-date with developments in education.
- Typically, a printed evaluation form does not deal specifically with the superintendent's work plan and emergent information requirements.
- Often, the form is not kept up-to-date in relation to changes in district priorities and superintendent duties and responsibilities.
- Use of printed forms is not conducive to addressing specific evaluation questions of parents, community, and other stakeholder groups beyond the notion of general feedback from the board and a summary assessment of performance.
- The printed form might not give weight to the various job criteria according to their relative importance.
- The form probably does not clearly define acceptable levels of performance.
- Typically, there are no provisions for training board members and other respondents to apply evaluation criteria consistently and objectively.
- There is no clear guideline to assure that board members will take into account the work environment as they evaluate superintendent performance.
- Printed forms typically are insensitive to the appropriateness and adequacy of funds, facilities, equipment, personnel, and materials that are available to support the functions of the superintendent.
- Likewise, printed forms are insensitive to community conditions, state support, parental support, and student characteristics as they affect superintendent performance.
- It is left to the discretion of the board whether or not the superintendent will obtain useful feedback from principals, teachers, students, parents, and other stakeholder groups.
- There are no provisions for documenting the information that board members and other respondents used to complete their evaluation of superintendent performance.
- Subjectivity is a concern because the data for making judgments are unknown, and the evaluation may be affected by the idiosyncracies and predilections of individual board members.
- There may be no provision for the superintendent to append to the filed report her or his assessment of its adequacy and defensibility.
- This kind of evaluation is unlikely to provide continuous feedback for improving the superintendent's performance.
- Typically, there are no provisions for immediate notification and assistance or intervention when the board first detects performance deficiencies.
- This model leaves open the question of whether or not the evaluation system should provide for professional development, remediation of deficient performance, or step-by-step termination.
- There is too little investment of resources to achieve a defensible evaluation.

- This model may not include provisions, budgetary or otherwise, for systematic evaluation and improvement of evaluation policies, printed forms, and procedures.
- Typically, the model does not invite input from school district stakeholders on how to improve evaluation policies, purposes, criteria, forms, processes, and data.
- It would be unusual for the board to formally adopt and hold itself accountable for meeting the professional standards of educational measurement and of personnel evaluation in selecting and employing the printed rating form.

Recommendations for Improving the Model

Boards intending to use this model are advised to make a sound evaluation form the centerpiece of a larger evaluation system. They should keep the superintendent's position description up-to-date and should regularly revise the evaluation form to keep pace with district priorities and changes in the superintendent's responsibilities. They should provide for developing, on an annual basis, a relevant file of information and should systematically use the information in completing the evaluation form. They should provide for stakeholder involvement and external review of the job description, evaluation criteria, printed rating form, provision for data, and analysis and summary procedures. Including both structured-response options and open-ended questions in the printed form will enhance the scope and depth of the information obtained. The model is strengthened when it includes interim evaluation feedback sessions during the school year as opposed to only issuing an end-of-year report. Users of the model should ask how it needs to be adapted in order to meet the professional standards of sound evaluation. They should then use this analysis to determine the needed procedures and budget. Periodically, they should use the *AERA, APA, and NCME Standards for Educational and Psychological Measurement* and the full set of Joint Committee *Personnel Evaluation Standards* to evaluate and improve the form, supporting information, and relevant data collection and analysis procedures.

Judgment Driven by Specified Criteria

MODEL LABEL
  REPORT CARDS

DISTINCTIVE FEATURES
  The superintendent is graded, usually along several dimensions (such as leadership), much like students receive grades in school subjects.

COMMON VARIATIONS
Grades may be assigned to the superintendent by the school board or, in some instances, by journalists from the local media.

PURPOSES/USES
Keeps the community informed of the board's and other groups' efforts to assess the superintendent, and facilitates discussion of the educational system among stakeholders in the community.

PERFORMANCE CRITERIA
Specified and explicit if performed by the school board. If left to the local media, the criteria may be ignored or discarded for the sake of a news story, possibly resulting in a more subjective rating.

PERFORMANCE STANDARDS
Unspecified

DATA COLLECTION METHODS
A report card that rates the superintendent's performance of various duties by assigning grades ranging from A (high) to F (low).

DATA SOURCES
May or may not be clear. Can include superintendent oral and written reports and school district data that relate to fiscal management and student achievement. Assessments regarding board relations and school climate may be included.

REPORTING
Usually in executive session, unless information is first given to the media for publication. Sometimes it is the representatives of the media who assign the superintendent's grades.

GENERAL TIMETABLE
Usually once a year, but may be more often or ongoing.

EVALUATOR/PARTICIPANTS
Board members, or in some cases, agents of the local media.

CONCEPT OF ADMINISTRATION
Sees the superintendent as the chief executive agent who serves at the pleasure of the board.

OVERSIGHT OF THE EVALUATION/PROVISIONS FOR APPEALS
None, other than legal channels, elections of board members, and, in some instances, using the local media to make a statement of appeal.

Evaluation of the Model

The Report Cards model for evaluating the superintendent has some major weaknesses but some strengths as well. The main strengths are in the Utility and Feasibility standards, which are largely met by this model. Additionally, the Report Cards model actively involves the board in the evaluation process, and it promotes interaction between the superintendent and the board. Also, the model is easy to use, inexpensive to implement, is based on established criteria, utilizes the evaluation to communicate district affairs to the community, and it may inadvertently assign to the media the role of watchdog, which may insure fair treatment of the superintendent.

This model has serious flaws in the Accuracy domain, however. It may lack a definition of the role of the superintendent, it may not be conducted within the context of the work environment, there are no provisions for documenting the processes used, the measurements are lacking in validity and reliability, it is prone to bias, and it is not clear how the board arrives at its decisions about the worth of the superintendent. This model is also very weak in the Propriety domain because it may not address the welfare of the superintendent, other stakeholders are not involved in the evaluation, and the established criteria may have little relation to the actual job of the superintendent.

Most Important Strengths

- There are provisions for the board, as the policy-setting body, to evaluate the superintendent.
- This model permits great flexibility in determining the criteria used in the evaluation.
- There are provisions for the board and the superintendent to agree on the criteria before the evaluation process begins.
- There is a clear authority base for acting on the evaluation results.
- Typically, this model is designed to accommodate the public's right to know and interest in this topic.
- This model provides an effective procedure for reporting evaluation results through the local media in terms that are familiar to the community.
- Involvement of the local media increases the utility of the evaluation results.
- The general timetable is known well in advance of the evaluation.
- This model is easy to implement.
- The evaluation is conducted at little or no cost to the district.
- This model is politically viable.
- The evaluation is efficient in its use of time and resources.
- Typically, the superintendent is given a copy of the final written report in advance of the formal meeting to review the material.
- Involvement of the local media may serve as a cross-check for many of the Accuracy standards.
- Board member involvement helps to consider multiple perspectives and to identify and address discrepant views of the superintendent's performance.

- This model motivates formal exchanges between the board and the superintendent.

Most Important Weaknesses

- There are no provisions for linking evaluation criteria to actual job requirements.
- There may be a lack of auditable data in this model.
- This model is prone to bias and to conflict of interest.
- There are no provisions for auditing the evaluation or for appeals.
- Evaluators may lack the necessary expertise and training to conduct the evaluation effectively.
- There is no explicit provision for multiple sources of evaluation information.
- There are no provisions for including other stakeholders in the evaluation process, apart from the local media in some instances.
- This model does not provide for ongoing feedback and assistance for improvement.
- There may be too little expenditure of resources to achieve a defensible evaluation.
- The evaluation may not consider the work environment.
- Sources of information are unclear.
- There is no provision for evaluating and improving the superintendent evaluation system.
- There are no provisions for documenting procedures.

Recommendations for Improving the Model

In order to improve the Report Cards model for evaluating the superintendent, major changes must be undertaken in order to meet all 21 of the personnel evaluation standards. For example, in the Propriety domain the model can be improved by establishing criteria that meet the needs of students and community and by linking these to the superintendent's administrative duties. Also, there is a need to include guidelines for designing, conducting, reviewing, and improving the system as part of the evaluation process, in addition to procedures for permitting the superintendent to review the evaluation report before it is released to the news media.

In the Utility domain, the Report Cards model can be improved by initiating a process to encourage the superintendent and board to reach agreement on the evaluation criteria, by encouraging interactions between the board and superintendent, by making provisions for improving those areas of performance deemed weak or inadequate, by involving other stakeholder groups in the evaluation process, and by providing training for board members in conducting the evaluation.

The model's Feasibility can be improved by developing more objective criteria for use in the evaluation of the superintendent, by involving other stakeholder groups both in the design and the application of the evaluation itself, and by monitoring the effectiveness of the evaluation process.

In the Accuracy category, the model can be strengthened by linking the evaluation criteria to actual performance, by specifying the procedures to be used, by utilizing valid and reliable measures of performance, by carefully managing the data, by controlling for bias, and by periodically reviewing the evaluation system.

It is important to recognize that this model is extremely weak in the Propriety and Accuracy domains, so much so that efforts to correct these shortcomings are tantamount to a complete rewriting of the model. The board must resolve the important issues of the welfare of the superintendent and fairness in the evaluation or stand the chance of not being able to recruit and keep fine candidates for the position.

Judgment Driven by Specified Criteria

MODEL LABEL
MANAGEMENT BY OBJECTIVES

DISTINCTIVE FEATURES
Uses preestablished, highly defined criteria for making judgments about the superintendent's performance. The evaluation criteria are the management objectives that have been established by the board and agreed to by the superintendent. The objectives are reviewed and adjusted regularly by the board and superintendent.

COMMON VARIATIONS
Variation is found in relation to the objectives, which may be very specific or much broader in nature. Examples of explicit standards are (1) the budget will not increase by more than 5 percent and (2) the percent of students failing the high school graduation test will decline. Also, variation is found in the degree to which the performance standards are made explicit. Examples of performance objectives currently used by superintendents and school boards are presented in Appendix B.

PURPOSES/USES
To establish exact and specific expectations for which the board holds the superintendent responsible, to help determine salary decisions as well as retention/extension decisions, to provide a forum for board/superintendent dialogue, to offer a systematic and credible procedure for judging superintendent performance.

PERFORMANCE CRITERIA
Specified and clear. May or may not consider student or system performance. The criteria are predetermined and can include variations the board deems important. Requires periodic review of performance.

PERFORMANCE STANDARDS

The objectives as defined in the agreement. Standards may or may not be explicitly stated. Tends to assure an objective evaluation of the superintendent. This model should guarantee that the objectives are based on current district needs and concerns.

DATA COLLECTION METHODS

Varied, depending on the objectives. For some highly specified objectives, it may be obvious what information is needed and how it is to be collected. Generally, board members serve as interviewers and observers.

DATA SOURCES

Superintendent's oral and written reports, school district data, input from staff and community, individual board member judgments, results of board/superintendent dialogue.

REPORTING

Usually in executive session; may be oral or written. Usually, reporting is oral and is followed by a written summation.

GENERAL TIMETABLE

Summative evaluation is once a year but formative sessions are held at least quarterly.

EVALUATOR/PARTICIPANTS

Board members. Sometimes an outside evaluator is invited to serve as a process person and to assist the board.

CONCEPT OF ADMINISTRATION

Sees the superintendent as the chief executive agent who serves at the pleasure of the board. The superintendent is responsible for the accomplishments of the school district--and so gets credit when these objectives are met, but is held responsible for when they are not met.

OVERSIGHT OF THE EVALUATION/PROVISION FOR APPEALS

None

Evaluation of the Model

The Management by Objectives (MBO) model for evaluating the superintendent has promise and, with modification and adjustment, can be a valuable tool for the adequate evaluation of the superintendent. There are concerns about a failure to meet standards, particularly in the Propriety, Utility, and Accuracy domains, but these can be corrected with minimum effort.

Most Important Strengths

- The board, as the top policy group in the organization, conducts the annual evaluation of the superintendent.
- The MBO model forces recognition of current priority objectives of the organization.
- The board has clear authority for acting on the evaluation of the superintendent.
- Provides for the collection of a variety of data to assist in the final judgment.
- There is flexibility in choosing which objectives to include in the process.
- This model encourages dialogue between the superintendent and board and focuses the dialogue on district concerns.
- This model forces the board and superintendent to meet periodically (at least annually) to discuss the superintendent's performance.
- This model meets legal requirements that boards evaluate their superintendent annually and that they oversee the affairs of the school district.
- Objectivity is enhanced because the performance objectives and standards are made explicit. It is therefore more difficult to bias evaluation outcomes.
- The evaluation is relatively easy to implement.
- There are provisions for reviewing the objectives and for adjusting them
- This model is politically viable.
- The reports and data are kept relatively secure.

Most Important Weaknesses

- MBO objectives could be watered down so as to become meaningless.
- MBO objectives could focus only on management issues and neglect those important issues of student learning and student concerns.
- Typically, board members lack the expertise and training to conduct such evaluations.
- The objectives chosen may not reflect current concerns.
- There is no provision for assisting the evaluatee to develop improvement plans.
- There are no provisions for involvement of stakeholders in the MBO process, either in designing the system or in understanding the results.
- The model may or may not consider the work environment.
- The objectives may not accurately reflect the actual job being performed.
- There is no provision for auditing the data or for a process of appeals.

Recommendations for Improving the Model

Boards wishing to use the Management by Objectives model are advised of the importance of and the need to meet the 21 personnel evaluation standards. Specific recommendations for improving the model include the establishment of a formal appeals process and adequate training of evaluators to enable them to perform their function effectively. In addition, boards, the superintendent, and other stakeholders should work to develop management objectives that are meaningful, tied to the actual requirements of the job--given current district needs and priorities--and that reflect the full range of the superintendent's responsibilities (readers interested in examples of the kinds of performance objectives currently in use should refer to Appendix B). Finally, evaluation using this model can be improved by involving other stakeholder groups in designing, implementing, reviewing, and understanding the appraisal system.

Judgment Driven by Specified Criteria

MODEL LABEL
PERFORMANCE CONTRACTING

DISTINCTIVE FEATURES
A legal contract between the board and the superintendent that stipulates explicit performance expectations. Criteria are outcomes based, rather than process oriented. Student outcomes are the focus of the evaluation. Includes consequences of success or failure in meeting these outcomes.

COMMON VARIATIONS
Found in the inclusion of a financial incentive as part of the performance contract, and as one of the consequences of the superintendent's success or failure in delivering contracted outcomes. See Appendix A for an example of an administrator compensation plan that is tied to evaluation.

PURPOSES/USES
Provides an assessment of the superintendent's performance relative to explicit criteria. Can be used in making personnel decisions, such as termination, continuation, remediation, determining salary levels, etc.

PERFORMANCE CRITERIA
Specified and explicit. Results or outcomes-oriented criteria are agreed upon by both the board and the superintendent in a legal contract. Appendix B includes examples of performance objectives and indicators in current use.

PERFORMANCE STANDARDS
Specified. May be expectations for student growth, e.g., an average gain in achievement test scores that exceeds a certain amount.

DATA COLLECTION METHODS
Observation, review of district records, and compilation of test scores indicative of student achievement.

DATA SOURCES
Superintendent oral and written reports; school district data that relate to district goals and priorities; and possibly data from teachers, principals, and members of other stakeholder groups.

REPORTING
Usually in executive session, may be oral and/or written.

GENERAL TIMETABLE
Usually once a year, may be specified in the legal contract.

EVALUATOR/PARTICIPANTS
Board members, possibly other stakeholders.

CONCEPT OF ADMINISTRATION
Sees the superintendent as the chief executive agent who serves at the pleasure of the board, but is granted the right to participate in the development of his or her own performance expectations.

OVERSIGHT OF THE EVALUATION/PROVISION FOR APPEALS
Provides a legal document, the contents of which can be upheld in court by either party, if necessary.

Evaluation of the Model

The Performance Contracting model for evaluating the superintendent meets some of the personnel evaluation standards but falls short of meeting a large number of them. In the Propriety domain, the standards that are met include regular meetings between the board and the superintendent and agreement on the expectations for the performance of the superintendent. Those areas left uncovered include the many aspects of the superintendent's responsibilities that may be neglected in this process and the failure to include other stakeholder groups in the evaluation process. In the Utility domain, the model's strengths include the involvement of the board, the top policy-making body, in the evaluation, and an evaluation structure that is conducive to encouraging board/superintendent dialogue. Utility domain weaknesses include the lack of provision for including other stakeholder groups in the evaluation and for providing ongoing feedback about performance. In the Feasibility category, the strengths include the cost-effectiveness of the model, the use of explicit criteria, and the political viability of the model. Feasibility weaknesses include a failure to allow for changing circumstances that affect district expectations, a lack of provision for stakeholder participation in the evaluation, and a lack of procedures for monitoring the evaluation process. In the Accuracy domain, the strengths include explicit performance criteria, provisions for multiple data sources, and the promotion of interactions between the board and the superintendent. Weaknesses in the Accuracy domain relate to the failure to consider the work environment, unclear sources of information, and a lack of provision for involving other stakeholder groups in the evaluation.

Most Important Strengths

- The model forces regular evaluations of the superintendent.
- The model is flexible enough to meet local conditions.
- There is a legal avenue for appeal.
- The board is involved in the evaluation of the superintendent.
- Contract negotiation may facilitate collaboration between the board and the superintendent on the design, implementation, and reporting of the evaluation.
- This model links employment decisions with evaluation results.
- The structure of the evaluation is conducive to promoting dialogue between the board and the superintendent.
- The board has due authority to evaluate the superintendent and to act on the results of the evaluation.
- This model is cost-efficient.
- The evaluation is based on explicit criteria.
- It is a politically viable model.
- Board member involvement helps to consider multiple perspectives of the superintendent's performance.

Most Important Weaknesses

- Outcomes-based criteria neglect the processes of the superintendent's work, so that unethical practices used to achieve outcomes may be ignored.
- Outcomes that are difficult to measure are likely to be omitted, so that the evaluation may not cover all key aspects of the job.
- Stipulation of expected outcomes may limit leadership behavior and judgment in relation to emergent issues.
- This model does not provide for ongoing feedback and assistance for improvement.
- The evaluation is unresponsive to changing district circumstances and unexpected or emergency situations.
- The model may not consider the work environment.
- Sources of information may not be clear.
- There is no involvement of other stakeholder groups.
- There is no provision for monitoring the evaluation system to make corrections and/or adjustments as needed.
- Board members usually lack the expertise and training to conduct such an evaluation.
- The criteria used may not reflect the district's priorities and therefore may not adequately measure the performance of the superintendent.
- The superintendent may be judged by factors over which she or he has no direct control, e.g., student achievement.
- This model may promote a narrowing of the curriculum.

Recommendations for Improving the Model

The Performance Contracting model for evaluating the superintendent has some major strengths as well as some major flaws. There are a number of standards that are not adequately met by the Performance Contracting model. These standards need to be addressed before this model can be effectively utilized to evaluate the performance of the superintendent.

The main strengths of the model are that it links employment decisions with expected results, it promotes active dialogue between the board and the superintendent, it places the responsibility for superintendent evaluation with the policy board, it is based on outcomes criteria, it is a legal mechanism for providing the evaluation, and it offers consequences and rewards for achieving the desired outcomes. Many of the deficiencies of this design can be addressed by making an effort to link the outcomes-based criteria as much as possible to the roles and responsibilities of the superintendent's job. In particular, steps should be taken to insure that all key aspects of the superintendent's job are included in the evaluation as well as safeguards against the use of unethical behavior to achieve performance objectives. In addition, the model can be improved by involving other stakeholders in the evaluation process, by monitoring the evaluation and making adjustments as necessary, and by making provision for addressing the full range of the 21 personnel evaluation standards.

Judgment Driven by Specified Criteria

MODEL LABEL
DUTIES/RESPONSIBILITIES-BASED EVALUATION

DISTINCTIVE FEATURES
   This model uses the duties and/or the responsibilities of the position as defined by the profession and modified by the board to account for local circumstances. A generic list of administrator duties is offered in Section 3 of this book for interested readers. Duties-based evaluation is highly structured, using clearly defined, preestablished, and ethically defensible criteria for judging performance.

COMMON VARIATIONS
   Found in the precise nature of the evaluation criteria, which may be the specific duties of the position or the broader responsibilities that a superintendent is expected to undertake. Appendix B lists examples of superintendent duties and responsibilities currently used by school boards and superintendents.

PURPOSES/USES
   Used to help the superintendent understand the specific expectations of the position. Assists in the development of improvement plans. Helps to determine salary decisions. Provides a forum for board/superintendent dialogue. Serves to delineate board and superintendent roles.

PERFORMANCE CRITERIA
Specified and clear. May or may not consider student performance or system performance. Can include variations the board deems important.

PERFORMANCE STANDARDS
The duties as defined. Insures that the criteria are applied consistently by every board member. The performance criteria may be implicit in the statement of duties (e.g., prepare a balanced budget for board approval) or may not be (e.g., serve as the instructional leader of the school).

DATA COLLECTION METHODS
Accountability records and observation by the board regarding the capacity of the superintendent to meet the duties criteria as established.

DATA SOURCES
Superintendent oral and written reports, school district data, input from staff and the community, individual board member judgments, board/superintendent dialogue.

REPORTING
Often in executive session; may be oral or written. Usually reporting is oral and is followed by a written summation.

GENERAL TIMETABLE
Usually once a year but can be more often and/or ongoing.

EVALUATOR/PARTICIPANTS
Board members. Sometimes an outside evaluator is invited to assist the board.

CONCEPT OF ADMINISTRATION
Sees the superintendent as the chief executive agent who serves at the pleasure of the board.

OVERSIGHT OF THE EVALUATION/PROVISIONS FOR APPEALS
None

Evaluation of the Model

The Duties/Responsibilities-Based Evaluation of the superintendent is flawed in some major areas, particularly in the Accuracy domain. However, this model has some strengths, particularly in the area of ethical evaluations and in meeting other Feasibility standards.

Most Important Strengths

- Regular evaluations of the superintendent by the district's top policy group.
- The evaluation is conducted in an ethical fashion.
- Judgments are based on the agreed-upon duties of the position.
- The board and superintendent discuss, at least annually, the adequacy of the superintendent's performance.
- This model meets the legal requirements for the policy board to evaluate the superintendent.
- Focuses on defined criteria.
- Forces the board to judge the degree to which the superintendent meets his/her assigned duties (e.g., provide leadership to the organization).
- The evaluation approach is politically viable.
- Facilitates clarification of the role of the board and the superintendent.
- The involvement of all board members allows for consideration of a much wider range of duties/responsibilities and forces consideration of disparate views of the superintendent's performance.
- Provides for collecting data from a variety of sources.

Most Important Weaknesses

- Typically, board members lack the needed expertise to conduct such evaluations, and there is no provision for training them in the evaluation process.
- The guidelines for collecting auditable data are inadequate.
- Such evaluations often do not consider job-related tasks that are important, perhaps not anticipated, but not included on the list of assigned duties and responsibilities.
- This model does not make adequate provision for the participation of other stakeholders in the development or process of the evaluation.
- There are no provisions as to whom and when the evaluation reports will be distributed.
- The evaluation lacks provision for auditing the evaluation or for an appeals process.
- This model does not provide information for anyone other than the superintendent and the board.
- The duties/responsibilities described in the model may be superficial and not adequately keyed to the needs of the district.
- The model does not provide adequate guidelines for the collection of relevant and valid evidence about how well the superintendent's duties/responsibilities were carried out.
- The evaluation may or may not consider the work environment.
- While judgments should be based on data regarding the superintendent's performance, it is not always clear how the board weights this evidence to arrive at a decision.

Recommendations for Improving the Model

Improving Duties/Responsibilities-Based Evaluation requires boards to insure that the model adequately meets the full range of the 21 personnel evaluation standards. This includes establishing a formal appeals process, training evaluators in effectively conducting Duties/Responsibilities-Based Evaluation, and involving stakeholders in designing, implementing, reviewing, and understanding the evaluation system. More specifically, stakeholder input should be used to improve the clarity and defensibility of evaluation procedures, criteria, data, judgments, and follow-up actions.

The duties or responsibilities of the position should be realistic in reflecting the actual job of the superintendent as well as district needs and priorities, and they should be developed through the joint efforts of the board, the superintendent, and other stakeholder groups. Furthermore, boards should ensure that data needs, sources, and methods of collection are clearly defined and delineated.

Judgment Driven by Data

MODEL LABEL
SUPERINTENDENT PORTFOLIO

DISTINCTIVE FEATURES
A collection of items or artifacts for demonstrating the performance of the superintendent. Usually printed, but may include videotaped or audiotaped evidence. Portfolio evaluation involves the systematic collection of data, generally by the superintendent, concerning the fulfillment of the duties or responsibilities of the office. Examples of items that may be included in a portfolio include surveys of stakeholder groups; descriptions of professional activities, for example, in the areas of human resources, community relations, and lecturing work; a videotape of the superintendent at work; letters from parents; newspaper clippings; and awards from professional organizations. See Appendix C for examples of evaluation documents that may form part of the superintendent's portfolio.

COMMON VARIATIONS
Variations include the degree to which the board takes responsibility for collecting specific parts of the portfolio, including input from stakeholder groups. Further, the evaluation guidelines may include directions for aggregating data to arrive at an overall summative judgment--an example of a summary evaluation form is included in Appendix C. There may also be variation in the final summary evaluation, which may be either quantitatively or qualitatively based.

PURPOSES/USES
Judgments are driven by a wealth of evidence, which often includes both a qualitative as well as a quantitative assessment of the superintendent's performance. The open-ended nature of the portfolio allows the board to cover

a wide agenda. This model provides a forum for board/superintendent dialogue on many topics and serves to delineate board and superintendent duties.

PERFORMANCE CRITERIA

The board can tailor the evaluation to school district goals and priorities. The use of a variety of measures is common. Expectations are established by the board for the performance of the superintendent.

PERFORMANCE STANDARDS

As established by the board and community. Use of various portfolio entries for such determination are common. Usually the performance standards are not clearly specified.

DATA COLLECTION METHODS

Entries to the portfolio are made by the superintendent, the board, and those stakeholders designated by the superintendent and the board.

DATA SOURCES

Varies, from newspaper clippings, to videotapes, to citizen's letters, to awards earned, to stakeholder surveys. Multiple sources are included in the portfolio model.

REPORTING

Usually at an executive session of the board that is prescheduled as the evaluation session. All data are provided for board review and for a summative evaluation of the superintendent's performance.

GENERAL TIMETABLE

Usually midyear and end of year.

EVALUATOR/PARTICIPANTS

Board members, with data provided by other stakeholders as agreed upon by the board and the superintendent.

CONCEPT OF ADMINISTRATION

Sees the superintendent as the chief executive of the organization who serves at the pleasure of the board.

OVERSIGHT OF THE EVALUATION/PROVISION FOR APPEALS

Generally, the superintendent provides much of the data on which the evaluation is based. Although no formal appeal process is defined, fairness in the evaluation can be promoted when other stakeholder groups are included in the process.

Evaluation of the Model

The analysis of the Superintendent Portfolio model for evaluating the superintendent suggests that this model has the potential for being one of the better methods of superintendent evaluation. This is because it utilizes a great variety of data sources, it provides for the involvement of other stakeholders, and it establishes a continuing dialogue between the board and the superintendent.

Deficiencies in certain areas can be easily corrected, so that Superintendent Portfolio evaluation has the potential to be an exemplary model for appraising the performance of the superintendent. As the board and superintendent enter into negotiations about evaluation procedures, the various shortcomings can be eliminated and the process can be improved to ensure that the superintendent's portfolio provides as complete and thorough an evaluation as possible.

Most Important Strengths

- This model provides for the regular evaluation of the superintendent by the district's top policy group.
- There is little room for conflict of interest when using the portfolio model.
- This model uses multiple sources of data.
- The evaluation serves to delineate board/superintendent roles.
- This model provides a useful basis for board/superintendent discussion about performance.
- There are provisions for using more than 1 evaluator in the process.
- There are provisions for follow-up conferences to be held within a reasonable time following data collection.
- There are provisions for flexibility in planning, with superintendent input, professional growth activities to reinforce strengths and to overcome identified weaknesses.
- There are provisions requiring that multiple criteria be used in evaluating the superintendent's performance.
- The board, as evaluators, meets legal requirements for the evaluation of the superintendent.
- There are provisions for encouraging the superintendent and other stakeholders to suggest ways by which evaluation procedures can be made more useful.
- There are provisions requiring that the policies established by the district governing board become the final authority in determining evaluation matters.
- There are provisions for funds to carry out mandated procedures.
- There are provisions for evaluating important responsibilities that are other than instructional.
- There are provisions for periodically reviewing and updating performance criteria and job descriptions.
- There are provisions for assessing whether or not students and staff receive fair treatment from the superintendent.

- There are provisions for considering and recording availability to the superintendent of professional, paraprofessional, and secretarial support services.
- There are provisions for informing the superintendent of the distribution (to whom, when, and why) of evaluation reports.

Most Important Weaknesses

- Collecting data for inclusion in the portfolio can be a time-consuming and administratively difficult process.
- There are no provisions for an appeal process.
- There are no provisions for designating an alternative evaluator if an unresolvable conflict exists.
- There are no provisions for the superintendent to respond, in writing, to evaluation feedback.
- There are no provisions for addressing only identified and agreed-upon professional responsibilities in the evaluation report.
- There are no provisions for training board members in evaluation techniques and skills.
- There are no provisions for monitoring the efficiency and effectiveness of the portfolio evaluation system.
- There are no provisions for a continuous search for new ideas that will result in achieving and maintaining the highest possible cost-effectiveness of the superintendent evaluation system.
- There are no provisions for comparing evaluation plans to actual evaluation practice.
- There are no provisions for testing the consistency of procedures across board members and making changes indicated by the findings.
- There are no provisions for assuring that the instruments and processes accurately evaluate what the system purposes and criteria intended they should evaluate.

Recommendations for Improving the Model

Portfolio evaluation is a feasible and readily adaptable model for evaluating the superintendent. Boards intending to adopt this model should take steps to ensure that it adequately meets the full range of the 21 personnel evaluation standards. More specifically, to address the main weaknesses of the model identified above, boards should insure that formal evaluation guidelines include provision for the superintendent to respond in writing to evaluation feedback, addressing only the agreed-upon responsibilities of the superintendent, an appeals process, and periodic review of the evaluation system. Steps should also be taken to provide adequate training of designated evaluators to enable them to carry out the evaluation of the superintendent as effectively as possible.

Judgment Driven by Data

MODEL LABEL
STUDENT OUTCOME MEASURES

DISTINCTIVE FEATURES
Use of districtwide scores on state and/or normative tests taken by the students of the district. Evaluation of the superintendent depends on the performance of the students on the prescribed tests.

COMMON VARIATIONS
The tests used may vary from state-mandated tests, to norm-referenced assessments, to locally developed criterion-referenced tests. Since comparisons of school districts are inherently unfair because of inequalities in student ability and readiness, the better implementations of this model use statistical techniques to create fairer comparisons.

PURPOSES/USES
To focus the superintendent's efforts directly on improving student learning. Used to determine salary levels, contract extension, and/or termination.

PERFORMANCE CRITERIA
Student test data that are adjusted for type of community, ability of students, and other background variables. Another basis for making judgments is to compare actual student gains with expected gains based on regression analyses.

PERFORMANCE STANDARDS
Specified in terms of expected scores or score gains, which are themselves often based on comparisons of the scores achieved in similar kinds of districts. May be unspecified.

DATA COLLECTION METHODS
Student testing and the collection of other student outcome information.

DATA SOURCES
District records of test administrations and analyses. State and locally generated test data.

REPORTING
Usually at an executive session of the board. Test data are provided to board members, which enable them to interpret how well the district is performing in relation to board projections.

GENERAL TIMETABLE
Usually once a year.

EVALUATOR/PARTICIPANTS
Board members

CONCEPT OF ADMINISTRATION
Sees the superintendent as the top teacher in the district and holds the
superintendent accountable for student growth.

OVERSIGHT OF THE EVALUATION/PROVISIONS FOR APPEALS
None, other than legal channels and elections of board members and, in rare
cases, recalls.

Evaluation of the Model

The analysis of the Student Outcome Measures model for evaluating the performance
of the superintendent indicates that it is highly flawed, but that it has potential for
use as part of the total evaluation of the superintendent. Use of student achievement
data can improve the district's performance in measurable outcomes and can provide
the basis for communicating with staff, the community, and students. This is an
excellent process for evaluating the organization's accomplishments over a given
period of time and provides valuable information about the effectiveness of the
superintendent in the instructional leadership domain. However, an appropriate
evaluation of the superintendent must include the many other duties for which the
position holder is responsible.

Most Important Strengths

- Focuses the work of the superintendent on what many would say is the
  essential purpose of schools, namely, the cognitive development of students.
- This model provides for the regular evaluation of the superintendent by the
  district's top policy group.
- The student data collected for use in the evaluation is exempt from personal
  bias.
- Typically, the board as the top policy-making body in the organization can
  adjust the allocation of resources to insure that there are enough resources to
  conduct the evaluation.
- Evaluation using this model is reasonably inexpensive.
- The board as evaluator meets the legal requirements for the evaluation of the
  superintendent.
- Reports are usually kept secure.

Most Important Weaknesses

- Student outcomes are not the total description of the superintendent's tasks.
  This model could lead, therefore, to a very narrow evaluation.
- Controlling for student background factors is difficult to achieve.

- The board is not trained to perform evaluations of the superintendent based on student outcomes.
- There are no provisions for training the board in the statistical skills needed to analyze student outcomes data.
- There are no provisions for an appeal process.
- There are no provisions for periodic examination of the tests included in the evaluation and for determining their validity and reliability.
- There are no provisions for the involvement of other stakeholders in either the process of the evaluation or in its development.
- The superintendent cannot be held directly responsible for student achievement. It is unfair, therefore, to judge the superintendent by factors not directly under her or his control.
- There are no provisions for limiting and focusing the test data so that it is only a part of the total evaluation.
- The data generated by this model may or may not provide an accurate measure of the superintendent's performance.
- There is no provision for basing the evaluation on the actual job performed by the superintendent.
- There is no provision for considering the work environment.

Recommendations for Improving the Model

If this model is used, it should be implemented in concert with other alternatives so that a complete evaluation can be achieved. The data utilized in the evaluation represent but a minor part of the superintendent's work, and to place all of the emphasis on student outcomes limits the performance evaluation of the superintendent. A comprehensive list of generic administrator duties is presented in Section 3 of this book, and examples of the range of superintendent duties and responsibilities that have recently been defined by school boards and superintendents are presented in Appendix B. While student outcomes are an important responsibility of the school organization, the superintendent does not have direct responsibility for teaching any of the students and, in fact, the legal and leadership responsibilities of the office of superintendent extend considerably beyond student test data. Boards should bear this in mind in developing an instrument and criteria for evaluating the superintendent. Boards wishing to use this model are also urged to formally involve other stakeholders in the development of the evaluation system and in the process of its implementation. In addition, boards are advised to pay close attention to and to attempt to maximize, as far as possible, the accuracy of data gathered through use of this model.

Judgment Driven by Data

MODEL LABEL
SCHOOL AND DISTRICT ACCREDITATION

DISTINCTIVE FEATURES
Involves the awarding of credentials to a school or district and to the superintendent in the process. Performed by an external organization.

COMMON VARIATIONS
Found in the nature of the accrediting body, which can be either a regional or a state accreditation organization. Variations also occur in the evidence considered, how it is weighted, and whether or not it is collected on-site.

PURPOSES/USES
Mainly provides an accreditation of the school and the district. Evaluation of the superintendent may be a by-product of the larger accreditation process.

PERFORMANCE CRITERIA
Determined by the focus of the accrediting body. Regional accreditors allow for district goals and priorities, whereas most state accreditors tend not to allow for district priorities.

PERFORMANCE STANDARDS
The superintendent is held to externally defined professional standards.

DATA COLLECTION METHODS
The school or district gathers and sends relevant data to the accrediting organization. Site visits may or may not be a part of the process.

DATA SOURCES
Selected by the school, the district, or the superintendent, under the direction of the accrediting organization.

REPORTING
Encompassed in the accreditation decision. Whether or not the report is formally presented to the school, district, or the superintendent is variable.

GENERAL TIMETABLE
Determined by the duration of the accreditation, e.g., every five years. May differ from one accrediting body to another.

EVALUATOR/PARTICIPANTS
State or regional accreditation bodies review the information. School or district personnel participate to the extent that they provide the data to the accrediting organization.

CONCEPT OF ADMINISTRATION
Sees the accreditation process as a mechanism for ensuring at least a minimally acceptable standard of education.

OVERSIGHT OF THE EVALUATION/PROVISIONS FOR APPEALS
None specified, other than those inherent within the state or regional accreditation policies. A different accrediting agent may be selected for subsequent evaluations.

Evaluation of the Model

Analysis of the School and District Accreditation model suggests that this is a partial approach to the evaluation of the superintendent. The focus of accreditation efforts are sometimes vastly different from the duties and responsibilities of the office of superintendent.

While the accreditation process can reveal many things about the school or district and can generate data that should and can affect the total evaluation of the superintendent, the specific tasks of the superintendent require a more focused examination of the activities of the office holder as an essential part of the evaluation effort.

Most Important Strengths

- There is periodic review of information designated by the accreditation organization.
- The board has a clear authority base for acting on the evaluation results.
- This model provides a mechanism for ensuring that students receive at least a minimally acceptable standard of education.
- The accreditation process may yield information that is important to the district.
- The accreditation process may help the district to set goals and priorities.
- Evaluation requires minimal staff, superintendent, and board time.
- Use of an external organization increases the model's political viability.
- Preselected accreditation criteria relieve the board and the superintendent of the task of establishing evaluation criteria.
- The model is fiscally viable.
- The superintendent and board together make decisions about the data that are collected and used.
- There are multiple data sources.
- The external accrediting organization may be more objective and may therefore lend credibility to the evaluation process.

Most Important Weaknesses

- The lack of local control may lead to the subordination of important district needs and priorities.

- Accreditation criteria may be inadequately linked to job requirements.
- Evaluation of the superintendent may not be a major part of the district accreditation process, if it is at all.
- There may be no provisions for auditing the evaluation or for an appeals process.
- There is no provision for including stakeholders in the evaluation process.
- Accreditors may lack the needed expertise and training to conduct personnel evaluations.
- This model does not provide for ongoing feedback and assistance for improvement.
- Accreditation does not necessarily lead to the improvement of educational leadership or of the quality of education.
- The evaluation may not serve the information needs of anyone other than the accreditation organization.
- There is too little participation for the board and the superintendent to value and have ownership of the process or the results.
- The evaluation may not be cost-effective.
- There are no provisions for monitoring the efficiency and effectiveness of the evaluation system.
- This model may not consider the work environment.
- Data used in the evaluation may not accurately measure performance.
- Data may not be a consistent measure of performance, and there is a chance of bias in the selection of data.
- There may be only occasional site visits.
- There are no provisions for documenting procedures.

Recommendations for Improving the Model

The School and District Accreditation model for evaluating the superintendent has some major weaknesses. The main focus of this design is to accredit the district, and the superintendent evaluation is performed as part of this process. As such, very few of the personnel evaluation standards are satisfied. The main strength rests in the fact that this model gives the superintendent a chance to be judged by outside evaluators who have political viability and credibility and who bring to the evaluation a set of performance criteria that a community of educators feel are important. It is perhaps the best model for insuring that cozy, comfortable, and easy-to-attain standards are not the basis of superintendent evaluation.

The model's weaknesses are many and can be improved in the following ways: by actively involving the board or other stakeholders in the design, implementation, and follow-up of the evaluation; by promoting interaction between the board and the superintendent; by making provisions for utilizing the results of long-term planning; by defining the role and responsibilities of the superintendent; by documenting the evaluation procedures; by providing for reliable and accurate performance measures; by periodically reviewing the evaluation system; by addressing the welfare of the superintendent, students, staff, community, and other stakeholders; by linking performance criteria to critical administrative functions; by assuring that the evaluation is conducted according to sound evaluation principles; by specifying legitimate audiences for reports; and by allowing for review of these reports. This model is keyed to minimally acceptable levels of education and performance, as are most accreditation processes.

The chart in Figure 1 presents summary descriptions for all 12 models. The chart in Figure 2 lists the models' main strengths and weaknesses.

Figure 1
SUPERINTENDENT PERFORMANCE EVALUATION
Summary Descriptions of Alternative Models

ORIENTATION	Global Judgment			Judgment Driven by Specified Criteria						Judgment Driven by Data		
	1	2	3	4	5	6	7	8	9	10	11	12
MODEL	Board Judgment	Descriptive Narrative Reports	Formative Exchanges About Performance	Stakeholder Evaluation	Printed Rating Forms	Report Cards	Management by Objectives	Performance Contracting	Duties-Based Evaluation	Superintendent Portfolio	Student Outcome Measures	School and District Accreditation
DISTINCTIVE FEATURES	Individual and collective board judgment	Board's end-of-year written report	Regular exchanges between board and superintendent	Assessment based on systematic querying of stakeholders	Assessments are gathered with a printed form	Board grades the superintendent's performance	Assessment against prespecified objectives	Contract specifying expected outcomes and consequences of success or failure	Comprehensive assessment against defined duties	Demonstration of performance using accountability records	Judgment of superintendent performance against student achievement	Judgment of superintendent performance based on district accreditation results
VARIATIONS	Verbal or written judgments	Structured or open-ended report; superintendent may also write a report	In scheduling of evaluation exchanges	Criteria may or may not be specified; methods of data collection and sampling may vary	In types of form, e.g., rating scale, checklist, or questionnaire. In groups completing the form	Other groups, e.g., media, assign grades	Objectives may be specific or broad	Sometimes includes a financial incentive	May use specific administrator duties or broader job responsibilities	Board may collect some of the data; may include aggregation guidelines	Tests vary; they may be state mandated, norm-referenced, or criterion-referenced	In evidence considered and how it is collected; accrediting body may be a regional or state organization
PURPOSES	Formative and summative	Formative and summative	Mainly formative	Mainly summative	Formative and summative	Summative	Formative and summative	Mainly summative	Formative and summative	Formative and summative	Summative	Summative
CUT SCORES/ STANDARDS	Unspecified	Unspecified	Unspecified	May be specified	Descriptive (e.g., "unsatisfactory") or numerical ratings	Unspecified	May be specified	Specified in the contract	May be specified	Usually unspecified	Norms may be used	Externally defined

Figure 1 (continued)

ORIENTATION	Global Judgment				Judgment Driven by Specified Criteria					Judgment Driven by Data		
	1	2	3	4	5	6	7	8	9	10	11	12
MODEL	Board Judgment	Descriptive Narrative Reports	Formative Exchanges About Performance	Stakeholder Evaluation	Printed Rating Forms	Report Cards	Management by Objectives	Performance Contracting	Duties-Based Evaluation	Superintendent Portfolio	Student Outcomes Measures	School and District Accreditation
DATA COLLECTION	Board members as participant observers	Board members as participant observers	Board members as participant observers	Varied, may include letters, questionnaires, rating forms, focus groups	Completion of the form by participant observers	Not always focused Observation/ review of records and test scores	Board members as interviewers and observers	Observation/ review of records and test scores	Observation, accountability reports, or data review	Portfolio compiled by superintendent and possibly board	Student tests and other outcome information	Self-study and site visits
REPORTING	Executive session; oral and written	Written report in executive session	Periodic discussions, usually in executive session	Oral or written, first in executive session followed by public report	Written report; public or private	May be in executive session or given to the media	Oral and/or written; usually in executive session	Oral and/or written; usually in executive session	Oral and/or written; often in executive session	Discussion in executive session	Interpretation of test scores; usually in executive session	Executive discussion of a public report
GENERAL TIMETABLE	Usually once a year; may be more often	Usually once a year	Periodic or as needs arise	Not more than once a year	Usually once a year	Usually once a year	Quarterly	Usually once a year	Usually once a year; can be more often	Usually mid-year and end of year	Usually once a year	Whenever accreditation report is due, e.g., every 5 years
EVALUATOR/ PARTICIPANTS	Board members	Board members and superintendent	Board members and superintendent	Board members and stakeholders, sometimes external evaluators	Board members and possibly other stakeholders	Board members; sometimes media or others	Board members and sometimes an outside evaluator	Board members and possibly other stakeholders	Board members and sometimes outside evaluators	Board members and superintendent with input from other stakeholders	Board members	District and accrediting personnel

Figure 2
SUPERINTENDENT PERFORMANCE EVALUATION
Main Strengths and Weaknesses of Alternate Models

ORIENTATION	Global Judgment				Judgment Driven by Specified Criteria					Judgment Driven by Data		
	1	2	3	4	5	6	7	8	9	10	11	12
MODEL	Board Judgment	Descriptive Narrative Reports	Formative Exchanges About Performance	Stakeholder Evaluation	Printed Rating Forms	Report Cards	Management by Objectives	Performance Contracting	Duties-Based Evaluation	Superintendent Portfolio	Student Outcome Measures	School and District Accreditation
MAIN STRENGTHS	Easy and inexpensive to use Ensures regular evaluation using board-approved procedures Grounded in direct board/superintendent exchange Provides scope to consider a wide range of criteria tied to district priorities Involves multiple judgments as a basis for making the summative evaluation	Inexpensive and easy to implement Ensures regular evaluation using board-approved procedures Encourages board reflection and a carefully considered evaluation Provides scope to consider wide-ranging criteria tied to district priorities Board and superintendent interact formally at least annually and directly Evaluation is flexible and responsive to district priorities and needs	Easy and inexpensive to implement Ensures frequent evaluation using board-approved procedures Much scope to consider a range of locally relevant criteria and to respond to changing district circumstances Provides continuous, formative feedback Board and superintendent interact formally, frequently, and directly about adequacy of the superintendent's performance	Regular evaluation using board-approved procedures Involvement of stakeholders in the evaluation process Provisions for collecting data from a variety of sources Encourages participation of the broader community in evaluation of the superintendent	Ensures regular evaluation by the district's top policy body Easy and inexpensive to implement Criteria are specified and applied consistently by all evaluators Provides for cross-checks of ratings and addressing conflicts of interest Well-developed forms ensure a comprehensive evaluation	Permits great flexibility in determining the criteria to be used Provides a familiar format for communicating evaluation results to the community Easy and inexpensive to implement Involvement of others may ensure fair treatment of the superintendent Provision for the superintendent and board to agree on criteria before the evaluation	Ensures regular evaluation using board-approved procedures Performance criteria/objectives are specified and periodically reviewed Recognition of and planning for current district priorities A more objective approach Easy to implement	Ensures regular evaluation using board- and superintendent-approved procedures Criteria are specified, and there is scope to incorporate district priorities There is a legal avenue for appeal Is cost-efficient and flexible enough to meet local conditions	Ensures regular evaluation using board-approved procedures Easy and not too costly to implement Includes ethical considerations A well-defined duties list will ensure a comprehensive evaluation Criteria for the evaluation are specified based on agreed-upon duties Facilitates clarification of superintendent and board roles Provision for collecting data from a variety of sources	Assures regular evaluation using board- and superintendent-approved procedures Helps delineate board/superintendent roles Data sources are clear, multiple and auditable Use of data reduces bias and conflicts of interest Flexibility to include (and review regularly) wide-ranging criteria tied to district needs Includes provision for stakeholders input	Assures regular evaluation using board-approved methods Use of learning measures reduces risk of bias and conflict of interest Reasonably inexpensive to implement Focuses the work of the superintendent on student achievement	Regular evaluation by an external organization, which may lend credibility Ensures that students receive a minimally acceptable level of education Requires minimal staff, superintendent, and board time May yield other information that is important to the district Data sources are clear May help district to set goals and priorities

Figure 2 (continued)

ORIENTATION	Global Judgment				Judgment Driven by Specified Criteria					Judgment Driven by Data		
	1	2	3	4	5	6	7	8	9	10	11	12
MODEL	Board Judgment	Descriptive Narrative Reports	Formative Exchanges About Performance	Stakeholder Evaluation	Printed Rating Forms	Report Cards	Management by Objectives	Performance Contracting	Duties-Based Evaluation	Superintendent Portfolio	Student Outcome Measures	School and District Accreditation
MAIN WEAKNESSES	Lack of prespecified evaluation criteria, procedures, and data Prone to bias and conflict of interest No procedures for resolving disputes among board members No provision for appeals or review and improvement of evaluation procedures Lack of involvement of other stakeholders	Lack of prespecified criteria, procedures, and data Prone to bias and conflict of interest No provision for appeals or review of evaluation procedures No explicit involvement of stakeholders	Lack of specified criteria, procedures, and data Prone to bias and conflict of interest No mechanisms for appeals and review of evaluation procedures No explicit involvement of stakeholders	Time consuming and difficult to implement No procedures for appeals and for monitoring the efficiency and effectiveness of the evaluation Criteria may be unclear and inconsistently applied May not be confined to agreed-upon performance criteria No explicit procedure for including student learning as a basis for evaluating the superintendent	Little involvement of stakeholders Criteria may be out-of-date, superficial, or inadequately keyed to job requirements Lack of auditable data No provision for appeals or review of evaluation procedures and forms Unlikely to provide continuous feedback for improving superintendent performance Printed form may emphasize general responsibilities to the exclusion of specific responsibilities (or vice versa)	Criteria may be inadequately linked to job requirements No provision for appeals or review of evaluation procedures Lack of auditable data No systematic involvement of stakeholders Prone to bias and conflict of interest No provision for multiple sources of information	Performance objectives may be poorly defined or neglect important issues or duties No involvement of stakeholders No procedures for appeals or data audits The model may or may not consider work environment	Performance objectives may neglect important job responsibilities Unintended outcomes, e.g. unethical behavior, and a narrowing of the curriculum Unresponsive to changing district circumstances and unexpected situations No involvement of stakeholders No provision for review of evaluation procedures May not consider the work environment	No provision for appeals and review of evaluation procedures Duties may be superficial and not keyed to district needs May or may not consider the work environment Inadequate guidelines for involving stakeholders and collecting auditable data	Can be time-consuming and administratively difficult to implement Lacks provision for appeals and periodic review of evaluation procedures May not be confined to identified and agreed-upon professional responsibilities	No provision for appeals or review of evaluation procedures and achievement tests No involvement of stakeholders Student outcomes are but one aspect of job responsibilities Student data may not provide a full range of performance duties Controlling for student background factors is difficult to achieve Unfair to judge the superintendent on factors not directly under her/his control	Superintendent evaluation may not be a major part of accreditation Lack of local control may lead to subordination of district priorities Accreditation criteria may be inadequately linked to job requirements No provision for appeals and data audit Little involvement of stakeholders Minimal involvement of board and superintendent May not be cost-effective

References

Joint Committee on Standards for Educational Evaluation.   (1988).   *The personnel evaluation standards*. Newbury Park, CA: Sage.

7 AN EMERGING MODEL FOR SUPERINTENDENT EVALUATION

This section presents the initial development of a new and improved model for the performance evaluation of the superintendent. The model recognizes the many facets of the superintendent's performance and attempts to provide for evaluating the superintendent's total performance.

The first part of Section 7 develops a theoretical model for consideration by explaining each piece of the proposed model and then incorporating these parts into a complete model. The second part of Section 7 presents a calendar for implementing the model with appropriate consideration for changes that are the result of state law and/or individual superintendent contracts. The third part of Section 7 offers some concluding comments and suggests uses for the evaluation model. In addition, a request for feedback is included.

It should be emphasized that we are not proposing a monolithic or rigid model of evaluation, but rather a flexible model that will permit a constellation of variations based on the context in which it is applied. Evaluations based on the model will take on different forms in different districts and in different years, depending on district circumstances, priorities, constraints, etc. Certainly, for instance, state performance mandates could significantly change or modify performance expectations and thus evaluation accountabilities. However, such externally imposed criteria can be accommodated in the proposed model. It does not specify, for all situations, which particular superintendent duties should be chosen for formal accountability.

In addition, the model is not intended to be viewed in a vacuum. Superintendent evaluation is part of the larger system of evaluation of all district personnel and programs and should be understood and implemented within this broader context.

Draft of an Improved Model

The preceding sections were designed to provide a firm foundation for developing a new superintendent performance evaluation model. They also provide a glimpse of the extreme complexity of the superintendent's job and the difficulties of evaluating superintendent performance in an accurate, fair, useful, and feasible manner. One implication of these complexities and difficulties is that board members might well require training in evaluation tasks. Many state school board associations, as well as the National School Boards Association, are initiating these developmental efforts. Gaining the necessary skills with which to properly and fairly perform superintendent evaluation will require of boards a commitment of time, energy, and human resources. In addition, many boards, recognizing the necessary commitment of time and other resources needed for adequate evaluation, will choose to employ, as a consultant, a trained external evaluator to assist them in this important enterprise.

While the need for better superintendent performance evaluation models is clear and while there are useful leads for model development, there is inadequate direction for integrating the concepts, standards, procedures, and constraints into a defensible model. The goal of this section is to make just such an integration and, thus, to outline a new and better model. Full development and validation of the desired new model for superintendent performance evaluation must await substantive reactions to this book and the subjection of the model to subsequent reworking, review, field testing, and revision of the subject model.

The model outlined in this section is designed to

a.   meet the requirements of *The Personnel Evaluation Standards* (Joint Committee on Standards for Educational Evaluation, 1988)
b.   build on the strengths of extant superintendent performance evaluation models and avoid their weaknesses
c.   embody and focus on the generic duties of the school district superintendent
d.   integrate established concepts of educational evaluation theory, including the basic purpose of evaluations (to assess merit and/or worth), the generic process of evaluation (delineating, obtaining, providing, and applying information), the main classes of information to be collected (context, inputs, processes, and products), and the main roles of evaluation (formative input for improvement and summative assessment for accountability)

A number of charts are used in this section to help the reader view the proposed model and underlying theory from a number of different perspectives, while sustaining the main message.

Tasks in the Evaluation Process

Figure 7-1 presents the general tasks involved in assessing the merit and worth of superintendent performance: **delineating, obtaining, providing,** and **applying** pertinent information. The school board that masters these task areas is doing a thorough and systematic job of superintendent performance evaluation, in a manner that should be valuable to the district, the board, the superintendent, and other right-to-know parties. To give some perspective to the entire process of developing the evaluation plan, it is useful to think of the task areas as the major responsibilities in creating an evaluation design with a variety of tasks included in each task area.

The **delineating** tasks provide the crucial foundation for the evaluation process. Here the board, in communication with the superintendent, clarifies the superintendent's duties and the basic ground rules for the evaluation. Decisions are made and recorded concerning such matters as whether the evaluation will address only merit or also worth, what audiences will have access to what evaluation results

Figure 7-1.   GENERAL   AND   SPECIFIC   TASKS   IN   EVALUATING
              SUPERINTENDENT PERFORMANCE

Delineate:

--Evaluation Uses and Users
--Accountabilities (Duties,
    Competencies)
--Indicators
--Weights
--Data Sources
--Performance Standards

Obtain Information on:

--District Context
--District & Superintendent
    Inputs
--District & Superintendent
    Process
--District & Superintendent
    Products

Apply:

--Professional Development
--Personnel Decisions
--District Improvement
--Public Accountability

Provide:

--Formative Feedback
--Summative Report

for what purposes, what superintendent accountabilities will undergird the collection of assessment information, how the different accountabilities will be weighted for importance, and what standards will be used to reach conclusions about merit and/or worth of the superintendent's performance. Evaluators should realize the importance of building in the capacity to recycle and modify the evaluation design as conditions change in a particular situation. In making these decisions, the board and superintendent will pay particular heed to the superintendent's contract and job description, the results of previous evaluations of the superintendent, current assignments given to the superintendent by the board and, especially, pertinent data on school system performance and needs, among other sources. The board and superintendent need to engage in productive communication and to make a written record of their agreements in order to prepare for the ensuing stages of the evaluation process.

The **obtaining** tasks include collecting, organizing, validating, and analyzing the needed information. In general, information is gathered about the district context (e.g., needs assessment data, including last year's student achievement, attendance, and graduation data), district and superintendent inputs (e.g., the district's strategic plan and budget and the superintendent's work plan), district and superintendent process (e.g., activity reports, financial data, and stakeholder judgments), and district and superintendent products (e.g., this year's student achievement and related data, special project outcomes, the superintendent's evaluations of district staff, and unexpected outcomes of superintendent activities).

Beyond these general classes of information, data should be collected in response to the specific information requirements determined in the delineating tasks. Both general and specific information should be organized to respond to the key evaluation questions determined in the delineating tasks, then analyzed in accordance with the given weights for different parts of the information and the rules for reaching judgments about merit and/or worth.

The **providing** tasks involve reporting the information obtained to the intended users in ways to best serve intended uses. These tasks may include a modicum of formative feedback from the board to the superintendent to provide guidance during the school year and are mainly concerned with products. However, the board should minimize this type of feedback lest it infringe on the day-to-day administrative authority delegated by the board to the superintendent. The providing tasks also include the compilation of 1 or more summative evaluation reports to serve accountability and decision-making purposes, and possibly to provide direction for the superintendent's professional improvement.

Basically, the board is the providing agent in the evaluation of superintendent performance. The board delivers information to the superintendent and, in accordance with prior decisions reached in the delineating stage, may also report to the press and the community. Formative evaluation reports are often oral and given only to the superintendent, while summative evaluation reports must be in writing, must address issues of merit and/or worth, and may be released at some level of detail to the public. Depending on prior decisions about intended uses and users, certain reports will be confidential and discussed in executive session, while others will be public. These are decisions to be made in advance and communicated, so that in reporting there will be no basis for dispute as to which audience should receive which report.

The **applying** tasks concern the uses of evaluation reports. These tasks are differentiated from the providing tasks in order to underscore the importance of assuring that evaluation findings are used in meaningful ways and not just collected and reported. Particular intended uses and users will have been determined in the delineating tasks. In general, boards and superintendents should plan to use reports to guide the superintendent's professional development, reach employment decisions (e.g., on salary, modification of assigned duties, continuation/termination), and as input for planning district improvement efforts (e.g., reorganization of the central office, employment of specialized personnel, and curriculum revision). The board should also consider how it can help other users to understand and apply reports (e.g., the press and community as they attempt to gain a better understanding of the superintendent's past performance and vision for improving the district).

Grounding Evaluation in Communication

The evaluation model described above relies heavily on sound communication. It is in the best interests of the board, superintendent, and members of the school community to develop an evaluation system that considers input from stakeholders, to maintain common understanding of the superintendent evaluation system among stakeholders, and to earn widespread respect for the evaluation system's integrity and value to the district. In order to make the evaluation system function effectively, it is also important to ground the process in effective ongoing communication between the board and the superintendent.

Communication to Help Develop or Improve the Evaluation System. The topic of evaluation makes many people nervous. Often they do not understand what is involved; view the process as highly subjective, secretive, and potentially corrupt; and/or see it as only a ritual with little or no value. Even the most rigorously designed and carefully executed evaluation system can engender such concerns if the stakeholders are not involved in setting up and periodically improving the evaluation system and if they are not kept informed about its purpose, structure, operations, findings, impacts, and quality.

When the board and superintendent decide either to develop a new superintendent evaluation system or to review and revise the present system, they should provide concrete opportunities for stakeholders to keep informed about the work and to provide input. For example, they might conduct announced meetings to hear and discuss input from interested parties.

It may strike some as unusual to single out the superintendent's evaluation system for public scrutiny when this is not done for other public employees. However, we argue that when a position so vital to the welfare of the community's children is being assessed, parents and community members have a right to be consulted.

Also, the district might engage a standing representative accountability commission, as recently seen in Dallas, Texas, and Lincoln, Nebraska, to provide systematic review and advisory assistance to the evaluation effort. Advisory commission membership might include parents, teachers, students, administrators, board members, and community representatives. Such persons can help to insure that views from a representative group of stakeholders are considered in designing and/or improving the evaluation system. The members of the accountability commission can also be asked to help explain the evaluation system to other stakeholders. This recommendation may have value beyond superintendent performance evaluation. An effective accountability commission might provide useful advisory and liaison services related to the district's other systems that evaluate student performance, programs, and teaching performance.

After the evaluation system is developed or refined, the board needs to achieve widespread understanding and respect for the system, beyond the persons who were involved in its development. The board should periodically inform the school district staff and community in a printed description of the criteria and procedures used to evaluate superintendent performance. In these releases the board should encourage, provide opportunities for, and give assurance that it will use input from stakeholders on how to improve the system. Accordingly, the board should maintain clear, accessible, and regular channels for receiving and using input from stakeholders. The board should keep the local press correctly informed about the nature of the superintendent performance evaluation system, so that newspaper and other media accounts of superintendent evaluation are based on accurate information.

Communication Required to Implement the Evaluation System. In addition to the communication needed to set up, periodically improve, and explain the superintendent evaluation system, there is also a need for productive communication within each evaluation cycle. Communication between the superintendent and board is the essence of the delineating stage in which they determine the evaluation questions, criteria, weights, and variables that will guide the collection, reporting, and use of information. Communication is also an essential part of the providing stage, in which the board presents both formative and summative feedback to the superintendent and sometimes summative reports to the diverse group of school district staff and constituents. Communication is also involved in the applying stage, especially when the board works out a relevant professional improvement plan for the superintendent and/or works with her/him to use the evaluation results to modify school district plans for the coming year.

The board should define, with the superintendent's participation, what information from the superintendent evaluation is appropriate for public release and what information should be kept confidential. Then the board should make sure that the appropriate information is obtained, verified for accuracy, and released only as prescribed by policy and formal agreements.

Clearly, the board and superintendent must engage in an ongoing process of effective communication if evaluations are to be keyed to important questions, to help the board and superintendent to work well together, and to be effective in bringing about improvements in the performance of the superintendent and district. As much as possible, the proposed model is designed to functionally integrate the performance evaluation process into the regular schedule of meetings between the board and superintendent.

Keying Evaluation to the Duties of the Superintendency

Just as superintendent performance evaluations should be grounded in effective communication, they should also be grounded in sound conceptualizations of superintendent duties. At a general level, these are the responsibilities--recognized in the U.S. society, in the local community, by the state education department, and by the pertinent educational professions--that superintendents have to fulfill in serving their communities and school districts. At a specific level, they are the particular leadership responsibilities required for addressing district/student needs and for preparing and implementing sound strategic plans. In the duties-based approach to evaluation, the board should assess the superintendent's fulfillment of the generic professional duties of all superintendents and the specific responsibilities in the particular superintendency.

In order to make the proposed model as useful as possible, this section recommends that boards adopt a particular set of general superintendent duties to undergird evaluations of superintendent performance. The duties presented in this section were determined through a careful integration of the duties identified in a study of administrator responsibilities in Texas school districts and the recently released AASA professional standards, which define a list of competencies for the superintendency. Both of these developments were reviewed in Section 3 of this publication. Figure 7-2 provides a matrix of these two lists. The broad duties of the superintendent form the rows of the matrix, and the general AASA superintendent competencies form the columns. The points of intersection indicate commonalities between the two lists and suggest what particular superintendent competencies are needed in fulfilling given duties.

The recommended set of superintendent duties is presented below in two levels under the heading "Proposed General and Illustrative Specific Duties of Superintendents." The first level includes duties recommended for adoption by boards as the general responsibilities of the superintendent. The second level is presented as an illustrative list of additional specific duties from which the board might choose and adapt the specific duties to be considered in a particular year's evaluation. This list is an improved version of the list of duties presented in Section 3.

Figure 7-2. MATRIX OF SUPERINTENDENT RESPONSIBILITIES

SUPERINTENDENT COMPETENCIES (AASA)

SUPERINTENDENT DUTIES (Texas)	1. Leadership and District Culture	2. Policy and Governance	3. Communications and Community Relations	4. Organizational Management	5. Curriculum Planning and Development	6. Instructional Management	7. Human Resource Management	8. Values and Ethics of Leadership
1. Foster Student Growth and Development	X	X	X	X			X	
2. Foster Equality of Opportunity	X	X	X	X	X	X	X	X
3. Foster a Positive School Climate	X		X	X			X	X
4. Lead School Improvement	X	X	X	X	X			
5. Foster Improvement of Classroom Instruction	X					X	X	
6. Lead and Manage Personnel		X		X			X	
7. Manage District Resources		X		X			X	X
8. Assure/Provide a Safe, Orderly Environment	X	X	X	X				X
9. Foster Effective School-Community Relations	X	X	X					X
10. Engage in Professional Development	X	X	X	X	X			X
11. Relate Effectively to the Board	X	X	X	X				X

Proposed General and Illustrative Specific Duties of Superintendents

1.   Promote and support **student growth and development**.

   1.1   Assess and report on student achievement, attendance, and graduation rate.
   1.2   Provide leadership for annually assessing and setting priorities on student and district needs.
   1.3   Evaluate and provide direction for improving school/district offerings.
   1.4   Motivate and assist students to develop a sense of self-worth.
   1.5   Provide leadership for improving parent involvement in the schools.
   1.6   Set priorities in the context of assessed student needs.

2.   Honor diversity and promote **equality of opportunity**.

   2.1   Recruit qualified minority and majority staff.
   2.2   Examine, communicate, and address gaps in achievement of different groups of students.
   2.3   Provide leadership necessary to fully integrate schools and programs.
   2.4   Serve as an articulate spokesperson for the welfare of all students in a multicultural context.
   2.5   Respect diversity of religion, ethnicity, and cultural values in students, staff, and programs.
   2.6   Insure equitable distribution of district resources.

3.   Foster a positive **school climate.**

   3.1   Assess and provide leadership for improving environments in and around each district school.
   3.2   Conduct school climate assessments.
   3.3   Articulate and disseminate high expectations for student learning and teaching quality.
   3.4   Promote a positive climate for learning and an atmosphere of acceptance for all students willing to participate in an orderly process of learning; do not tolerate chronic disruptive and/or criminal behavior from students.
   3.5   Promote, demonstrate, and support clear 2-way communication at all levels of the district.
   3.6   Promote academic rigor and excellence for staff and students.
   3.7   Encourage and foster self-esteem in staff and students.
   3.8   Manifest multicultural and ethnic understanding.
   3.9   Assess individual and institutional sources of stress and apply methods for reducing stress.

4.   Provide leadership in **school improvement** efforts.

    4.1   Develop, communicate, and implement a collective vision of school improvement.
    4.2   Encourage, model, and support creativity and appropriate risk taking.
    4.3   Provide direction and support for periodic review of curriculum and school policies and procedures.
    4.4   Formulate strategic plans, goals, and change efforts with staff and community.
    4.5   Formulate procedures for gathering, analyzing, and using district data for decision making.

5.   Stimulate, focus, and support **improvement of classroom instruction**.

    5.1   Provide encouragement, opportunities, and structure for teachers to design better learning experiences for students.
    5.2   Evaluate and provide direction for improving classroom instruction.
    5.3   Develop and offer opportunities that respond to teachers' needs for professional development.
    5.4   Encourage and facilitate the use of new technology to improve teaching and learning.

6.   Lead and manage **personnel** effectively.

    6.1   Define and delegate administrative authority and responsibility effectively.
    6.2   Evaluate performance of subordinates and take appropriate follow-up actions.
    6.3   Recognize and reward exemplary performance of subordinates.
    6.4   Encourage and support personal and professional growth among staff.
    6.5   Comply with applicable personnel policies and rules.
    6.6   Recruit and select competent district personnel.

7.   Manage **administrative, fiscal, and facilities functions** effectively.

    7.1   Obtain competent fiscal/financial analysis.
    7.2   Keep informed of funding sources.
    7.3   Prepare appropriate budgets and cost estimates.
    7.4   Manage the district budget.
    7.5   Create and implement an internal/external audit system.
    7.6   Maintain accurate fiscal records.
    7.7   Ensure that facilities are maintained and upgraded as necessary.
    7.8   Manage attendance, accounting, payroll, transportation.
    7.9   Manage personal and district time effectively.

7.10 Conduct sound evaluation to guide decisions, e.g., in selecting office equipment and planning building construction or fund-raising campaigns.

7.11 Identify and evaluate alternative employee benefits packages.

7.12 Effectively apply the legal requirements for personnel selection, development, retention, and dismissal.

8. Assure/provide a **safe, orderly environment**.

8.1 Develop and communicate guidelines for student conduct.

8.2 Ensure that rules are uniformly observed and enforced.

8.3 Discipline students for misconduct in an effective and fair manner.

8.4 Promote a collaborative approach to discipline, involving staff, students, and parents.

9. Foster effective **school-community relations**.

9.1 Formulate and implement plans for internal and external communication, including communication of the school district mission, student and district needs, and district priorities to the community and mass media.

9.2 Write and speak clearly and influentially in order to recruit community support for school programs.

9.3 Involve parents and other community members in serving school programs.

9.4 Provide service to the community and leadership for developing rapport between the schools and the community.

9.5 Obtain and respond to community feedback.

9.6 Implement consensus building and conflict mediation.

9.7 Align constituencies and build coalitions to support district needs and priorities and to gain financial and programmatic support.

9.8 Maintain constructive communication with employee organizations, including but not restricted to unions.

9.9 Understand and be able to communicate with all cultural groups in the community.

9.10 Institute, nurture, and improve the district's cooperative relationships with other districts, intermediate education units, the state education department, federal education agencies, etc., including sharing scarce resources, facilitating student transfers, conducting staff development, and obtaining grants.

9.11 Apply formal and informal techniques to assess external perception of the district by means of surveys, advisory groups, and personal contact.

9.12 Form alliances with other groups concerned with the welfare of children and youth, e.g., the police and fire departments and the juvenile courts.

9.13 Be knowledgeable about the community, including its history, culture, resources, and services.

9.14 Identify and analyze the political forces in the community.

9.15 Design effective strategies for passing referenda.

9.16 Successfully mediate conflicts related to the district.

9.17 Respond in an ethical and skillful way to the electronic and printed news media.

9.18 Involve stakeholders in educational decisions affecting them.

9.19 Exhibit environmental awareness and be proactive in such efforts as recycling and preserving natural resources.

10.   Embody and promote **professionalism**.

10.1 Participate in professional education organizations, e.g., AASA, AERA, ASCD.

10.2 Conduct oneself in an ethical and professional manner.

10.3 Stay abreast of professional issues and developments in education.

10.4 Disseminate professional ideas and new developments to other professionals.

10.5 Know and employ appropriate evaluation and assessment techniques, e.g., performance assessment, standardized testing, and educational statistics.

10.6 Obtain and use evaluation information as a basis for improving performance; conduct a systematic annual self-evaluation, seeking and responding to criticism of performance.

10.7 Maintain an understanding of international issues affecting education.

10.8 Maintain personal, physical, and emotional health.

11.   Relate effectively to the **school board**.

11.1 Meet the board's needs for information about district performance.

11.2 Interact with the board in an ethical, sensitive, and professional manner.

11.3 Communicate clearly and substantively to the board.

11.4 Educate the board about professional education issues and approaches.

11.5 Recommend policies to improve student learning and district performance.

11.6 Provide leadership to the board for defining superintendent and board roles, mutual expectations, procedures for working together, and strategies for formulating district policies.

11.7 Recognize and apply standards involving civil and criminal liabilities, and develop a checklist of procedures to avoid civil and criminal liabilities.

11.8 Recommend district policy in consideration of state and federal requirements.

11.9 Draft a district policy for external and internal programs.

The next section moves from consideration of what duties should be assessed when examining superintendent performance to consideration of what information will be required to assign particular responsibilities and assess their fulfillment.

General Framework to Guide Collection and Use of Information for Evaluating Superintendent Performance

In the development of a general framework on which to base the evaluation of the superintendent, the authors considered a variety of data and needs. First, it seemed to the authors that an evaluation of the performance of the school superintendent must include several elements in order to make it a viable evaluation. It became apparent that among the common threads to be included in any model development were such elements as the communications between the evaluator and the evaluatee as well as the generic personnel evaluation standards developed by the Joint Committee on Standards for Educational Evaluation.

Second, it became important to relate the evaluation of the superintendent to the evaluation of the district since he/she is the chief executive officer of the organization and cannot escape the responsibility for the performance of the entire organization. Therefore, the evaluation of the superintendent is carried out on 2 levels, with the evaluation of the organization providing the important baseline data with which to evaluate the superintendent. This includes the district and campus plans, test and other student evaluative data, which are recycled as needed to provide current data for the evaluation, as well as such parameter-establishing information as board policies and state statutes.

Third, with the careful examination of the district and campus data, a well-grounded itemization of student and system needs can be developed. This is the basis for establishing the "accountabilities" for which the superintendent is responsible during the current evaluation cycle. In addition, the generic duties of the position, supplemented by the particular and unique duties added through board/superintendent agreement, are to be considered in the evaluation.

The general categories of context, input, process, and product evaluation can assist the board to obtain both the general year-to-year comparison information and the specific information needed in given years. These concepts are discussed here in terms of pertinent questions relating to superintendent assignments and performance, and the information needed to answer these questions.

Context evaluation provides information on system and student needs, system problems, opportunities that the district might use to improve programs and other aspects of the district, and assessments of school district goals and objectives. This information is useful for determining job and school district targets early in the school year, for examining the significance of accomplishments near the end of the school year, and for placing the year-end assessment of effectiveness within the proper context of constraints that may have impeded achievement plus opportunities that did or could have enhanced accomplishments.

At the beginning of the evaluation year, the board and superintendent need to examine whether or not the superintendent's previously assigned responsibilities and job targets are focused sufficiently on addressing the school district's current and projected leadership needs and problems. Data on needs, opportunities, and problems in the district should be employed early in the year to help the superintendent appropriately update responsibilities and job targets. These same data will be useful later in the year for contrasting data on accomplishments (product evaluation) with the previously identified needs.

For both early target setting and later examination of the significance of accomplishments, the board and superintendent should review available district data, which might include any or all of the following:

- Student achievement data disaggregated by grade, content area, and race, and contrasted to previous years and to results from similar school districts
- Student attendance
- Student graduation rate
- Incidents of crime in the schools
- Records of student immunization
- Up-to-date data on diversity and extent of integration of the student body and school district staff
- Survey results on school climate from each school
- Report on the dispersion of ratings of effectiveness of teachers and other categories of school staff
- Records of complaints about the district received in previous years
- Difficulties as indicated in most recent school principal reports

Near the end of the school year the board and superintendent should review these same context evaluation data plus information on environmental constraints on what the district and superintendent could accomplish. This helps them to see the superintendent's accomplishments (product evaluation) in the appropriate context: e.g., were the accomplishments significant in comparison to previously identified district needs and priorities, and were they basically what could be expected in light of budgetary and other constraints?

The following examples are among the context data on constraints and opportunities to be reviewed in interpreting product evaluation results:

- Student mobility rate in each school for each of the past 3 years
- Percent of school district families below the poverty line
- Percent of free and reduced lunches, disaggregated by school
- The district's per pupil expenditure compared to that of similar districts in the region
- Crime rate statistics, disaggregated by school attendance area
- Data/editorials on school attitudes toward the district
- Community's record in passing school funding issues over the past 5 years
- Data on teen pregnancies for each of the past 3 years
- Data on low birth weight babies disaggregated for each of the last 10 years
- Percentage of single parent families, by school

Quite obviously, school districts vary widely on the environmental factors listed above. Depending on their status on these and related factors, some districts have a much easier time than others in raising achievement levels. It is reasonable and fair for districts to at least consider what environmental conditions affected the performance of the superintendent and district. Ideally, districts could do this systematically by statistically removing the influence of background variables from the year-to-year gains in student achievement data, as is being conducted on a statewide basis in Tennessee (Sanders & Horn, 1993; 1994). However, until all the states reach this level of sophistication in collecting and analyzing school district data, school boards should at least perform a "clinical" analysis of background environmental information in order to reach reasoned and properly cautious judgments of the accomplishments of the superintendent and school district.

Input evaluations provide information and judgments concerning district budgets, strategic plans, personnel assignments, calendars of events, and superintendent work plans, as well as information on potentially relevant educational and administrative strategies used elsewhere or recommended in the literature. This information is instrumental early in the fiscal year for developing a clear understanding between the board and superintendent of the plans for the coming year. The information is also useful for clarifying and otherwise improving the district's long-range strategic plan and the superintendent's annual work plan. Input evaluations can also be useful late in the year when the board may need to decide whether shortfalls in district and/or superintendent performance are due to inadequate planning.

The main information that is designed to guide planning activities includes the following:

1. Plans from previous years

   1.1 District strategic plans
   1.2 Superintendent work plans
   1.3 Board and superintendent assessments of implementation and results of plans from previous years

2. Financial information from previous years

   2.1 District budgets
   2.2 Audited financial reports
   2.3 Board and superintendent assessments of the adequacy of budgets in previous years

3. Plans for the present year

   3.1 Overall district plan
   3.2 Specific plans keyed to priority needs and problems
   3.3 Campus plans
   3.4 School district calendar for the year
   3.5 Superintendent work plan and schedule of main events

3.6   Board agenda for the year
3.7   Independent evaluations of the planning documents

4. Reports on effective practices in other districts

4.1   Example strategic plans, budgets, and year-long calendars from similar districts with reputations for excellence
4.2   Evaluation reports from projects that addressed problems being faced in the present district
4.3   Reviews of literature on educational and administrative strategies that might be adopted by the district

5. Approach to planning in the district

5.1   Description of the district's approach to strategic planning
5.2   Records of the involvement of stakeholders in the planning process
5.3   Evaluation reports on the district's planning process

As a part of their regular communication, the board and superintendent need to review plans, budgets, accounting reports from previous years, work plans, and calendars. They should do so in the interest of assuring that plans appropriately address unmet student needs. In addition to reviewing and judging district plans, the board can be assisted by learning what plans, planning processes, and particular improvement strategies are working well in other districts. Consistent with the need to ground planning as well as evaluation in sound communication, the board should also assure that the district's planning process includes appropriate involvement of stakeholders.

The superintendent has a major and ongoing responsibility to provide the board with **process evaluation** information. Essentially, this includes documentation and progress reports on the implementation of district and superintendent plans and use of district funds and other resources. The information should also include any noteworthy modification in plans, schedules, assignments, and budgets. Much of the needed process information will be given to the board in the form of written and oral progress reports by both the superintendent and other school district staff. These reports will cover progress in carrying out special projects; updates on the development of curriculum materials, the development of funding proposals, staff recruitment, staff training, meetings with stakeholder groups, etc.; delivery of instruction and other district services; and expenditures compared to budget. The superintendent can and should expect to receive the board's evaluations of the adequacy of the reported progress during these meetings. Such process evaluations by the board can provide the superintendent and staff with direction and stimulation for appropriate problem-solving activities.

In addition to this regular exchange, superintendents are advised to maintain portfolios of up-to-date information on the implementation of plans. Such an up-to-date information source can assist the superintendent to address unexpected questions from the board. The information will be invaluable to the board when it conducts its summative evaluation of the superintendent's performance. If the superintendent defines a clear structure for the portfolio, staff can be engaged to regularly supply the needed documentation as it becomes available.

Product evaluation will be a primary concern of the board when it develops its summative evaluation report on the superintendent's performance. In addition to the process evaluation record on the extent to which targeted needs were addressed by the superintendent, the board will need evidence on the extent of improvements and shortfalls, i.e., product information. Primarily, the product evaluation indicators will be a function of the previously identified priority needs. For example, were improvements seen in such targeted need areas as those listed below:

1. Teacher attendance
2. Involvement of stakeholders in the district's planning process
3. Racial balance of staff across the schools
4. Maintenance of school buildings
5. Constructive coverage of the district's programs by the media
6. Measures of school climate across the district
7. Dropout rate
8. Percentage of students having needed immunizations
9. Achievement test scores of all students, disaggregated by sex, race, and socioeconomic status
10. Student attendance, disaggregated by sex, race, and socioeconomic status
11. Physical fitness of students
12. Foundation and government grants and contracts
13. Replacement of science text materials

The preceding list is only illustrative. It suggests that, in any given year, the outcomes expected of a superintendent are likely to be keyed to clear directives from the board or to past disappointments, limited in number, and heavily dependent for interpretation on past measurements in both the present district and similar districts. It is likely that the board will be more interested in the direction of outcomes (improvement versus deterioration or maintenance of the status quo) than in whether or not some targeted values are met or exceeded.

Certainly, the board and superintendent may previously have set clear standards for the expected level of improvement, but such determinations at the precise cut-score level are invariably arbitrary. On the other hand, agreements between the board and superintendent that performance must improve are not arbitrary. The emphasis on reaching the summative judgment must be on whether the unmet needs were professionally and substantially addressed and whether the current year's measure was decidedly in the direction of improvement (or at least halting a previous negative trend). Also, the board will be interested in learning whether the district's performance is comparable to what is seen in similar districts known for excellent programs and achievements. Of somewhat less pertinence but nevertheless high interest to the community is how the district compares to state and national norms.

In addition to the targeted variables, product evaluations must look for positive and negative side effects or unexpected outcomes. The superintendent can determine some of this by maintaining a section on unexpected accomplishments, as well as the one on expected accomplishments in the superintendent performance portfolio. In addition, the board might conduct a hearing in which stakeholders are invited to submit evidence and judgments about the accomplishments of the school district. Such a hearing is likely to reveal both positive and negative side effects.

To supplement or as an alternative to the hearing, the board might survey different stakeholder groups, asking them to identify and assess the significance of the superintendent's accomplishments. The board could then analyze and use the judgments, along with other information, in arriving at its summative assessment of the superintendent's performance.

When feasible the board and superintendent should obtain and analyze a broad scope of information pertinent to developing a summative evaluation of the superintendent's accomplishments. This could include current and past student outcomes, pertinent external comparisons and norms, previously set standards, unexpected outcomes, student body characteristics, the superintendent's activities during the year, the superintendent's accomplishments compared to generic duties and specific responsibilities, judgments of superintendent performance and accomplishments by a panel of stakeholders, and district constraints. The board could then analyze and use the judgments, along with other information, in arriving at its summative assessment of the superintendent's performance.

As the process and product evaluations are accomplished, it is important to note that these results become the baseline data to be recycled for the development of the next cycle's context evaluation.

The foregoing discussion of context, input, process, and product evaluation is summarized in Figure 7-3. For each type of evaluation, the chart identifies pertinent information to be obtained, methods for obtaining the information, and uses of the obtained information. Board presidents and superintendents may find this chart useful for informing new board members about the kind of information they should be seeking and using to evaluate superintendent performance, as well as the performance of the overall district.

Figure 7-3. FOUR TYPES OF EVALUATION

	CONTEXT EVALUATION	INPUT EVALUATION	PROCESS EVALUATION	PRODUCT EVALUATION

INFORMATION	1. Multiyear district data:
	  • test results
	  • student attendance
	  • graduation
	  • dropouts
	  • student characteristics
	  • staff characteristics
	  • staff evaluations
	  • school environment
	  • school programs
	  • student services
	  • district finances
	  • district facilities
	  • complaints
	2. Data from comparable districts
	3. Pertinent national & state norms
	4. Conclusions re needs, problems, opportunities
		1. District strategic plan
		2. Staff assignments
		3. District calendar
		4. Budget
		5. Accounting reports from prior plans
		6. Superintendent duties
		7. Superintendent salary
		8. Superintendent work plan
		9. Parent & community involvement
		10. Promising new strategies & associated evaluations
		11. Independent assessment of the district's plans, strategies, assignments, & budgets
			1. Progress reports on:
			  • special projects
			  • staffing
			  • product development
			  • delivery of instruction
			  • delivery of student services
			  • stakeholder involvement
			2. Accounting reports
			3. Exception reports, e.g., modifications in
			  • plans
			  • assignments
			  • schedules
			  • budgets
			4. Independent assessment of operations
				1. Comprehensive identification of outcomes
				2. Comparison of outcomes to
				  • assessed needs
				  • assigned duties
				  • previous trends
				  • achievements in similar districts
				  • pertinent norms
				3. Judgments of outcomes in consideration of
				  • needs
				  • opportunities
				  • problems
				  • constraints
				  • costs

METHOD	1. District data banks 2. Stakeholder panel 3. School climate surveys 4. Annual principal reports 5. Clippings file 6. Hearings 7. Quantitative & qualitative analysis	1. Strategic planning process 2. Budget planning process 3. Records of stakeholder involvement in planning 4. Site visits to other districts 5. External evaluators	1. Staff/superintendent progress reports 2. Accounting reports 3. Superintendent portfolio of activities 4. Records of stakeholder involvement in programs	1. District data bank 2. School climate surveys 3. Superintendent portfolio of accomplishments 4. Survey of stakeholders 5. Independent ratings by board members 6. Synthesis report by board president/committee

Figure 7-3. FOUR TYPES OF EVALUATION (continued)

	CONTEXT EVALUATION	INPUT EVALUATION	PROCESS EVALUATION	PRODUCT EVALUATION
USE	1. Set district priorities 2. Set superintendent job targets 3. Provide basis for judging significance of accomplishments 4. Consider district constraints in judging superintendent performance 5. Target pertinent opportunities for use in school improvement	1. Clarify board/superintendent understanding of plans, assignments, budgets 2. Improve plans, assignments, budgets 3. Involve stakeholders in planning 4. Provide clear guidance for superintendent performance	1. Keep board & community informed about implementation of plans 2. Maintain fiscal accountability 3. Provide early warning system for identifying & addressing implementation problems 4. Maintain record of implementation for use in interpreting outcomes	1. Help board assess merit and/or worth of superintendent's accomplishments 2. Help board develop outcome-based decisions on superintendent's • salary • continuation • professional development plan 3. Help board be accountable to community for oversight of superintendent's accomplishments

Putting the Pieces Together

Figure 7-4 provides an overview of the evaluation model outlined in this chapter, configured to suggest the broader context of overall district assessment and evaluation. This flow model uses shaded rectangles to denote the main task areas and unshaded boxes to denote the more specific tasks in the evaluation process. The arrows indicate influential relationships and their direction(s). Some are 1-way, as in the influence of district-level context and inputs information on determining the superintendent's accountabilities; others are reciprocal, as in the contribution from district-level evaluations to the information required for superintendent evaluation and vice versa.

The rectangle to the left includes the driving forces required in any evaluation. These are communication between evaluator and evaluatee and, as appropriate, with district personnel and constituents, plus adherence to the professional standards of sound evaluation. These forces are intended to drive all aspects of the evaluation process.

The large rectangle encompassing the superintendent evaluation activities denotes the larger system of school district evaluation. The top part of this rectangle includes district-level context and input evaluation. The context evaluation variables, as seen in individual unshaded boxes, include needs, community climate, public expectations, and statutes and policies from which are developed the inputs seen in the remainder of the unshaded boxes. These inputs include plans, budgets, and specified superintendent duties. This district-level information, denoted in the Context and inputs part of the large shaded rectangle, provides an assessment of the district's needs, opportunities, plans, problems, and constraints, and is the basis for developing superintendent accountabilities.

The bottom part of this large rectangle denotes that district-level process and product evaluation are potential sources of information for superintendent evaluation. Those charged with carrying out the superintendent evaluation process should keep in mind that district-level evaluations are sources of information for superintendent evaluation, both for addressing main questions about superintendent performance and for interpreting performance data in light of the dynamics and constraints in the larger district.

The interior shaded rectangles of the model denote the 4 main task areas involved in superintendent evaluation: delineating accountabilities, obtaining information, and reporting and applying evaluation results. In delineating the superintendent's accountabilities, decisions are made on the following items, as noted in the boxes: uses and users of the evaluation, data sources, indicators, weights, and standards. These matters are decided in accordance with district policies and in light of district needs, plans, and budgets plus other context and input evaluation information. The generic duties common to all superintendents and the more specific superintendent duties previously defined by the school board provide the initial baseline for review and updating of superintendent duties.

Obtained information concerning the superintendent's implementation of duties and the superintendent's accomplishments feeds into both formative feedback to the superintendent during the year and to a summative report at the end of the year.

Figure 7-4

SUPERINTENDENT EVALUATION MODEL

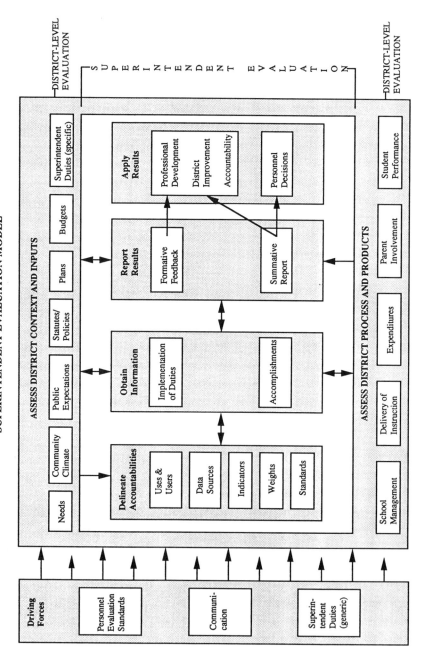

Arrows from the district-level assessment rectangle indicate that both formative and summative findings should be interpreted in light of the broader district context.

Four areas of application served by evaluation results are identified in the Apply Results rectangle. Personnel decisions require summative evaluations; the other 3 foci of application (professional development, district improvement, and accountability) can be addressed either for the purpose of improving the application area (a formative process) or for making a summative judgment or decision about it.

We emphasize that it is crucial for all of the above to be grounded in sound communications. A district accountability commission may be appointed to oversee the development and periodic review and improvement of the evaluation system. Also, the district must provide school personnel and the public with clear and up-to-date information on the structure, implementation, and results of the superintendent evaluation system. Channels should be defined and kept open so that stakeholders can have input into the improvement of the evaluation system. Finally, board/superintendent evaluative exchanges must be ongoing and functionally integrated into their regular flow of work together, especially in their regularly scheduled meetings.

Implementing the Model Within Normal School Year Calendars

Scheduling and assigning responsibilities for the evaluation tasks entails developing a work schedule that corresponds to the board's annual agenda. No one sequence and set of assignments will fit all situations. Some districts will need to start the evaluation cycle at the beginning of the fiscal year, while others will need to start it in April, at the beginning of the school year, or at some other starting point.

Also, the evaluation work must be integrated into the regular flow of superintendent-board interactions. Typically, the school board and superintendent are involved in formal, planned communications at least once a month at the regularly scheduled board of education meetings. Many school districts schedule 2 or more meetings a month, so the opportunity for superintendent-board dialogue is ample.

The following suggestions are provided as a calendar in which to conduct an adequate superintendent performance evaluation. There is no intention in these suggestions that the board should micromanage the superintendent's work. In suggesting an annual calendar of evaluation tasks, the intent is to provide a mechanism that boards can use to conduct a complete and fair performance evaluation as part of the district's normal governance/administrative calendar. In the event that state law and/or contractual arrangements require the summative evaluation of the superintendent to be completed by the end of February, the cycle would be adjusted to conform to legal or contractual requirements. In that case, the first quarter would start in April.

Superintendent/Board Interactions in the Context of an Annual Evaluation Calendar

The annual evaluation calendar can be a fiscal or any other year according to the nuances of the district. Below we list the tasks required in each quarter so that the district can adjust the evaluation calendar according to its needs. While we recognize that districts vary in the flow of board/superintendent interactions and that projected schedules are subject to interruption as unforeseen issues arise, it is nonetheless important for boards to define and schedule a sequence of evaluation tasks to be undertaken. The following is offered as an illustration and guideline of how this might be accomplished.

TASKS

QUARTER #1

- Review prior year's activities and results (especially student performance data, performance evaluations of school staff, and system needs)
- Set preliminary strategic plan
- Set general priorities; review duties
- Set preliminary superintendent objectives and work plan/duties

QUARTER #2

- Accept campus improvement plans
- Set priorities for the year/update duties
- Adjust strategic plan
- Adjust superintendent objectives and work plan as needed
- Establish superintendent evaluation design (including intended uses and users, performance indicators and weights, performance standards, data sources and procedures, and reporting schedule)

QUARTER #3

- Progress report on implementation of strategic plan and assigned superintendent duties
- Formative evaluation exchanges between board and superintendent
- Adjust superintendent priorities and tasks
- Set improvement targets

QUARTER #4

- Accountability report from the superintendent
- Gather data from community, students, schools
- Summative evaluation of superintendent
- Development of professional improvement plan if needed
- Pertinent personnel decisions

- Summary report to community
- Recycle strategic plan

Dialogue about the listed tasks should occur sometime during the quarter under which they are listed. The district's strategic plan should be adopted as early in the first quarter as possible. This provides the structure needed to develop a comprehensive and pertinent list of superintendent priorities and tasks. Also, the summative evaluation should be completed as late as is feasible in the fourth quarter, so that it can reflect a comprehensive set of data about superintendent and district performance, in the context of district needs and pertinent constraints.

Main Superintendent/Board Performance Evaluation Activities in Each Quarter

As seen in the task list, evaluation of superintendent performance is a small but important part of superintendent/board interactions during the year. It is important to integrate superintendent performance evaluation functionally into the regular flow of board/superintendent activities, so that evaluation facilitates rather than impedes collaboration.

However, for purposes of studying superintendent performance evaluation, it is useful to filter out nonevaluative activities in order to focus on the main superintendent performance evaluation activities in each quarter. Figure 7-5 is provided for this purpose. While the figure depicts a parsimonious separation of context, input, process, and product evaluation, by quarter, the intent is only to show what the main emphasis is in each quarter, not to indicate that only one kind of evaluation occurs in each quarter. In general, context and input evaluation are most important early in the year, and process and product evaluation take on prominence past midyear.

As shown in the figure, the first quarter **emphasis**, relating to superintendent evaluation is on **Context Evaluation**. The board and superintendent review the prior year's activities and results especially to identify unmet needs in both student accomplishments and district offerings. Review of context evaluation information is keyed to setting general priorities for the year and updating the district's strategic plan. Such review is useful to the board for defining the superintendent's main responsibilities and accountabilities for the year.

During the second quarter, the emphasis relating to superintendent evaluation is more on **Input Evaluation** than the other 3 types. The superintendent evaluates campus plans and provides feedback to help schools improve the plans. The board and superintendent also review and adjust the district's strategic plan in light of the assessment of campus plans. Based on the adjusted strategic plan and the previously defined superintendent responsibilities and accountabilities, the board also establishes the design and schedule for evaluating superintendent performance during the remainder of the year, including intended uses and users, questions to be addressed in formative and summative evaluation reports, and needed process and product information.

Figure 7-5. MAIN EVALUATION EMPHASIS IN EACH QUARTER

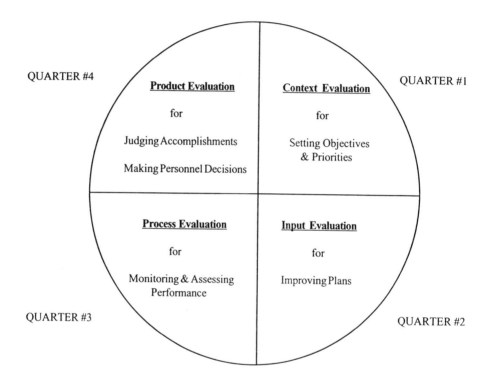

QUARTER #4

Product Evaluation

for

Judging Accomplishments

Making Personnel Decisions

Context Evaluation

for

Setting Objectives
& Priorities

QUARTER #1

Process Evaluation

for

Monitoring & Assessing
Performance

Input Evaluation

for

Improving Plans

QUARTER #3

QUARTER #2

The third quarter evaluation of superintendent performance emphasizes **Process Evaluation**. The superintendent maintains a portfolio of information on the implementation of district plans and provides progress reports to the board. The board reacts to the reports by providing formative feedback to the superintendent. The board and superintendent adjust priorities and plans as appropriate.

During the fourth quarter, the superintendent evaluation emphasizes **Product Evaluation**. The superintendent maintains a portfolio on accomplishments (throughout the year) and provides an accountability report to the board near the end of the year. The board may gather additional data, e.g., judgments from the community, schools, and students. The board completes a summative evaluation of the superintendent's performance. The board may use the summative evaluation for any or all of the following purposes: to make decisions on continuation/termination and salary, to work with the superintendent to develop a professional improvement plan, to report to the community, to begin revision of the district's strategic plan.

As seen in the above discussion, the relative emphases, by quarter, on Context, Input, Process, and Product (CIPP) evaluation correspond quite closely and differentially to what steps the board of education needs to take in each quarter in evaluating superintendent performance. Therefore, boards of education might usefully adopt the CIPP concepts as the bottom line concepts that guide evaluations of superintendent performance. The simplicity of these four concepts, at the general level, facilitates training new board members in the district's general approach to superintendent evaluation. The fact that each CIPP concept fits in a particular quarter of the school year provides a parsimonious scheme to guide data collection.

Finally, context, input, process, and product evaluations are keyed to

1. helping boards and educators focus district efforts on meeting district and student needs
2. assigning professional responsibilities in order to best address district and student needs
3. monitoring progress to help assure that responsibilities are being implemented professionally and effectively
4. assessing outcomes and taking actions focused on improving performance in meeting student and district needs

Differentiating Board and Superintendent Responsibilities for Superintendent Performance Evaluation

In addition to sequencing evaluation tasks, it is also useful to define the individual and collective evaluation responsibilities of the superintendent and board. Figure 7-6 is a general guide to assigning such responsibilities, which include applying evaluative information as well as delineating, obtaining, and reporting it. The responsibilities are differentiated by the collective efforts of the superintendent and board, plus the independent responsibilities of each. Also, the responsibilities are organized according to the applicable quarter of the year. Within each quarter, the

Figure 7-6. EVALUATION-RELATED RESPONSIBILITIES OF SUPERINTENDENT AND BOARD IN EACH QUARTER

	QUARTER #1	QUARTER #2	QUARTER #3	QUARTER #4
Superintendent and Board	1. Review Context Evaluation data 5. Discuss superintendent evaluation plan for the year	2. Discuss campus plans	3. Review progress in implementing plans (Process Evaluation)	3. Gather data from community, students, schools 6. Develop Professional Improvement Plan 8. Recycle strategic plan
Superintendent	3. Update strategic plan	1. Evaluate campus plans (Input Evaluation) 3. Adjust strategic plan	1. Maintain portfolio of key activities 2. Provide progress reports	1. Maintain portfolio of accomplishments (Product Evaluation) 2. Provide accountability report to Board
Board	2. Set general priorities 4. Approve strategic plan 6. Update superintendent duties	4. Approve revised strategic plan 5. Establish superintendent evaluation design	4. Formative evaluation of superintendent performance	4. Summative evaluation of superintendent performance 5. Personnel decisions 7. Report to community

Note: Within each quarter, the listed responsibilities are numbered to indicate their approximate sequence.

listed responsibilities are numbered to indicate their approximate sequence. An underlying principle in the chart is differentiation of evaluation tasks, in accordance with the board's governance and policy-making authority and the superintendent's responsibilities for carrying out the board's directives. Essentially, the superintendent provides advice and data to the board, and the board uses the input to evaluate superintendent and district performance and to take appropriate follow-up action. In addition, the board and superintendent jointly use the evaluative information to engage in collaborative planning. The chart should be self-explanatory in view of the description of tasks provided earlier in this section.

Managing the Evaluation Process

In reaction to a draft of this section, Dr. Darrell K. Root pointed up a key omission regarding the implementation of the proposed new model. He, quite correctly, noted that school districts need advice and support regarding the management of the superintendent's evaluation process. In fact, he stated that the entire process would lose credibility if the superintendent were to manage his/her own evaluation. While the board and particularly the board president is often charged by statute and/or policy with the responsibility of conducting and managing the evaluation of the superintendent, typically these people do not have the expertise needed to do this task. Therefore, the following options are culled from Dr. Root's recommendations as viable options for districts to consider:

1. Some credible body, such as the state department of education, CREATE, or the Joint Committee on Standards for Educational Evaluation, should create and maintain a list of professionals capable of managing the process of evaluating the superintendent's performance. These professionals would assist the board in establishing its model and help identify the needed tasks to be accomplished during the various phases of the evaluation. These professionals would also teach the board the basic techniques needed to implement the chosen model.
2. Boards could employ persons from the approved list for assistance and guidance in establishing their superintendent's performance evaluation system. The main task of the professional would be to teach the board president and other board members how to implement the system of superintendent performance evaluation.
3. CREATE, the Joint Committee, state education departments, NSBA, AASA, and the various state level organizations for superintendents and board members could usefully offer training sessions for board presidents and other board members to learn the evaluation process.

Dr. Root is correct when he indicates that "the process is too important not to have it guided by someone knowledgeable enough about evaluation and its implications." Districts spend more on the superintendent's salary than on that of any other employee, and for a small fee they can contract with an outside facilitator to appropriately guide the process. This seems to be a wise investment of school district resources to meet a real need--that of meaningful and accurate evaluation of the chief executive officer of the district.

While the engagement of an outside expert would simplify the process for the board, there are other options that the board could consider:

1. Arranging with the state department of education to present a workshop on superintendent evaluation for all boards and board presidents in the area, region, and/or state
2. Having an expert on evaluation present at a state and/or national boards conference
3. Pooling their resources with other districts and engaging an expert to conduct seminars for the various districts included in the sharing of the cost
4. Sending representatives to meetings of AERA and other national evaluation groups to learn how to develop and implement the evaluation process
5. Providing user-friendly evaluation materials to boards

Concluding Comments

Superintendent performance evaluations do not distinguish precisely between superintendent performance and district performance, nor between superintendent performance and board performance. While this can be problematic (if roles are not carefully delineated), it is also appropriate and desirable. For the board and superintendent to benefit maximally from superintendent performance evaluation, they need to evaluate needs, plans, processes, and outcomes--keyed not just to improving the superintendent's performance of duties, but more fundamentally to improving the collaborative work of the board and superintendent and ultimately district functioning, particularly in areas affecting student achievement. Since the superintendent serves as the district's chief administrator, it is reasonable to key judgments of her/his performance to judgments of the district's functioning and achievements. Of course, the constraints in the setting must be taken into account, and the superintendent should not be held accountable for shortfalls not under her/his control.

Clearly, the superintendent cannot control poverty in the district, nor can the superintendent control limited school finances. Such factors severely restrict the resources available to the superintendent in attempting to meet student needs and improve school district services. It is important, therefore, for boards to consider constraints on the superintendent when interpreting evaluation-related data and in the process of arriving at judgments about superintendent performance. By thoroughly considering contextual factors when making evaluative judgments, boards can be assured of providing a fair and defensible evaluation of superintendent performance. Finally, the board should take into account its own role and performance when evaluating the superintendent. This will require, at a minimum, some self-evaluation by the board.

Despite the brief section on implementation of superintendent performance evaluation, this publication's recommendations for a new superintendent performance evaluation model are largely theoretical. The model introduced and discussed in this chapter provides conceptual tools to guide both discussion and field work toward improving superintendent evaluation. We hope the manuscript will be useful to interested parties for further examining and improving the concept and procedures of superintendent performance evaluation. The next step, and a future Evaluation Center project, will be to operationalize and field test the model as developed.

In its present form, school boards and other groups might find CREATE's draft superintendent performance evaluation model useful for several purposes:

- As a conceptual organizer for discussing the characteristics of sound superintendent evaluation systems
- As an experimental model to be adapted, operationalized, and tested
- As an overlay for developing a superintendent performance portfolio
- As a set of checklists for examining the completeness of an existing superintendent evaluation system
- As a guide to defining school district policy on superintendent evaluation
- As a template for a school district committee to use in designing a new superintendent evaluation system

The authors need feedback on the draft superintendent performance evaluation model in order to improve and prepare it for field testing. Pertinent reactions and recommendations will be welcomed. We would also like to hear from any groups with interest in helping to field test the model.

References

American Association of School Administrators. (1993). *Professional standards for the superintendency.* Arlington, VA: Author.

Joint Committee on Standards for Educational Evaluation. (1988). *The personnel evaluation standards.* Newbury Park, CA: Sage.

GLOSSARY

The following glossary terms are defined as they are used in this monograph and in the context of evaluating the performance of school administrators. Some of the terms may have less specialized or different meanings in other settings.

Accountabilities   The areas of performance that are to be given priority in the evaluation and for which the evaluatee will be held accountable.

Accountability   The responsibility for implementing a process or procedures, for justifying decisions and expenditures made, and for the results or outcomes of professional activities.

Accreditation   The awarding of credentials to a school or school district by an external accrediting body.

Accuracy   The extent to which an evaluation conveys technically adequate information about the performance of an evaluatee.

Administration   Management of an organization through such actions as planning, staffing, motivating, directing, controlling, communicating, and evaluating.

Administrative processes   Sequences of behaviors or activities that are part of the job of administrator: e.g., planning, leading, and communicating.

Assessment   The act of rating or describing an individual on some variable of interest.

Assessment center   A process (not necessarily a location) employing simulation techniques to identify and measure a wide variety of administrative job skills. Most centers are designed to identify or select individuals for advancement into or within school administration. The participants engage in a number of activities that simulate behaviors typically found in management or administrative positions.

Behavior   Specific, observable actions of an individual in response to internal and external stimuli.

Bias   Any constant error; any systematic influence on measures or on statistical results irrelevant to the purpose of measurement.

Board of education   The group of local citizens, usually but not always elected, who are empowered by state law to administer a public school system.

Career ladder scale   An incremental pay scale through which an administrator advances as a result of favorable evaluations.

Checklist   A printed form consisting of a series of statements for marking the presence or not of specific indicators of performance, such as traits, processes, or outcomes.

Cognitive ability   The psychological element consisting of such mental processes as perceiving, knowing, recognizing, conceptualizing, judging, and reasoning.

Competency   A skill, knowledge, or experience that is suitable or sufficient for some purpose.

Constituents   The groups, such as parents and the community, on whose behalf administrators act.

Content domain   A body of knowledge and/or a set of tasks or other behaviors defined (usually for a specific job or function) so that given facts or behaviors may be classified as included or excluded.

Context   The set of circumstances or acts that surround and may affect a particular job situation.

Contextual variables   Indicators or dimensions that are useful in describing the facts or circumstances that surround a particular job situation and influence a person's performance of that job.

Credibility   Worthy of belief or confidence by virtue of being trustworthy and possessing pertinent knowledge, skills, and experience.

Criteria (evaluation)   The dimensions of performance on which administrators are judged; e.g., traits, processes, and outcomes.

Data   Material gathered during the course of an evaluation, which serves as the basis for information, discussion, and inference.

Data collection methods   Any technique or set of steps used to obtain information about the performance of an individual.

Design (evaluation)   A representation of the set of decisions that determine how an evaluation is to be conducted; e.g., data collection schedule, report schedules, questions to be addressed, analysis plan, management plan, etc. Designs may be either preordinate or emergent.

Diagnosis   The determination of strengths and weaknesses, usually in response to an identified need for improvement and as a basis for preparing a professional development plan.

Dimension   An aspect or element of administrator performance or of an evaluation system.

Duties   The obligatory tasks, conduct, service, or functions enjoined by order, ethical code, or usage according to rank, occupation, or profession.

Duties-based evaluation   An evaluation model based on what the administrator can be legally and professionally required to do as the position holder.

Evaluatee   The person whose performance is evaluated.

Evaluation   Systematic investigation of the merit or worth of something; e.g., a person's qualifications or performance in a given role.

Evaluation model   A distinctive and comprehensive conception, approach, system, or method for producing data and judgments relating to the performance of an administrator.

Evaluation system   A regularized structure and set of procedures by which an institution initiates, designs, implements, and uses evaluations of its personnel or programs.

Evaluator   Anyone who accepts and executes responsibility for planning, conducting, and reporting evaluations.

Evidence   Information (often documentary) given by credible witnesses, such as students, teachers, and members of the board, to generate and support judgments about an administrator's performance.

External evaluation   Evaluation conducted by an evaluator from outside the organization in which the evaluation is occurring.

Feasibility   The extent to which an evaluation is appropriate and practical for implementation.

Feedback   The information and recommendations given to an administrator, based on the results of an evaluation, which are designed to help improve performance.

Formal evaluation   Evaluation conducted in accordance with a prescribed plan or structure.

Formative evaluation   Evaluation designed and used to promote growth and improvement in a person's performance or in a program's effectiveness.

Goal   An intended outcome that an individual or group works to achieve. Usually general in nature in contrast to *objectives*, which are more specifically defined. Goals may differ among stakeholder groups, and they may change over time.

Informal evaluation   Evaluation conducted without a prescribed plan or structure.

Instrument   An assessment device adopted, adapted, or constructed for the purposes of evaluation.

Interview   A process in which a series of verbally delivered questions are posed to elicit information about the qualifications, competencies, and/or job performance of an administrator.

Job description   A summary of the qualifications, role, responsibilities, duties, and working conditions associated with a specific position.

Joint Committee on Standards for Educational Evaluation   A group representing the major professional educational organizations, which convened to develop a series of standards for use in assessing educational evaluation systems.

Management by objectives-based evaluation (MBO)   An evaluation model based on predetermined objectives set for and usually agreed upon by the administrator.

Merit   Evaluatee excellence as assessed by intrinsic qualities or performance, in contrast to extrinsic value or worth to the organization.

Merit pay   Monetary compensation in the form of higher wages or salaries awarded to deserving employees--who may have the same job descriptions and responsibilities as other employees not receiving merit pay--on the basis of verifiable superiority in the *quality* of their work performance.   The differences in compensation, which may be one-time bonuses or permanent pay increases, are usually based on annual systematic evaluations of employee performance.

Objectives (performance)   A specific description (often written) of intended outcomes that an individual or group works to achieve. Objectives are specified so that they are observable and measurable.

Objective evaluation   Evaluation carried out in a way that minimizes error or bias due to the predilections of the evaluator.

Observation   The recording of notes and evidence about performance while watching the administrator on the job. This may involve direct observation or the use of videotapes.

Observer   The person who makes notes about performance while watching the administrator on the job. This individual is not necessarily the evaluator.

Outcomes   The results of an administrator's professional activities; e.g., new curricula, student achievement scores, and teacher morale. Outcomes are the products of both administrator traits and processes.

Performance   The execution of the job of administrator. Performance is a function of administrator competency as well as the specific context of the job.

Performance contract   An agreement, usually written, between the board and the superintendent stipulating the results or outcomes that the superintendent is expected to achieve and the consequences of success or failure in doing so.

Performance indicator   An observable or measurable sign of executing the job of administrator.

Performance standard   A formal specification of the expected level of achievement in fulfilling a performance objective or job function.

Personnel evaluation   The systematic assessment of a person's performance and/or qualifications in relation to a role and some specified, defensible institutional purpose.

Portfolio   A collection of documents or artifacts gathered to show aspects of the administrator's performance, such as surveys of stakeholder groups, descriptions of professional activities, a videotape of the superintendent at work, letters from parents, and awards from professional organizations.

Propriety   The extent to which an evaluation is conducted legally, ethically, and with due regard for the welfare of those involved in the evaluation as well as those affected by its results.

Questionnaire   A printed form consisting of a series of queries or statements that are designed to produce information about aspects of administrator performance, including traits, processes, and outcomes.

Random sampling   Drawing a number of items or individuals from a larger group or population so that every item or individual has the same (and independent) chance of being chosen.

Rating scale   A printed form designed to elicit judgments on a graduated scale (usually of 3-9 points) about aspects of administrator performance. The scale may be numerical or descriptive.

Reliability   The extent to which an evaluation provides consistent information about the performance being assessed.

Responsibilities   The areas of activity that define what an administrator is expected or obliged to do as the position holder. More specific and localized than duties.

Role definition   Specification of the behavior that is characteristic and expected of the occupant of a defined position in a group.

Sample   A part of a defined population of items or individuals.

School district   A legally constituted collection of institutions, within defined geographic boundaries, that collaborate in teaching persons under college age.

Score   Any specific value in a range of possible values describing the assessment of an individual.

Self-evaluation   The process of reviewing one's own performance.

Skill   The ability to use knowledge effectively and readily in the execution of a task or activity.

Stakeholders   Those individuals who have a vested interest in the results of administrator evaluation.

Standard   A principle commonly agreed upon by experts in the conduct and use of evaluation, by which to measure the value or quality of an evaluation.

Student outcomes   Measures of the results of professional activities on students; e.g., test scores, attendance rates, and college entrants.

Subjective evaluation   An evaluation not open to verification by others; not using public or communicable standards.

Summative evaluation   Evaluation designed to present conclusions about the merit and/or worth of a person's performance.

Superintendent presentation   A process whereby the superintendent gives information about and discusses aspects of his or her own job performance and the performance of the school district.

Traits   Characteristics or competencies seen as possessed by an individual; e.g., attitudes, training, experience, knowledge, and skills.

Utility   The extent to which an evaluation serves the relevant information needs of evaluatees and other users.

Validity   The degree to which evidence supports the inferences that are drawn from an evaluation.

Worth   The extrinsic value of the evaluatee to the organization or in relation to a purpose or need. Merit is a necessary, but not a sufficient, condition for worth.

APPENDICES

Superintendent Performance Evaluation

Examples of Evaluation Materials

Appendix A. Example Policies

     1.   Board Policy Statements

     2.   Compensation Plan Tied to Evaluation

Appendix B. Responsibilities of the Superintendent

     1.   Job Descriptions

     2.   Statements of Objectives and Performance Indicators

Appendix C. Evaluation Forms

     1.   Anchored Rating Scales

     2.   Checklist

     3.   Questionnaires

     4.   Interview Evaluation Form

     5.   Superintendent Presentation Evaluation Forms

     6.   Descriptions of Professional Activities

     7.   Summary Evaluation Form (For Multiple-Data-Collection Model)

Appendix D. Professional Development Plan

     1.   Postevaluation Development Plans

Superintendent Performance Evaluation

<u>Examples of Board Policy Statements</u>

Planned Evaluation of the Superintendent

Evaluation of Superintendent

Superintendent: Evaluation and Appraisal

Evaluation of Superintendent: Board Policy

Evaluation of Administrative Staff

ALEXANDRIA CITY PUBLIC SCHOOLS

POLICY FILE:	# 0343
POLICIES ARE ON WHITE PAPER, EXHIBITS ON GREEN PAPER.	

PLANNED EVALUATION OF THE SUPERINTENDENT

General Statement

Through planned evaluation of the Superintendent, the School Board shall strive to accomplish the following:

(1) Clarify for the Superintendent his role in the school system as seen by the Board.

(2) Clarify for all Board members the role of the Superintendent in light of his job description and the immediate priorities among his responsibilities as agreed upon by the Board and the Superintendent.

(3) Develop harmonious working relationships between the Board and the Superintendent.

(4) Provide administrative leadership for the school system.

The School Board shall periodically develop with the Superintendent a set of performance objectives based on the needs of the school system. The Superintendent's performance shall be reviewed according to specified goals. Additional objectives shall be established at intervals agreed upon with the Superintendent.

Procedure for Evaluation

The School Board shall evaluate the Superintendent's performance as follows:

(1) Once each year in May the Board and Superintendent will jointly review the Superintendent's job description to ensure that it accurately reflects both Board expectations and the realities of the Superintendent's day-to-day responsibilities. Insofar as there are discrepancies, the job description will be modified.

Policy # 0343   Page 1 of 2

164

(2) Also each May, the Board will review the Superintendent's progress toward agreed-upon objectives and prepare a written evaluation of his performance based on:

    (a) The Superintendent's results in achieving Board approved objectives.

    (b) Strengths and weaknesses identified by the Board in fulfilling responsibilities set forth in the job description.

    (c) Other concerns agreed on by the Board.

It will be signed by the Board Chairman and the Superintendent and one copy shall be placed in the Superintendent's personnel file. A duplicate copy will be retained in the confidential files of the Board maintained by the Clerk of the Board.

(3) The evaluation report also shall contain agreed-upon objectives for the coming year that are designed to correct deficiencies in the Superintendent's performance or to achieve specific Board goals for the school district. These new objectives will be developed at least once a year as a part of the Board's evaluation of the Superintendent's performance.

(4) The Board and Superintendent shall meet at least one other time during the year to review the Superintendent's progress toward objectives. Progress meetings may be held more often at the option of the Superintendent or Board.

(5) All evaluation meetings will be in executive session and all evaluation reports will be considered confidential, as permitted under the Virginia Freedom of Information Act.

(6) As made necessary by the seating of new members on the Board and other changing conditions, the Board and Superintendent will review both the Board-Superintendent relationship and the appraisal process. Such review will include discussion of management responsibilities and the respective roles of the Board and Superintendent.

Date of Adoption: 4/15/93

Policy # 0343   Page 2 of 2

Evaluation of Superintendent

Through the evaluation of the superintendent, the board will strive to accomplish the following:

1. Clarify for the superintendent his/her role in the school system as seen by the board.
2. Clarify for all board members the role of the superintendent in light of the job description and the priorities among the responsibilities as agreed upon by the board and the superintendent.
3. Develop harmonious working relationships between the board and the superintendent.
4. Provide administrative leadership for the district.

The board will develop, with the superintendent, a set of performance objectives based on the needs of the district. The performance of the superintendent will be reviewed quarterly in accordance with these specified goals. During the quarterly meetings, additional objectives can be established.

The following guidelines and procedures will be observed throughout the evaluation process:

1. The primary purpose of the evaluation will be to effect improvements in the administrative leadership of the district.
2. Annually in March, the board will devote a closed session to conducting a summative evaluation of the superintendent's performance.
3. The standards to be used in the evaluation will be agreed to by both the superintendent and the board.
4. The board will not limit its evaluation to those items that appear on the evaluation form, but will use performance objectives, personality traits, and routine minimal job performances.
5. The evaluation will be a composite of the evaluations by individual board members, but the board, as a whole, will meet with the superintendent to discuss the composite evaluation.
6. The evaluation will include a discussion of strengths as well as weaknesses.
7. The written evaluation will be a summative checklist and narrative results of performance according to the stated objectives. It will be signed by the board president and the superintendent and one copy will be placed in the superintendent's personnel file. A copy will be given to the superintendent.
8. All evaluation reports will be considered confidential.
9. Following the summative evaluation session, the board will follow the procedures established for extension of the superintendent's contract.

Pleasant Plains C.U.D. #8
Pleasant Plains, IL

NEPN: CB1
EPS: CBG
~~BJCD~~

SUPERINTENDENT:
EVALUATION AND APPRAISAL

PERIODIC WRITTEN EVALUATIONS	The Board shall have an evaluation system that provides periodic written evaluations of the Superintendent at annual or more frequent intervals. Such evaluations shall be considered by the Board prior to any decision not to renew the Superintendent's contract. *Education Code 21.202, 21.208*

APPRAISAL
PROCESS

The Board shall establish an annual calendar that provides for the following activities, in which both the Board and the Superintendent shall participate:

1. A goal-setting procedure that defines expectations and sets priorities for the Superintendent.

2. Formative conference(s).

3. Summative conference(s).

4. A written professional growth plan that is based on assessment, formative input, and self-assessment. The professional growth plan shall be confidential and under the control of the Board and the Superintendent.

The Superintendent shall be involved in developing, selecting, and/or revising the appraisal instrument and process.

STAFF INPUT

The Board may implement a process for collecting staff input for the Superintendent's evaluation and/or for the Superintendent's professional growth plan. If such a process is implemented for use in the Superintendent's evaluation, staff input shall not be anonymous.

APPRAISER
TRAINING

Before conducting the Superintendent's appraisal, Board members shall have evidence of training in appropriate personnel evaluation skills related to the locally established criteria and process.

19 TAC 149.45(d), 149.46

APPRAISAL
CRITERIA

The criteria used to evaluate the Superintendent shall include, but not necessarily be limited to, the following:

1. Instructional management.

2. School/organizational climate.

CR 1

SUPERINTENDENT: ~~BJCD~~
EVALUATION AND APPRAISAL

3. School/organizational improvement.

4. Personnel management.

5. Administration and fiscal/facilities management.

6. Student management.

7. School/community relations.

8. Professional growth and development.

9. Board/Superintendent relations.

In developing indicators and descriptors for the criteria, the Board shall use the Superintendent's job description in concert with the criteria descriptors adopted by the State Board.

19 TAC 149.45

168

P4044   EVALUATION OF SUPERINTENDENT   EPS: CBG

BOARD POLICY:

The Board of Education shall be responsible for completion of formal evaluations to document the quality of professional performance provided by the Superintendent of Schools.

Administrative Implemental Procedures:

1. The Superintendent of Schools shall be evaluated no less frequently than required by law.

2. The Division Director of Personnel Services shall assist the Board President by providing a schedule of the activities and by making available the evaluation documents.

3. Approximately March 1 of each year, the Superintendent of Schools shall be evaluated by the Board of Education.

4. The following procedures shall be applicable in completing the evaluation:

    a. Evaluation conditions in excess of the requirements of state law (if any) set forth in the Superintendent's employment contract shall take precedent over any administrative implemental procedures herein set forth.

    b. Each member of the Board of Education shall prepare an evaluation of the Superintendent and give it to the President of the Board.

    c. The President of the Board shall prepare a tentative composite evaluation of the Superintendent and then schedule time with the Board to discuss the composite and reach consensus on a single composite evaluation for the Superintendent.

    d. The Superintendent shall submit to the Board a self-evaluation regarding his/her performance which may include a plan for the improvement of that performance.

    e. The President shall schedule a conference(s) with the Superintendent and the Board of Education members to provide the following:

        (1) Common understanding of the Board's evaluation of the Superintendent and the basis for the evaluation.

        (2) Opportunity for discussion with the Superintendent regarding any area(s) of concern and any recommendations that the Board may anticipate.

        (3) Give a copy of the Board's composite evaluation to the Superintendent.

    f. The Superintendent shall be given the opportunity to review and sign the completed form(s). He/she may submit a written response to any part of the evaluation within 14 calendar days following the presentation of the formal evaluation. The written response will be signed by the Superintendent and the President of the Board of Education.

    g. Evaluation documents and responses thereto shall be forwarded to the Division Director of Personnel Services and shall be maintained in the administrator's personnel file.

5. The Division Director of Personnel Services shall make available to individuals and agencies evaluation documents and responses thereto in accordance with state statutes.

Administrative Responsibility: Personnel Services
Latest Revision Date: November 1987
Previous Revision Date: July 1986

ADMINISTRATION

Evaluation of Administrative Staff

A. Purpose of Evaluation: The primary purpose of evaluation is the improvement of the educational program. The process has secondary functions which may include one or more of the following: modifying the assignments, validating the administrative staffing process, providing feedback on performance and establishing a basis for professional growth and development. The relationship between the evaluator and administrator should be characterized by open communication, helpfulness and a sharing of responsibility for improved performance.

B. Evaluation Model

1. Administrators shall be evaluated openly and with full knowledge by the superintendent, his/her designee, or their immediate supervisor (in case of assistant principals.)

2. A year-end rating of "does not meet expectation" will be accompanied by the evaluator's narrative explaining the reason(s) or cause for the rating.

3. The evaluator may, upon the evaluation criteria ratings, recommend to the superintendent probationary status per RCW 28A.67.065, fourth paragraph.

C. Data Collection: Information for verification of criteria should be collected from a variety of sources. The evaluator has the responsibility to weigh and document all data as to its validity, reliability and objectivity. Based upon information gathered, the evaluator shall make judgments as to both the results and process of performance. The evaluator shall take into consideration situational factors which affect performance, i.e., enrollment, facilities, resources.

D. Reporting Procedures:

1. Conferences between the evaluator and administrator

a. Conferences may be initiated by either the evaluator or administrator.

b. The evaluator will initiate a timely communication upon receipt of derogatory information which may adversely affect the administrator's final evaluation.

c. A minimum of three (3) conferences shall be held annually.

   1. The first conference shall be scheduled on or before October 1 each year. This conference shall be for the purpose of reviewing evaluation procedures and identifying the administrator's performance indicators related to specified criteria where appropriate.

   2. An evaluation conference shall be scheduled on or before February 1. The purpose of this conference shall be to review performance based on the evaluation criteria. An evaluation report form shall be completed at this time.

   3. The second evaluation conference shall be held on or before June 1. This conference shall be for the purpose of assessing performance on the evaluation criteria.

2. The two evaluation conferences shall be documented by the evaluator on the established evaluation report forms. Administrators shall sign and receive a copy of the evaluation report within ten (10) days of the conference. The original copy shall become a part of the administrator's personnel file. The administrator's signature does not necessarily imply agreement with the contents of the report. The signature signifies the administrator has read and received a copy. The administrator has the right to attach an addendum to the original evaluation report in explanation of any disagreement with its contents.

E. Probation

1. In the event the superintendent establishes that an administrator's performance warrants probationary status as determined in B-3, the superintendent shall notify the administrator in writing of his/her probationary status on or before February 1. The notice of probationary status shall include an evaluation report covering the year to date and shall:

a. specifically identify the deficiencies of the administrator's performance
b. delineate expected performance
c. suggest a reasonable program and time line for improvement
d. identify district resources available to help achieve the expected performance level.

2. There shall be at least two progress conferences per month during the period of probation. These conferences shall be for the purpose of assessing progress toward meeting the expected performance levels as specified in the notice of probation report. Both the

172

evaluator and the administrator may have another individual of their choosing be a party to conferences held during the probationary period. The notice of probation and any subsequent reports during the probationary period shall be removed from the administrator's personnel file after three years of successful performance following the probationary period.

3. On or before May 15, the superintendent shall notify the administrator of the status of his/her probation:

    a. The probationary administrator has demonstrated sufficient improvement in his/her performance in the stated areas of deficiencies to warrant removal of probation status.

    b. The administrator has demonstrated sufficient improvement to justify a continuance of the probationary period for the following school year.

    c. The administrator has not demonstrated sufficient improvement in the areas of deficiency as stated in the notice of probation to warrant a continued contract in his/her present position. In such cases, the superintendent will recommend to the board on or before May 15 that:

        1. the administrator be re-assigned to a subordinate position for which he/she is qualified, or

        2. the administrator's contract be non-renewed.

F. Right to Appeal

If the administrator/supervisor is in disagreement with the procedures used to reach the supervisor's evaluation of his/her performance, he/she may proceed as follows:

1. He/she may write a statement of disagreement with the evaluator's conclusions on the evaluation form and request an appeal conference with the evaluator. The evaluator shall respond to this request, holding an appeal conference within five (5) working days and providing a written decision to the appellant within five (5) working days after the conference.

2. If the administrator/supervisor and evaluator cannot come to mutual agreement through the above procedure, the administrator/supervisor may request a conference with the superintendent or his/her designee to appeal the evaluator's conclusions. This request must be submitted to the superintendent within five (5) days of receipt of the evaluation report. Within five (5) working days of receipt

of this request, the superintendent or his/her designee shall meet with the evaluator and the appellant alone or with another member of the administrator/supervisor group to seek resolution of the above disagreement. The superintendent or his/her designee shall provide to the appellant a written decision and the reason(s) on which such decision was based within five (5) working days from the conclusion of the meeting. This procedure will be bypassed should the evaluator of the administrator/supervisor be the superintendent.

3. If the appellant is not satisfied with the decision reached by the superintendent or his/her designee, he/she may appeal this decision to a board of appeals composed of a board member (designated by the board president), a district-level administrator (designated by the superintendent) and a member of the administrator/supervisor group (designated by the group). It shall be the function of the board of appeals to hold a hearing within ten (10) working days of the appointment of its members. Ten (10) working days' notice shall be given to both parties of the time and place of the hearing. Within ten (10) days after the hearing, the board of appeals will provide to the appellant and his/her supervisor its findings of fact, reasoning and conclusions on the issues submitted by the parties. The findings and conclusions of the board of appeals shall be final.

Superintendent Performance Evaluation

<u>Example of Compensation Plan Tied to Evaluation</u>

Administrators' Evaluation - Compensation Plan (District Scheme)

MONTROSE AREA SCHOOL DISTRICT

ADMINISTRATORS' EVALUATION - COMPENSATION PLAN

I. INTRODUCTION:

In compliance with Section 1164 of the Public School Code of 1949, as amended, (Act 93 of 1984) and in recognizing the need for a strong administrative management team, the Montrose Area School District Board of Directors establishes this administrators' evaluation - compensation plan.

II. TERM OF PLAN:

A. The Administrative Evaluation - Compensation Plan will be for a term of three (3) years. The following is an explanation and application of this three year plan.

(1991-92   Last year of previous Compensation Plan)
1991-92   First year of evaluation phase
1992-93   First year of compensation phase
1992-93   Second year of evaluation phase
1993-94   Second year of compensation phase
1993-94   Third year of evaluation phase
1994-95   Third year of compensation phase

During the 1994-95 year, meet and discuss process begins for new Evaluation/Compensation Plan.

III. PROCEDURES FOR MEET AND DISCUSS:

Administrators may request in writing a meet and discuss meeting.

A. Session #1

An informal meeting should be conducted between the Finance/Compensation Committee and a committee of administrators or a representative for the purpose of sharing ideas and concerns pertaining to the evaluation - compensation plan.

B. Session #2

An informal meeting should be conducted between the Finance/Compensation Committee and a committee of administrators or a representative for the purpose of presenting specific proposals for new compensation plans or altering the compensation plan already in force.

C. Session #3

The administrative evaluation - compensation plan should be presented to the entire board in a formal setting for their approval.

D. Additional sessions would be held if needed.

IV. THE EVALUATION PROCESS:

    A. An evaluation system is an important part of our administrators' compensation plan. Administrators are evaluated and rated in order to determine their success related to job performance criteria and management objectives. They are also rated to improve their performance and to establish appropriate building and program goals to maximize student achievement.

    B. Guidelines for a Good Evaluation System

        1. Should be accepted by everyone.
        2. Evaluation carried out in an atmosphere of mutual trust and benefit.
        3. Evaluation should focus on growth and development.
        4. Evaluation should involve self-evaluation and evaluation by immediate supervisor.
        5. Evaluation should be monitored to determine its effectiveness.

    C. Developing Goals

        Management goals/objectives are developed and agreed upon by the administrator and the evaluator.

    D. Job Description Criteria (attachment #1)

    E. Management Objectives (attachment #2)

V. SALARY ADJUSTMENT SCHEDULE:

    A. By mid-July the administrator and evaluator meet to discuss the administrator's management objectives and review the administrators's job description for the coming school year.

    B. By mid-August all management objectives and job description criteria will be finalized for the coming school year.

    C. Three meetings will be held during the year to discuss the progress of the administrator's management objectives and job description.
        First session   — November
        Second session — February
        Third session   — April

    D. The Superintendent will review each administrator's status with the Finance/Compensation Committee following each meeting throughout the year.

    E. The beginning of April each person included in this plan shall submit a final report on his/her management objectives and a self-evaluation on his/her job description to their respective evaluatee.

    F. By mid-April each evaluatee will meet with the Superintendent to discuss the recommended salary increases and job performance for their respective evaluees. (This meeting will take place before the evaluatee discusses the final recommended salary increase and job performance with the evaluee.)

G. End of April, after meeting with the Superintendent, the evaluatee will meet with their respective evaluees and review the final evaluation and salary recommendation.

H. Each administrator will have the opportunity to request a follow up meeting with their respective evaluator within two weeks of their final evaluation for any items they feel require clarification. If an evaluation rating or total score is changed as a result of this meeting, the administrator will be notified.

I. Subsequent to receiving his/her final performance score, the administrator may request, through the Finance/Compensation Committee, a meeting with the Board or its designated members to appeal the rating or its component scores. This meeting will be scheduled during the month of May to allow time for subsequent meetings prior to the end of the fiscal year. All compensation factors used in the administrators's salary calculation must be finalized by the Board, by the last Board meeting of the fiscal year.

J. Board approval should be gained at the June School Board meeting so that salary adjustments will be effective July 1.

VI. EVALUATION – COMPENSATION SCALE:

The following criteria should be used when utilizing the administrators's job description and yearly goals:

Achieved – Dependable and conscientious in fulfillment of the job description criteria for their administrative position. (Two points for achieved)

1. Achieves most short range goals.
2. Stimulates effective growth within area of responsibility.
3. Organizational skills are clearly evident.
4. Communicates clearly and effectively with all groups.
5. Performs well according to job description.

Partially Achieved – Could be more dependable and conscientious in fulfilling the responsibilities of the job description criteria for their administrative position. (One point for partially achieved)

1. Short range goals in various stages of completion.
2. Contribution to growth in area of responsibility is marginal.
3. Lack of adequate organizational skills.
4. Clear and effective communication with all groups is inconsistent.
5. Partially achieved job description criteria.

Not Achieved – Inadequately fulfills the administrative responsibilities of their position. (Zero points for not achieved)

VII. FRINGE BENEFITS:

Each administrator shall be provided with a fringe benefit package which includes those benefits as described in each individual's compensation plan booklet. These benefits shall be continued through the third year of the compensation phase (1994-95).

VIII. POSITIONS INGLUDED IN THE PLAN AND EVALUATOR'S RESPONSIBILITY:

 A. Superintendent – evaluates positions B, D, G, H, I, J, and K
 B. Principal of Business Affairs – evaluates position C
 C. Business Manager
 D. High School Principal – evaluates positions E and F
 E. Assistant High School Principal (Attendance and Discipline)
 F. Assistant High School Principal (Athletics and Activities)
 G. Elementary Principal/Director of Elementary Education
 H. Elementary Principal
 I. Director of Transportation
 J. Director of Food Services
 K. Director of Maintenance, Buildings and Grounds

IX. EVALUATION SCALE AND NUMERICAL RATING SYSTEM:

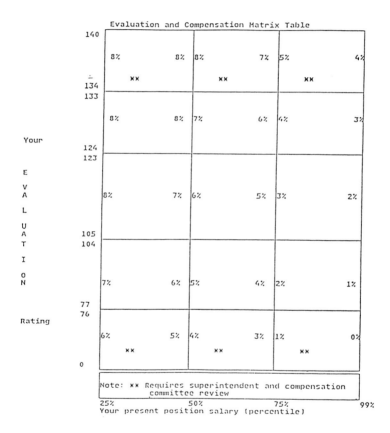

Evaluation and Compensation Matrix Table

Your EVALUATION Rating

140						
	8%	8%	8%	7%	5%	4%
134	XX		XX		XX	
133	8%	8%	7%	6%	4%	3%
124 / 123	8%	7%	6%	5%	3%	2%
105 / 104	7%	6%	5%	4%	2%	1%
77 / 76	6%	5%	4%	3%	1%	0%
	XX		XX		XX	
0						

Note: XX Requires superintendent and compensation committee review

25%   50%   75%   99%
Your present position salary (percentile)

The administrator's evaluation and compensation plan agreement is based on the following criteria:

1. The previous years' PA OMNI Data for the respective administrative position is used as the base figure (ref: PA OMNI, Table ALL-10).

2. The administrator's current salary for the respective position will fall within the 25% - 99% sector range of the base.

3. The administrator's "evaluation rating" and the administrator's current salary sector placement, according to the evaluation and compensation matrix table, determines the percentage increase to his/her current salary for the coming school year.

4. If the administrator's base salary falls between the 25%-50%, 50%-75%, or 75%-99%; the determination of the percentage increase will be based on the amount of the base salary in relationship to the mid salary amount between the two percentages. If the base salary is above the midpoint, the administrator would get the lower percentage, and if the base salary is at or below the midpoint they get the higher percentage.

5. It is the intent of this matrix design to cause the salary placement of the respective administrator or director to be driven towards the 75% of the PA OMNI Report, Table ALL-10.

The following formula will be used in determining the administrator's rating for the year. The administrator's job description criteria plus the four management objectives/goals will equal their final rating score.

The rating score will be converted, using the administrator's respective matrix, to obtain a percent increase. The percent increase will be multiplied by the current salary to obtain the new year's salary.

The job criteria consists of fifty (50) items with a weighted value of 0 (not achieved), 1 (partially achieved), or 2 (achieved) points and there will be four (4) management objectives each weighted at 0 (not achieved), 5 (partially achieved), or 10 (achieved) points.

Example: Job Description Criteria + Management Objectives = Rating
          Possible points   100   +   40   =   140

Special Note: Gross mismanagement or any extenuating circumstances in any single area may be grounds for deviating from the Evaluation Compensation Plan

AG/dlt

Superintendent Performance Evaluation

<u>Examples of Job Descriptions</u>

Job Description: Superintendent of schools

Qualifications and Duties of Superintendent (Job Description)

Job Description: Superintendent

KALAMAZOO PUBLIC SCHOOLS

Job Description
Superintendent of Schools

The Superintendent of Schools is the chief administrator of the School System and is directly responsible to the Board of Education.

MAJOR DUTIES

① Responsibilities to the Board of Education

1. The Superintendent attends all regular and special meetings of the Board of Education (excluding Library Board meetings). He/She is responsible for submitting an agenda for each School Board meeting.

2. The Superintendent administers the School System within the policies established by the Board of Education and the State. He/She recommends to the Board new policies and keeps the Board informed on matters of importance to the School System.

② Duties Prescribed by State Statutes

1. The Superintendent puts into practice the educational policies of the State and the Board of Education in accordance with the method provided by the Board.

2. He/she recommends those teachers selected for contracts and suspends any teacher for cause until the Board may consider action on the charges.

3. He/She classifies and controls the promotion of pupils.

4. The Superintendent recommends to the Board the best methods of arranging the course of study and the proper textbooks to be used.

5. He/She reports to the State Superintendent of Public Instruction all matters pertaining to the educational interests of the School District.

6. He/She supervises and directs the work of administrators, teachers, and other employees of the Board of Education.

7. The Superintendent assists the Board in all matters pertaining to the general welfare of the School System and performs such other duties as the Board may determine.

③ Educational Program

1. The Superintendent organizes, plans, and directs the educational program for the School System.

2. He/She works cooperatively with staff members to plan the curriculum.

3. He/She ensures that the curriculum for the School System is implemented.

MAJOR DUTIES

Educational Program (continued)

4. The Superintendent determines that the curriculum is adapted to the needs of individual students.

5. He/She approves proposed experimental and innovative programs.

6. He/She ensures that the educational program is evaluated.

7. He/She supervises and evaluates the work of administrators.

8. The Superintendent works with staff, parents, students, and outside agencies to develop and maintain acceptable standards of behavior in the School System.

9. He/She implements personnel skills development programs for staff.

10. He/She encourages the development of appropriate co-curricular and inter-scholastic activities.

④ Staff and School-Community Relations

1. The Superintendent interprets the school philosophy and School System policies and procedures to the staff and the community.

2. He/She coordinates the activities of school personnel.

3. He/She promotes satisfactory communications between the staff and parents.

4. The Superintendent involves staff, students, and community in decision making.

5. The work of community agencies is coordinated with school activities by the Superintendent.

6. The Superintendent or his/her designee hears and responds to grievances.

7. He/She understands and implements the terms and conditions contained in the various master agreements.

8. He/She investigates and recommends action to the Board of Education concerning student expulsions and exclusions.

9. Recommendations are made to the Board of Education for changes in administrative organization, additional administrative staff needs, and applicants to fill administrative vacancies.

10. He/She meets regularly with administrative staff to inform them of activities and to solicit their input.

⑤ Business Affairs

1. The Superintendent oversees the business affairs of the School District.

2. He/She establishes an annual budget.

3. He/She makes sure that all funds are accounted for.

QUALIFICATIONS AND DUTIES OF SUPERINTENDENT
(Job Description)

POSITION: Superintendent of Schools

QUALIFICATIONS: 1. State Superintendent's certification
                 2. Successful experience as an educational
                     leader and administrator
                 3. Other qualifications as determined by the
                     Board

REPORTS TO: Board of Education

SUPERVISES: Central office administrators and school
                 principals; through them all District personnel.

JOB GOAL: To provide for effective administration of all
                 schools and departments and to provide
                 educational leadership throughout the school
                 system and community

PERFORMANCE RESPONSIBILITIES:

1. The Superintendent of schools shall be the executive officer of
    the Board of Education and shall be responsible to it for the
    execution of its policies and the observation of its rules.
    He/she shall attend all Board meetings except at such times
    when consideration may be given to his/her employment or
    salary.

2. The Superintendent shall develop administrative principles and
    procedures for implementing Board policies.

3. The Superintendent shall have the supervision of all schools of
    the District, their organization, classification, and
    management. The Superintendent shall be the representative of
    the Board, and all directions from the Board to employees or
    pupils shall be communicated through him/her. Directions
    the Superintendent may give for the management of the schools
    to these employees and pupils, on points not covered by the
    printed rules, shall be valid until disapproved by the Board.

4. At the January meeting preceding the opening of school, the
    Superintendent of schools shall submit a school calendar for
    Board approval.

184

5. Purchasing: Purchases of $10,000 or more shall generally be let by bid except special items of instructional material of equipment and supplies which have been found through experience to be superior or to meet the needs of the Lee's Summit R-7 School District shall become standard equipment or a supply item and will be bought directly from the firm supplying such material upon indication of price. At equal cost and quality, local merchants will be given preference when purchases are made.

6. The Superintendent of schools shall ensure maintainence of an accurate system of records and reports for the District as may be required by the Missouri Department of Elementary and Secondary Education, by law, or the Board of Education. The Superintendent may in turn hold principals, supervisors, and teachers responsible to him/her for the same.

7. Assignment of Staff Members: Organization and assignment of members shall be under the direction of the Superintendent, subject to the approval of the Board of Education.

8. Extracurricular Activities: The extracurricular activities shall be managed in such a manner as to bring out their maximum benefits with a minimum of interference with the regular curricular program.

9. Substitute Teachers: The Superintendent of schools shall have the power to select substitute teachers and fill temporary vacancies and report such appointments to the Board at the next regular meeting.

10. Continuing Census: The Superintendent of schools shall cause to be kept a continuing census according to methods prescribed by the Board.

11. The Superintendent and his/her staff shall prepare such financial reports as may be necessary to keep the Board properly informed about the financial plans and conditions of the District. The operating budget shall be approved by the July meeting.

12. Agenda: The agenda for the meeting of the Board of Education shall be prepared jointly by the Superintendent and the secretary of the Board of Education. Members of the Board of Education may request additional items be added to any such agenda. This agenda shall be mailed by the secretary so as to reach Board members two days in advance of the meeting.

13. He/she shall recommend employees for appointment, promotion, demotion, transfer, or dismissal in accordance with the policies of the Board.

14. He/she shall approve for adoption all textbooks, supplementary instructional materials, all courses of study, and co-curricular programs to be offered in the District.

15. He/she shall be active in the civic affairs of the community and be responsible for the general public relations program of the school. He/she shall perform such other duties as the Board may determine.

16. The Superintendent of schools or a person designated by him/her shall establish needed rules and regulations for the effective operation of all divisions.

17. The Superintendent of schools shall furnish to the Board of Education at each regular meeting a budget summary showing the income and expenditures of the District in relation to the adopted budget. He/she shall also keep the Board informed at least quarterly regarding the financial standings of the cafeteria and the various school activity accounts.

18. He/she shall attend national, state, and regional professional meetings for the welfare of the schools where public education is concerned.

19. He/she shall evaluate those administrators who report directly to the Superintendent of schools.

Adopted: September 11, 1986

Revised: May 11, 1989

Reorganized School District No. 7, Jackson County, Lee's Summit, Missouri

186

DES MOINES PUBLIC SCHOOLS

JOB DESCRIPTION

DEPARTMENT: Superintendent's Office

JOB TITLE: Superintendent

D.O.T. # 099.117-022   FULL TIME X   PART TIME

D.O.T. CLASS:
Sedentary   Light X   Medium   Heavy   Very Heavy

REQUIREMENTS:
A.   Education Level: Master's degree in school administration ÷ 30 approved graduate hours. Doctor's degree desired.

B.   Certification or Licensure: Iowa administrator/superintendent certificate; Drivers license.

C.   Experience Desired: 5 years as superintendent or assistant superintendent required; 8 years desired.

D.   Other Requirements: Understanding of complex organizational systems; knowledge of Iowa law and school finance, effective schools research, technology and strategic planning related to change and demographics. Availability for extended hours of work.

REPORTS TO: School Board

RECEIVES GUIDANCE FROM: School Board, Central Cabinet and Administrative Council.

ESSENTIAL FUNCTIONS:

Provides directions for four member Central Cabinet. Serves as chief executive officer for School Board; charged with responsibility of implementing district policy, maintaining a focus on the district's mission and general administration of the school district.

Frequent:

Establishes systematic process for evaluating programs .
Recommends new programs, courses of study, textbooks, technology and instructional materials for Board approval.
Establishes advisory groups on a regular and systematic basis for planning and receiving information for determining future changes.

187

- 11 -

Utilizes central administrative team (including cabinet) as sounding board for all district
    proposals.
Initiates staff selection processes and salaries, and makes recommendations for Board
    approval.
Assigns and transfers personnel as well as suspensions in accord with Board policies and
    procedures.
Submits for Board approval possible policy statements, procedures, regulations and
    programs related to effective, efficient and equitable District leadership and
    management issues.
Provides leadership in maintaining all provisions of the law relating to schools as well as
    observance of school policies by staff.
Participates in a variety of community organizations and serves as the District's
    representative.
Provides leadership in areas of facility maintenance, renovation and replacement projects.
Provides leadership in the areas of staff assessment process, including correction and
    removal of those not meeting District standards.
Manages conflicts inherent in complex educational organizations.
Provides leadership in maintaining a system sensitive to diversity and desegregation patterns
    in accord with state guidelines.

Occasional or Periodic:

Prepares and implements District referendums approved by the Board.
Provides leadership in the establishment of a school district marketing plan with a
    marketing team for each school as well as individual building plans.
Develops an annual District Improvement Plan, including goals and objectives.
Provides an annual improvement plan including goals and objectives.
Provides an annual "State of the Schools" presentation to selected business, community
    and staff leaders.
Develops an annual strategic planning progress report for the District.
Provides an annual assessment of student achievement growth.
Conducts a biennial survey of general public's perception of District's effectiveness.
Prepares a progress report on superintendent's objectives through the annual
    administrative evaluation process.

PHYSICAL REQUIREMENTS:

		Never 0%	Occasional 1-32%	Frequent 33-66%	Constant 67%+
A.	Standing		X		
B.	Walking			X	
C.	Sitting		X		
D.	Bending/ Stooping	X			
E.	Reaching/ Pushing/ Pulling	X			
F.	Climbing		X		
G.	Driving		X		
H.	Lifting 10 #Max		X		
I.	Carrying 20 Ft.		X		
J.	Manual Dexterity Tasks:			X	

Specify: Telephone
Calculator

OTHER REQUIREMENTS (Intellectual, Sensory):

Exemplary oral and written communications skills.
Ability to work well with others and motivate them.
Sensitivity in applying theories of sound education to meet District needs.
Outstanding leadership and decision making skills.
Conflict resolution skills.

WORKING CONDITIONS:

A. Inside   X   Outside   Both

B. Climatic Environment:

Primary work area is an air-conditioned office.
Visits to schools and other facilities involve extremes of temperature and humidity.

C. Hazards: Stairs in most buildings.
Stress caused from managing conflicts.

Signature of Supervisor: _____

Date: _April 30, 1992_

Superintendent Performance Evaluation

Examples of Statements of Objectives and Performance Indicators

Superintendent's Role and Responsibility (including objectives for the year)

Superintendent Performance Objectives (including methods of measurement)

Superintendent Responsibilities and Performance Indicators

DES MOINES PUBLIC SCHOOLS — 13 —

SUPERINTENDENT'S ROLE AND RESPONSIBILITY

Title: Superintendent of Schools   Year: 1992-93

Responsibility Statement:
The responsibility of the chief professional officer or superintendent of the Des Moines Public Schools is to: (1) maintain the integrity of the school district's "mission" and (2) provide the necessary leadership for the district to operate as an effective, equitable, and efficient organization.

Organizational Tasks:
The organizational tasks to be performed by the superintendent include planning, implementing, and evaluating the district's programs, as well as interacting with individuals and groups interested in district services. Successful performance is expected by the Board of Education in program management of teaching and learning activities, human and fiscal resources, instructional support services, and public relations. In addition, each of the organizational tasks and management functions must be interpreted in terms of established Board of Education policies and procedures. The Board of Education expects the superintendent to maintain a positive working relationship with the body as a whole.

Organizational Relationships:
The superintendent reports to the Board of Education. The superintendent chairs the Administrative Council and directly supervises the executive staff. The executive staff includes the Associate Superintendent for Teaching and Learning, Associate Superintendent for Management Services, Executive Director for Business and Financial Services and Director for Board and Public Relations.

Personnel Resources:

Category	Funding Source Local	Federal/State	Amount
Superintendent	1		$ 89,760
Administrators	4		336,795
Office Personnel	1		26,648
Total	6		$453,203

Objectives:
WEIGHT (%)

50% 1. During the 1992-93 school year, the superintendent of schools will meet the organizational expectations of the Board of Education, staff, students, parents, and general citizenry by:
- Being visible and accessible
- Focusing district educational direction
- Sharing in day-to-day experiences.

15% 2. During the 1992-93 school year, the superintendent will continue to refine roles and responsibilities of administrators by:
- Assisting in the development of the administrative excellence program including a focus on leadership, evaluation, recruitment and retention of administrators.
- Assisting principals with school-based management through shared decision making process and outcome determinations.
- Continuing to revise superintendent's evaluation process as a model for future development for other administrative positions.

15% 3. During the 1992-93 school year, the superintendent will continue the development of the district's strategic plan by:
- Adjusting current programs to projected reductions in 1992-93 and 1993-94 budget revenues.
- Addressing the issue of developing a school district "Report Card."
- Extending program evaluation to selected instructional and non-instructional areas; focus on completing first round of evaluations.
- Expanding school/business alliance cooperative efforts

•Extending "At-Risk" program services through coalitions with outside agencies (e.g., United Way, Human Services, etc.); focus on SUCCESS program.

10%   4.   During the 1992-93 school year, the superintendent of schools will continue to implement the 1992-93 district Improvement Plan by:
•Focusing staff effort on the activities listed under the eight (8) major components of the plan.
•Marketing the district's teaching and learning achievements in relation to "open enrollment" issues.

10%   5.   During the 1992-93 school year, the superintendent will continue to implement the schoolhouse extension and bond levy by:
•Developing, monitoring, and completing plans for building additions, new school(s), and general building improvements.

NAPE-like continuous assessment data will be used for grades P, 5, 6, 7, 9, 10 and 11.

7. The dropout rate for Henderson County students will be equal to or less than the dropout rate for the average of the five contiguous districts, the average of comparable size districts in Kentucky, and the state average.

Measurement: 1991-92 dropout data from the Kentucky Department of Education will be used.

8. Henderson County students will have a successful graduate transition rate equal to or better than that of the five contiguous districts, the average of Kentucky districts of comparable size, and the state average.

Measurement: Department of Education transition data will be used.

2

II. SUPERINTENDENT/BOARD RELATIONS

Goal:
To promote a positive, productive working relationship between the Superintendent and the Board of Education.

Objectives:
1. The Superintendent shall:

    a. establish a positive working relationship between himself and the members of the Board;

    b. provide for open, two-way communication between himself and the. Board;

    c. operate within board policy, and

    d. effectively articulate the needs of the school system and provide adequate data for decision making.

Measurement: Board questionnaire (and follow-up interviews if warranted), and independent assessment of communication process and materials.

3

III. SUPERINTENDENT LEADERSHIP AND STAFF RELATIONS

Goal:
The Superintendent shall demonstrate effective professional leadership.

Objectives:
1.   The Superintendent shall be seen as providing positive vision and direction for the school district.

2.   The Superintendent shall effectively communicate district goals and expectations to staff*. (staff members will understand where the district is going and what is expected of each.)

3.   The Superintendent shall promote and maintain positive staff morale.

4.   The Superintendent shall promote high moral and ethical standards for all district personnel.

5.   The Superintendent shall maintain a positive, professional working relationship with teachers, principals, and central office personnel.

6.   The Superintendent shall provide constructive, beneficial staff development programs.

7.   The Superintendent shall demonstrate a participatory leadership style.

8.   The Superintendent shall encourage and assist staff members to achieve their professional potential.

Measurement: Staff questionnaire; analysis of formal communications

* Staff means all district employees.

IV. SCHOOL/COMMUNITY RELATIONS

Goal:
To secure community support for the public schools.

Objectives:
1. The Superintendent will develop and implement systems for keeping parents and non-parents well informed regarding the Henderson County Schools.

2. The Superintendent will maintain a positive level of public support for the Henderson County Schools.

3. The Superintendent will provide opportunities for legitimate community participation in the schools.

4. The Superintendent will be a viable and active member of the community.

Measurement: Analysis of formal communication systems with parents, news media and other. Analysis of newspaper clips and notation of Superintendent's community participation.

V. FISCAL MANAGEMENT AND GENERAL ADMINISTRATION

Goal:
To utilize the fiscal resources of the district for the maximum benefit of the children and taxpayers of Henderson County.

Objectives:

1. The Superintendent shall manage the school district in compliance with Kentucky Revised Statutes and the Administrative Regulations of the State Board of Education.

2. The Superintendent shall initiate and implement an effective long-range planning program.

3. The Superintendent shall conduct a program of capital improvements which provide adequate facilities within budgetary limitations.

4. The Superintendent shall implement a maintenance system which provides for: a safe learning and working environment for all students and employees; a functional environment conducive to learning; and a cost effective use of maintenance dollars.

5. The Superintendent shall provide a transportation system in compliance with all state safety standards. The transportation system shall be efficient and cost effective.

6. The Superintendent shall develop and implement a systematic reporting procedure to keep the Board informed about school district business transactions.

7. The Superintendent shall propose a balanced budget and manage the fiscal affairs of the district within the budget.

Measurement: This could range from relatively simple to very complex. Need to discuss.

VI. SUPERINTENDENT'S PROFESSIONAL GROWTH AND DEVELOPMENT

Goal:
To ensure that the Superintendent stays current regarding local, state, and national education issues, and to ensure that he stays professionally active.

Objectives:
1. The Superintendent shall maintain an active reading list of state and national educational publications.

2. The Superintendent shall maintain membership in appropriate state and national educational organizations and shall assume a leadership role in those organizations.

3. The Superintendent shall maintain statewide recognition as an educational leader.

Measurement: Measurement shall consist of an analysis of: professional reading; membership, attendance and participation level in professional organizations and groups; publications, presentations, recognition, and offices held.

198

Superintendent Responsibilities and Performance Indicators

Below is a list of 13 statements that reflect the major responsibilities of the superintendent in managing the district. The board will assess the superintendent's performance in fulfilling each of these responsibilities.

For ease of deliberation, the 13 statements are grouped by required categories of appraisal. Each statement is followed by a list of indicators that represent some of the behaviors a superintendent will exhibit in fulfilling the responsibility statement. The sets of indicators are not exhaustive. They are provided to board members as a common reference in assessing the superintendent's performance.

| Organizational Climate | 1. The superintendent displays effective personal leadership attributes.
Indicators
a. Demonstrates ability to gain staff support and commitment to district goals.
b. Maintains poise and emotional stability in the full range of professional activities.
c. Demonstrates ability to work well with individuals and groups.
d. Demonstrates the ability to speak and write effectively.
e. Demonstrates sensitivity in dealing with staff, student, and community members from diverse cultural backgrounds.
f. Maintains high standards of ethics, honesty, and integrity in all personal and professional matters.

2. The superintendent effectively delegates authority and responsibility.
Indicators
a. Clearly communicates performance expectations to staff.
b. Provides those responsible for delegated tasks with ample authority and support.
c. Effectively monitors progress of delegated tasks.
d. Uses collaborative decisionmaking with staff when appropriate and feasible. |

21

Board/Superintendent Relations	3. The superintendent maintains a positive and productive working relationship with the board of trustees. *Indicators* a. Keeps board adequately informed on issues, needs, and operations of the school system. b. Prepares board agendas and meeting materials with the board president. c. Presents pertinent and objective facts and explanations in assisting the board with its policy decisions. d. Is responsive to the concerns of board members. e. Supports board policies and actions in a positive manner. --- 4. The superintendent assists in the development of and effectively administers board policy. *Indicators* a. Recommends effective policies on organization, finance, instructional programs, personnel, school plant, and related functions of the district. b. Communicates and interprets board policies to the staff and community and executes them as communicated. c. Effectively and promptly initiates administrative procedures necessary to implement board policy. d. Ensures compliance with all laws and state regulations in district policies and procedures.
Organizational Improvement	5. The superintendent effectively plans district programs and services to meet identified needs. *Indicators* a. Recommends appropriate goals and objectives for the district. b. Develops effective long- and short-range plans to implement district goals and improve programs. c. Uses collaborative planning processes when appropriate and feasible. d. Evaluates progress toward established program goals in a systematic fashion. e. Organizes resources, personnel, and facilities for the effective implementation of district goals.

Administration and Fiscal/Facilities Management	6. The superintendent directs the preparation and expenditure of the district budget within the district's fiscal capabilities. *Indicators* a. Anticipates and plans for long-range financial needs. b. Prepares sound recommendations and priorities for the annual budget. c. Provides for effective management of financial accounting and investment systems. d. Ensures that funds are expended in accordance with the approved budget. 7. The superintendent anticipates the district's needs for facilities and materials and establishes an effective system for their use. *Indicators* a. Keeps informed on physical needs of school programs including facilities, equipment, and supplies. b. Anticipates facility needs and administers building projects effectively and efficiently. c. Ensures that school plant and facilities are efficiently maintained.
Instructional Management	8. The superintendent coordinates a program of instruction that supports the philosophy and goals of the district. *Indicators* a. Keeps informed regarding all aspects of the instructional program. b. Communicates high expectations for student achievement. c. Involves appropriate groups in instructional goal setting. d. Initiates the planning for development and evaluation of new programs and services designed to achieve specific instructional goals and objectives.

Student Management	9. The superintendent oversees a system of student services and student discipline that is effective and equitable. *Indicators* a. Recommends sound discipline policies and ensures that they are equitably administered. b. Ensures that student rights are protected. c. Promotes support services for students that encourage student growth.
Personnel Management	10. The superintendent provides for personnel practices that promote high-quality staffing and job performance. *Indicators* a. Anticipates and recommends the number, types, and organization of positions needed to effectively and efficiently implement district programs. b. Maintains employment practices that provide for high-quality staff. c. Recommends equitable pay systems and appropriate pay increases for personnel. d. Effectively evaluates the performance of district administrative personnel. --- 11. The superintendent initiates and promotes an effective employee relations program. *Indicators* a. Provides for the development and execution of fair and effective personnel procedures and practices. b. Provides for clear lines of authority and communication in district's management organization. c. Displays sensitivity to the needs and concerns of staff. d. Promotes a positive work environment that supports high staff morale. e. Supports the professional development of all personnel through a well-planned comprehensive training program.

School/Community Relations	12. The superintendent promotes positive community relations through effective communication and involvement of community members. *Indicators* a. Develops and implements a planned program for communication between the schools and the community. b. Promotes districtwide community support and involvement with the schools. c. Gains community support for bond issues, tax issues, and other referenda that promote the district's goals and objectives. d. Represents the district in activities involving other school systems, institutions, agencies, and professional or community groups. e. Maintains a cooperative relationship with the news media.
Professional Growth and Development	13. The superintendent seeks opportunities for continued professional growth. *Indicators* a. Plans for specific improvement in professional performance. b. Pursues continuing professional development through reading, attending conferences, and involvement with related agencies.

Superintendent Performance Evaluation

Examples of Anchored Rating Scales

Four-Point Numerical Rating Scale

Five-Point Numerical Rating Scale

Nine-Point Numerical Rating Scale

Two-Point Descriptive Rating Scale (with comment sections)

Three-Point Descriptive Rating Scale (with comment sections)

Five-Point Descriptive Rating Scale (with comment sections)

Four-Point Descriptive Rating Scale (with strengths/weaknesses/suggestions for improvement sections)

Superintendent, Four-Point, Self-Assessment Numerical Rating Scale

ALABAMA PROFESSIONAL EDUCATION PERSONNEL EVALUATION PROGRAM

SUPERINTENDENT'S QUESTIONNAIRE
FOR COMPLETION BY LOCAL BOARD OF EDUCATION

Evaluatee: _____ Evaluator: _____ Date: _____

This questionnaire should be completed by the members of the local board of education. Each board member should complete the questionnaire individually. Then the scores from each board member's questionnaire should be averaged for each indicator. The averaged scores will be recorded on the Evaluation Summary Report.

The definition items listed under each indicator define that indicator. These should be used to formulate a response at the indicator level. Following the last indicator of each competency, a space is provided for the board member to write notes which justify the assigned scores. **The following rating scale should be used to determine a rating for each item and indicator assessed:**

1 - Unsatisfactory	Indicates the evaluatee's performance in this position requirement is not acceptable. Improvement activities must be undertaken immediately.
2 - Needs Improvement	Indicates the evaluatee's performance needs improvement in this position requirement. Improvement activities are required for performance to meet standards.
3 - Area Of Strength	Indicates the evaluatee always meets, and sometimes exceeds expectations for performance in this position requirement. Performance can be improved in the area(s) indicated, but current practices are clearly acceptable.
4 - Demonstrates Excellence	Indicates the evaluatee does an outstanding job in this position requirement. No area for improvement is readily identifiable.
L - Limited Responsibility	Indicates the evaluatee has limited **(L)** responsibility in this indicator/competency area. When an "L" is indicated, a numerical rating (1-4) should also be assigned.

Use Definitional Items to Determine Indicator Ratings

(KEY)   1 - Unsatisfactory   3 - Area of Strength   [L - Limited Responsibility]
               2 - Needs Improvement   4 - Demonstrates Excellence

1.0 CHIEF EXECUTIVE OFFICE OF THE SCHOOL BOARD

1.2 Reports to the School Board the Status of Programs, Personnel, and Operations   1   2   3   4 | L

	1	2	3	4	L
- prepares and presents to the board an annual written report					
- reports to the board at the beginning of each school year the certification/ licensure status of all professional staff	1	2	3	4	L
- reports regularly to the board the status of school system operations; e.g., budget, financial conditions, support services, policy implementation efforts	1	2	3	4	L
- reports to the board school system and school problems of which they should be aware and plans for correcting them	1	2	3	4	L
- reports and interprets to the board new or modified federal and state laws and state board policies and regulations	1	2	3	4	L
- appraises the board of current trends and developments in education	1	2	3	4	L

F32-0991

KEY	1 - Unsatisfactory	3 - Area of Strength	L - Limited Responsibility
	2 - Needs Improvement	4 - Demonstrates Excellence	

1.3 Performs Duties as Chief Executive Officer   1 2 3 4   L

- ensures that schools are operated in accordance with applicable federal and state laws and the rules and regulations of the state and local boards of education   1 2 3 4   L
- prepares, when necessary, plans for consolidation of schools and submits them to the board for approval   1 2 3 4   L
- prepares courses of study in accordance with state board rules and regulations, submits them to the local board for approval, and supplies printed copies to all staff and interested citizens   1 2 3 4   L
- prepares rules and regulations for grading and standardizing the schools and submits them for approval to the local board   1 2 3 4   L
- visits the schools regularly   1 2 3 4   L
- directs the taking of the city/county quadrennial school census   1 2 3 4   L
- prepares and submits the annual report to the state superintendent of education   1 2 3 4   L
- serves as a liaison between the school board and school personnel   1 2 3 4   L
- ensures that approved board minutes are maintained and available to the public   1 2 3 4   L

NOTES FOR JUSTIFICATION OF SCORES:

2.0 EDUCATIONAL LEADERSHIP OF THE SCHOOLS

2.1 Communicates Vision/Mission to Staff, Students, and Parents/Guardians   1 2 3 4   L

- prepares and seeks board approval of a mission and goals statement   1 2 3 4   L
- disseminates (orally and in writing) the mission and goals of the school system to staff, students, and parents/guardians.   1 2 3 4   L
- speaks regularly to community organizations, civic and church groups, and parent groups about vision, mission, programs of the schools   1 2 3 4   L

NOTES FOR JUSTIFICATION OF SCORES:

4.0 FINANCIAL MANAGEMENT

4.1 Seeks Sufficient Funding for the School System   1 2 3 4   L

- identifies long-range and short-range financial needs of the school system   1 2 3 4   L
- communicates (orally and in writing) specific financial needs of the schools regularly to the local board, local government, community, state board, and state legislature   1 2 3 4   L
- identifies sources of potential funding beyond the state and local budget and applies for them   1 2 3 4   L
- seeks resources and assistance through collaboration with business and industry   1 2 3 4   L

4.2 Prepares Budget   1 2 3 4   L

- prepares and submits to the board for approval an annual budget and salary schedule   1 2 3 4   L
- involves administrative and teaching personnel in budget preparation   1 2 3 4   L
- prepares for the board and publishes in a newspaper an annual statement of receipts and disbursements   1 2 3 4   L

4.3 Ensures Compliance with Federal, State, and Local Laws and Policies   1 2 3 4   L

- communicates (orally and in writing) to all school personnel federal and state laws and policies regarding receipt and expenditures of funds   1 2 3 4   L
- reviews expenditures by central office personnel and building administrators   1 2 3 4   L

206

KEY	1 - Unsatisfactory 2 - Needs Improvement	3 - Area of Strength 4 - Demonstrates Excellence	L - Limited Responsibility

4.4 Establishes and Maintains Procedures for Procurement and Fixed Assets Control of Equipment and Supplies

1 2 3 4   L

- prepares and disseminates written procedures for procurement and fixed assets control of equipment and supplies in accordance with local board policies, state laws, and State Board of Education rules and regulations   1 2 3 4 L
- assigns specific responsibilities for procurement and control to appropriate persons   1 2 3 4 L
- reviews procurement and control processes regularly and adjusts as necessary   1 2 3 4 L
- maintains a current fixed assets inventory   1 2 3 4 L

NOTES FOR JUSTIFICATION OF SCORES:

5.0 COMMUNITY RELATIONS

5.3 Models Positive Community Involvement

1 2 3 4   L

- participates actively in civic organizations and community activities   1 2 3 4 L
- makes school facilities available to the community   L 2 3 4 L
- invites and provides opportunities for community participation in planning and problem solving   1 2 3 3 L

NOTES FOR JUSTIFICATION OF SCORES:

6.0 MANAGEMENT OF SCHOOL SYSTEM RESOURCES

6.1 Manages School Facilities

1 2 3 4   L

- establishes and implements both long-range and short-range plans for financing, construction, renovation, maintenance, and demolition of buildings   1 2 3 4 L
- ensures the protection of property   1 2 3 4 L
- monitors and evaluates facilities utilization, construction, and maintenance   1 2 3 4 L
- provides adequate human and fiscal resources to ensure the protection of property, and the adequacy and appearance of facilities   1 2 3 4 L

NOTES FOR JUSTIFICATION OF SCORES:

7.0 COMMUNICATION AND INTERPERSONAL RELATIONS

7.1 Speaks Clearly, Correctly, and Coherently

1 2 3 4   L

- uses standard speech   1 2 3 4 L
- pronounces words correctly   1 2 3 4 L
- adjusts rate of speaking when needed/requested   1 2 3 4 L
- adjusts speaking volume when needed/requested   1 2 3 4 L
- organizes presentations   1 2 3 4 L
- uses vocabulary and style appropriate to level of audience   1 2 3 4 L
- speaks fluently without hesitations   1 2 3 4 L

F32-0991

KEY	1 - Unsatisfactory 2 - Needs Improvement	3 - Area of Strength 4 - Demonstrates Excellence	L - Limited Responsibility

7.2 Writes Clearly, Correctly, and Coherently

1 2 3 4 | L

- spells words correctly — 1 2 3 4 | L
- uses correct grammar and mechanics — 1 2 3 4 | L
- writes legibly — 1 2 3 4 | L
- uses vocabulary and style appropriate to level of audience — 1 2 3 4 | L
- organizes written information — 1 2 3 4 | L

7.3 Establishes Effective Communication Processes and Interpersonal Relations

1 2 3 4 | L

- develops and maintains systematic, two-way communication with school personnel, students parents/guardians, board, and community — 1 2 3 4 | L
- brings factions together to resolve issues — 1 2 3 4 | L
- demonstrates skill in conducting conferences and interviews — 1 2 3 4 | L
- listens to other people — 1 2 3 4 | L
- uses nonverbal behaviors to establish positive climate and affect — 1 2 3 4 | L
- demonstrates fair and equitable treatment of all school personnel, students, and parents/guardians — 1 2 3 4 | L
- demonstrates respect and consideration for those with whom he/she interacts — 1 2 3 4 | L
- discusses problems and concerns directly with their sources rather than talking about them to others — 1 2 3 4 | L

NOTES FOR JUSTIFICATION OF SCORES:

9.0 PROFESSIONAL RESPONSIBILITIES

9.1 Implements Federal, State, and Local Laws, Policies, and Procedures

1 2 3 4 | L

- monitors implementation of applicable laws, policies, and procedures — 1 2 3 4 | L
- establishes procedures for maintaining up-to-date files of applicable laws, policies, and procedures — 1 2 3 4 | L
- communicates relevant information to all personnel to ensure accurate decision making and implementation of policies and procedures — 1 2 3 4 | L
- seeks clarification of policies, procedures, regulations as needed — 1 2 3 4 | L
- makes decisions in accordance with applicable policies and regulations including policies and guidelines on student promotion and retention — 1 2 3 4 | L
- supports established laws, policies, and procedures to school personnel, students, parents/ guardians — 1 2 3 4 | L

9.2 Peforms Duties In An Effective Manner

1 2 3 4 | L

- performs duties in accordance with established job description — 1 2 3 4 | L
- completes tasks on time — 1 2 3 4 | L
- responds to requests for service in a positive manner — 1 2 3 4 | L
- considers the interests of all persons when making decisions — 1 2 3 4 | L
- makes decisions in a timely manner — 1 2 3 4 | L
- performs duties accurately — 1 2 3 4 | L
- is punctual for work, meetings, and appointments — 1 2 3 4 | L
- provides data to school board and other agencies as requested — 1 2 3 4 | L

NOTES FOR JUSTIFICATION OF SCORES:

SUPERINTENDENT EVALUATION FORM

5 - the administrator exceeds job requirements
4 - performance is above average
3 - administrator is doing a satisfactory job
2 - administrator needs to take action to improve
1 - performance does not meet job requirements

RELATIONSHIP WITH THE BOARD

[   ]   Keeps board informed of school activities, programs and problems

[   ]   Is receptive to board member ideas and suggestions

[   ]   Makes sound recommendations for board action

[   ]   Maintains a friendly and courteous attitude toward board members

[   ]   Facilitates the decision making process for the board

[   ]   Accepts board criticism as constructive suggestion for improvement

[   ]   Gives constructive criticism in a friendly, firm and positive way

[   ]   Follows up on all problems and issues brought to her attention

EFFECTIVE LEADERSHIP OF STAFF

[   ]   Maintains a highly qualified staff

[   ]   Encourages staff development

[   ]   Deals with staff honestly and fairly

Page 2

[ ]   Maintains open, concerned and congenial relations with staff

[ ]   Delegates effectively

[ ]   Involves staff in appropriate decision making

[ ]   Communicates well with staff

[ ]   Assesses the performance of employees fairly and reasonably

MANAGEMENT SKILLS AND ABILITIES:

[ ]   Maintains a smooth-running administrative office

[ ]   Prepares all necessary reports and keeps accurate records

[ ]   Speaks and writes acceptably

[ ]   Proposes organizational goals prior to each fiscal year

[ ]   Plans well in advance

[ ]   Is progressive in attitude and action

PERSONAL AND PROFESSIONAL ATTRIBUTES:

[ ]   Displays good grooming

[ ]   Projects professional demeanor

[ ]   Participates in professional activities such as association activities

[ ]   Participates in community activities

[ ]   Displays a good sense of humor

FISCAL MANAGEMENT:

[　]　Presents a balanced budget

[　]　Completes the year with a balanced budget

[　]　Displays common sense and good judgment in business transactions

[　]　Adequately supervises physical plant operations

[　]　Adequately supervises food service operations

[　]　Adequately supervises transportation operations

COMMUNITY AND PUBLIC RELATIONS

[　]　Represents the school in a positive and professional manner

[　]　Actively promotes the school to the public

[　]　Accepts public criticism and responds appropriately

SILVERDALE, WASHINGTON

SUPERINTENDENT'S EVALUATION FORM

Scoring Instructions: Please assess the administrator's performance by scoring each item. A score of (1) is the lowest possible score and connotes gross incompetence; a score of (9) indicates excellent and/or commendable performance. Your appraisal is a serious and responsible assignment. The superintendent wants to know his level of performance as perceived by the Board.

Areas of Responsibility	Unsatis-factory			Satis-factory			Commend-able		
	1	2	3	4	5	6	7	8	9
A. RELATIONSHIPS WITH THE BOARD									
1. Keeps the Board informed on issues, needs and operation of the school system based on thorough study and analysis.									
2. Offers professional advice to the Board on items requiring Board action.									
3. Interprets and executes the intent of Board policy.									
4. Seeks and accepts constructive criticism of his/her work.									
5. Supports Board policy and actions to the public and staff.									
6. Has a harmonious working relationship with the Board.									
7. Understands his/her role in administration of board policy, makes recommendations for employment or promotion of personnel in writing and with supporting data; and accepts responsibility for his/her recommendations. If the recommendation is not accepted by the Board, he/she willingly finds another person to recommend.									
8. Receives recommendation for personnel from Board Members and applies the same criteria for his/her selection for recommendation as he/she applies to applications from other sources.									
9. Accepts his/her responsibility for maintaining liaison between the Board and personnel, working toward a high degree of understanding and respect between the staff and the Board and the Board and the staff.									
10. Remains impartial toward the Board, treating all Board Members alike.									
11. Refrains from criticism of individual or group members of the Board.									
12. Goes immediately and directly to the Board when he/she feels an honest, objective difference of opinion exists between him/her and any or all members of the Board in an earnest effort to resolve such difference immediately.									

212

Areas of Responsibility	Unsatis-factory			Satis-factory			Commend-able		
	1	2	3	4	5	6	7	8	9
13. Bases his/her position with regard to matters discussed by the Board upon principle and is willing to maintain that position without regard for its popularity until an official position has been reached, after which time he/she supports the decision of the Board, as long as he/she remains in its employ.									
B. COMMUNITY RELATIONSHIPS									
14. Gains respect and support of the community on the conduct of the school operation.									
15. Solicits and gives attention to problems and opinions of all groups and individuals.									
16. Develops friendly and cooperative relationships with news media.									
17. Participates actively in community life and affairs.									
18. Works effectively with public and private agencies.									
C. STAFF AND PERSONNEL RELATIONSHIPS									
19. Develops and executes sound personnel procedures and practices.									
20. Develops good staff morale and loyalty to the organization.									
21. Treats all personnel fairly, without favoritism or discrimination.									
22. Delegates authority to staff members appropriate to the position each holds.									
23. Recruits and assigns the best available personnel in terms of their competencies.									
24. Encourages participation of appropriate staff members and groups in planning, developing procedures for implementation and policy interpretation.									
25. Evaluates performance of staff members, giving commendation for good work as well as constructive suggestions for improvement.									
26. Takes an active role in development of salary schedules for all personnel and recommends to the Board the levels which, within budgetary limitations, will best serve the interests of the District.									

Areas of Responsibility	Unsatisfactory			Satisfactory			Commendable		
	1	2	3	4	5	6	7	8	9
27. At the direction of the Board, meets and confers with leaders of the teachers' association representing to the best of his/her ability and understanding the interest and will of the Board.									
D. EDUCATIONAL LEADERSHIP									
28. Understands and keeps informed regarding all aspects of the instructional program.									
29. Implements the District's philosophy of education.									
30. Participates with staff, Board and community in studying and developing curriculum.									
31. Organizes a planned program of staff evaluation and improvement.									
32. Provides democratic procedures in curriculum work, utilizing the abilities and talents of the entire professional staff and lay people of the community.									
33. Inspires others to highest professional standards.									
E. BUSINESS AND FINANCE									
34. Keeps informed on needs of the school program -- plant, facilities, equipment and supplies.									
35. Supervises operations, insisting on competent and efficient performance.									
36. Determines that funds are spent wisely and adequate control and accounting are maintained.									
37. Evaluates financial needs and makes recommendations for adequate financing.									
F. PERSONAL QUALITIES									
38. Defends principle and conviction in the face of pressure and partisan influence.									
39. Maintains high standards of ethics, honesty and integrity in all personal and professional matters.									
40. Earns respect and standing among professional colleagues.									
41. Devotes his/her time and energy effectively to his/her job.									
42. Demonstrates his/her ability to work well with individuals and groups.									

	Unsatis-factory			Satis-factory			Commend-able		
	1	2	3	4	5	6	7	8	9
43. Exercises good judgment and democratic processes in arriving at decisions.									
44. Possesses and maintains the health and energy necessary to meet the responsibilities of his/her position.									
45. Maintains poise and emotional stability in the full range of his/her professional activities.									
46. Is suitably attired and well groomed.									
47. Uses language effectively in dealing with staff members, the Board and the public.									
48. Writes clearly and concisely.									
49. Speaks well in front of large and small groups, expressing ideas in a logical and forthright manner.									
50. Maintains his/her professional development by reading course work, conference attendance, work on professional committees, visiting other districts and meeting with other superintendents.									

COMMENTS

Pleasant Plains Community District #8

Superintendent Evaluation

	Performs Adequately	Needs Improvement	Comments
Traits & Skills			
1. Attitude - projects a positive image to staff, community, students and others.			
2. Decision Making - makes timely and correct decisions without over reliance on others.			
3. Judgment and Perception - adapts to new and changing situations. Ability to recognize and define what is important.			
4. Leadership and Responsibility - motivates and influences others to do their best. Sets and applies high standards and goals.			
5. Progressiveness - keeps abreast and communicates current happenings in field. Initiates projects to improve school district.			
Management Responsibilities			
District Management			
1. Assesses district needs and develops goals and objectives.			
2. Develops management and leadership skills.			
3. Organizes staff and assignment of responsibilities.			
4. Delegates responsibility and reviews appraisal of staff performance.			
5. Communicates effectively to the school board.			
6. Provides information to school board to develop goals, policies, procedures, and evaluation of superintendent.			

CBI-CBG/AF

	Performs Adequately	Needs Improvement	Comments
Educational Programs			
1. Complies with legal requirements.			
2. Responsive to community needs and aspirations.			
3. Encourages research and development.			
4. Coordinates curriculum planning.			
5. Analyzes program standards and evaluation.			
6. Monitors grade-level articulation and departmental coordination.			
7. Promotes basic skills development.			
8. Monitors special programs such as special education, gifted.			
9. Monitors extra-curricular programs.			
Budget/Finance			
1. Researches potential revenue sources.			
2. Develops budget based on program priorities.			
3. Supervises accounting, auditing, and control procedures.			
4. Controls and approves purchasing.			
5. Prepares long range financial forecasts.			
Personnel Management			
1. Prepares written employment policies and procedures.			
2. Develops job descriptions.			
3. Recruits and selects employees.			

	Performs Adequately	Needs Improvement	Comments
4. Initiates training and development of staff.			
5. Advises board in collective bargaining and contract administration.			
Support Operations			
1. Advises on facility planning and development.			
2. Supervises plant operations, buildings, and group maintenance.			
3. Monitors transportation.			
4. Monitors food services.			
5. Supervises central office management.			
Communications/Public Relations			
1. Provides interim reports and board packets in a timely manner.			
2. Disseminates public information.			
3. Encourages citizen involvement in school matters.			
4. Coordinates special projects such as referendums.			

ADOPTED: JULY 20, 1992

ATTACHMENT E

DES MOINES ADMINISTRATOR PERFORMANCE EVALUATION INSTRUMENT *

*NOTE: Adjustments have been made to be superintendent specific

COMPOSITE PERFORMANCE RATING

		DOES NOT MEET	NEEDS IMPROVEMENT	MEETS
Performance Area I	Common Tasks			
Performance Area II	Job Specific Tasks			
Performance Area III	Objectives			
Summative Rating				

EVALUATEE'S SIGNATURE _____ DATE _____

ASSIGNMENT _____ DATE _____

EVALUATOR'S SIGNATURE _____ DATE _____

N - PERSONNEL FILE   Y - EVALUATOR COPY   P - EVALUATEE COPY

DES MOINES SUPERINTENDENT
PERFORMANCE EVALUATION INSTRUMENT

EVALUTEE_____ Evaluation Period _____ DATE_____

PERFORMANCE AREA II: Position Specific Tasks for Superintendent

A. RELATIONS WITH THE BOARD OF EDUCATION

LEVELS OF PERFORMANCE

	Inadequate (1)	Below Standard (2)	Standard (3)	Above Standard (4)	Exceptional (5)	Don't Know (DK)
1. Prepares adequately for board meetings.	❑	❑	❑	❑	❑	❑
2. Provides sufficient information to enable board members to make decisions.	❑	❑	❑	❑	❑	❑
3. Is responsive to concerns of board members.	❑	❑	❑	❑	❑	❑
4. Keeps board informed about school operations.	❑	❑	❑	❑	❑	❑
5. Implements board policies.	❑	❑	❑	❑	❑	❑
6. Advises board on need for new and/or revised polices and procedures.	❑	❑	❑	❑	❑	❑

COMMENTS:

B. MANAGEMENT OF PUBLIC RELATIONS

LEVELS OF PERFORMANCE

	Inadequate (1)	Below Standard (2)	Standard (3)	Above Standard (4)	Exceptional (5)	Don't Know (DK)
1. Handles media relations skillfully.	❑	❑	❑	❑	❑	❑
2. Maintains effective relations with local business/governmental leaders.	❑	❑	❑	❑	❑	❑
3. Is effective in working with state legislative leaders.	❑	❑	❑	❑	❑	❑
4. Maintains effective working relationships with State Department of Education personnel..	❑	❑	❑	❑	❑	❑
5. Presents a positive image of the schools to the public.	❑	❑	❑	❑	❑	❑
6. Handles parent concerns effectively and politely.	❑	❑	❑	❑	❑	❑
7. Is accessible to staff, students, parents and other citizens.	❑	❑	❑	❑	❑	❑

COMMENTS:

C. INTERACTION: RELATES EFFECTIVELY WITH OTHERS

LEVELS OF PERFORMANCE

	Inadequate (1)	Below Standard (2)	Standard (3)	Above Standard (4)	Exceptional (5)	Don't Know (DK)
1. Contributes to harmony and unity of human resources within the district.	❑	❑	❑	❑	❑	❑
2. Models appropriate human relation skills.	❑	❑	❑	❑	❑	❑
3. Maintains effective two-way (oral & written) communications.	❑	❑	❑	❑	❑	❑
4. Represents the school district appropriately outside the organization.	❑	❑	❑	❑	❑	❑
5. Motivates others to accomplish professional and district goals.	❑	❑	❑	❑	❑	❑
6. Participates as a member of the district's administrative team.	❑	❑	❑	❑	❑	❑
7. Participates in personal growth activities.	❑	❑	❑	❑	❑	❑
8. Displays a professional attitude toward work.	❑	❑	❑	❑	❑	❑
9. Places a high priority on personal integrity.	❑	❑	❑	❑	❑	❑

COMMENTS:

D. ASSESSING OUTCOMES: ASSESSES RESULTS OF PROGRAMS, ACTIVITIES, EVENTS AND STAFF PERFORMANCE

LEVELS OF PERFORMANCE

	Inadequate (1)	Below Standard (2)	Standard (3)	Above Standard (4)	Exceptional (5)	Don't Know (DK)
1. Recognizes and/or establishes standards and criteria to judge program value or worth.	❑	❑	❑	❑	❑	❑
2. Applies standards and criteria to assess results of processes and programs.	❑	❑	❑	❑	❑	❑
3. Arrives at reasoned decisions and makes recommendations and/or judgments based on assessment.	❑	❑	❑	❑	❑	❑
4. Recognizes the importance of focusing on student outcomes.	❑	❑	❑	❑	❑	❑
5. Utilizes staff performance evaluations as part of making changes in their roles and responsibilities.	❑	❑	❑	❑	❑	❑

COMMENTS:

C. MANAGEMENT OF TEACHING AND LEARNING

LEVELS OF PERFORMANCE

	Inadequate (1)	Below Standard (2)	Standard (3)	Above Standard (4)	Exceptional (5)	Don't Know (DK)
1. Is knowledgeable and up-to-date in curriculum and instructional trends and developments.	❏	❏	❏	❏	❏	❏
2. Monitors the effectiveness and equity issues related to the educational program.	❏	❏	❏	❏	❏	❏
3. Devotes adequate time and effort to strategic or short/long-range planning.	❏	❏	❏	❏	❏	❏
4. Recommends instructional improvement programs to the school board.	❏	❏	❏	❏	❏	❏
5. Prepares an annual strategic planning report on achievement of district goals and objectives.	❏	❏	❏	❏	❏	❏
6. Works with board and staff to develop district improvement plan and program priorities.	❏	❏	❏	❏	❏	❏

COMMENTS:

D. MANAGEMENT OF STAFF, BUSINESS AND PHYSICAL RESOURCES

LEVELS OF PERFORMANCE

	Inadequate (1)	Below Standard (2)	Standard (3)	Above Standard (4)	Exceptional (5)	Don't Know (DK)
1. Defines and delegates responsibility.	❏	❏	❏	❏	❏	❏
2. Ensures a system of staff development.	❏	❏	❏	❏	❏	❏
3. Establishes and monitors procedures for evaluating staff performance.	❏	❏	❏	❏	❏	❏
4. Plans, organizes and recommends an annual budget to the school board.	❏	❏	❏	❏	❏	❏
5. Monitors district revenues and expenditures.	❏	❏	❏	❏	❏	❏
6. Conducts and directs studies and planned activities related to school organization, attendance area boundaries and school facility requirements.	❏	❏	❏	❏	❏	❏
7. Plans plant and equipment fund budget strategy and recommends priorities.	❏	❏	❏	❏	❏	❏

COMMENTS:

E. PROFESSIONAL QUALITIES

LEVELS OF PERFORMANCE

	Inadequate (1)	Below Standard (2)	Standard (3)	Above Standard (4)	Exceptional (5)	Don't Know (DK)
1. Writes effectively.	❑	❑	❑	❑	❑	❑
2. Speaks effectively.	❑	❑	❑	❑	❑	❑
3. Has good judgment, perception and common sense.	❑	❑	❑	❑	❑	❑
4. Makes timely and justifiable decisions backed by supportive rationale.	❑	❑	❑	❑	❑	❑
5. Demonstrates leadership by accepting responsibility for addressing complex district issues.	❑	❑	❑	❑	❑	❑
6. Demonstrates fairness and consistency in the handling of problems.	❑	❑	❑	❑	❑	❑
7. Remains calm and poised in difficult situations.	❑	❑	❑	❑	❑	❑
8. Has a sense of humor.	❑	❑	❑	❑	❑	❑
9. Improves through positive participation in professional growth activities.	❑	❑	❑	❑	❑	❑

COMMENTS:

DES MOINES SUPERINTENDENT
PERFORMANCE EVALUATION INSTRUMENT

EVALUTEE_____   Evaluation Period _____   DATE_____

PERFORMANCE AREA III: Annual Objectives for Superintendent

ANNUAL OBJECTIVES MAY BE DEVELOPED FROM DISTRICT, DEPARTMENTAL, BUILDING, PERSONAL, AND/OR PROFESSIONAL GOALS.

OBJECTIVES:

LEVELS OF PERFORMANCE

	Inadequate (1)	Below Standard (2)	Standard (3)	Above Standard (4)	Exceptional (5)	Don't Know (DK)
Refer to superintendent's district issues and responsibility statement for 1996-97 (attachments C and D).	❑	❑	❑	❑	❑	❑

The superintendent's 1995-96 weighted objectives are on the following pages.

MID-YEAR COMMENTS:

_____
Evaluatee's Signature   Date

ANNUAL COMMENTS:

_____   _____   _____
Evaluatee's Signature   Evaluator's Signature   Date

1. The following aspects should be included in any annual objective: A) Who is to accomplish annual objective; B) What is to be accomplished; C) Date of attainment; D) How attainment is to be documented or measured; and E) (When appropriate) what contributes acceptable levels of performance.
2. At the time the annual objectives are adopted, evaluatee should discuss procedures, time lines and resources necessary to achieve stated objectives with the evaluator.
3. The evaluator is responsible for scheduling mid-year and annual conferences.
4. Summative evaluation reports should be completed in triplicate. Copies should be completed for the evaluator, evaluatee, and personnel office.

Sample

Summary Appraisal Report

Name _____ Date of Review _____

Appraisal Period: From _____ To _____

Directions

Based on cumulative performance information, evaluate the superintendent's effectiveness in meeting each responsibility. Next to each statement, assign the rating that most closely represents your judgment.

Any rating of CO, EE, or U should be accompanied by written comments specifying the reasons for the rating. The board member has the option of attaching an addendum.

Rating Scale

CO   Clearly Outstanding: Performance is consistently far superior to what is normally expected.

EE   Exceeds Expectations: Performance demonstrates increased proficiency and is consistently above expectations.

ME   Meets Expectations: Performance meets expectations and presents no significant problems.

BE   Below Expectations: Performance is consistently below expectations and significant problems exist.

U   Unsatisfactory: Performance is consistently unacceptable.

Performance Responsibilities   *Rating*

Organizational Climate

1. The superintendent displays effective personal leadership attributes.   _____

2. The superintendent effectively delegates authority and responsibility.   _____

Board/Superintendent Relations

3. The superintendent maintains a positive and productive working   _____
relationship with the board of trustees.

4. The superintendent assists in the development of and effectively   _____
administers board policy.

Performance Responsibilities   *Rating*

Organizational Improvement

5. The superintendent effectively plans district programs and services _____
to meet identified needs.

Administration and Fiscal/Facilities Management

6. The superintendent directs the preparation and expenditure of the _____
district budget within the district's fiscal capabilities.

7. The superintendent anticipates the district's needs for facilities and _____
materials and establishes an effective system for their use.

Instructional Management

8. The superintendent coordinates a program of instruction that sup- _____
ports the philosophy and goals of the district.

Student Management

9. The superintendent oversees a system of student services and stu- _____
dent discipline that is effective and equitable.

Personnel Management

10. The superintendent provides for personnel practices that promote _____
high-quality staffing and job performance.

11. The superintendent initiates and promotes an effective employee _____
relations program.

School/Community Relations

12. The superintendent promotes positive community relations through _____
effective communication and involvement of community members.

Professional Growth and Development

13. The superintendent seeks opportunities for continued professional _____
growth.

Comments by board member(s): _____

_____
_____
_____
_____
_____
_____
_____
_____
_____
_____
_____
_____

Comments by superintendent: _____

_____
_____
_____
_____
_____
_____
_____
_____
_____
_____
_____

_____   _____
Superintendent's Signature   *Date*

_____   _____
Board President's Signature   *Date*

CENTRAL KITSAP SCHOOL DISTRICT NO. 401
Silverdale, Washington 98383   YEAR _____

ADMINISTRATIVE EVALUATION REPORT - Form 1

NAME _____

SCHOOL/LOCATION _____

ADMINISTRATIVE ASSIGNMENT _____

If other than annual evaluation, indicate period
of time covered by report _____

Progress Conference Date Prior To
Feb. 1 _____

Year-End Conference Date Prior To
June 1 _____

Other Conference Date

_____

_____

It is my judgement, based upon the adopted criteria and the (individual's specified **
objectives) that this administrator's overall performance has _____
expectations during the evaluation period covered by this   (met or not met)
report.

_____
(Supervisor's Signature)

CRITERIA	STRENGTHS, WEAKNESSES SUGGESTIONS FOR IMPROVEMENT

EVALUATION OF PERSONNEL
Rating:
  Exceeds expectations _____
  Meets expectations _____
  Does not meet expectations _____
  Undetermined at this time _____	

SCHOOL/DEPARTMENT ADMINISTRATIVE/MANAGEMENT
Rating:
  Exceeds expectations _____
  Meets expectations _____
  Does not meet expectations _____
  Undetermined at this time _____	

SCHOOL/DEPARTMENT FINANCE
Rating:
  Exceeds expectations _____
  Meets expectations _____
  Does not meet expectations _____
  Undetermined at this time _____	

** added by Cabinet to Evaluation Committee working draft 10/1/80

PROFESSIONAL PREPARATION AND
SCHOLARSHIP

Rating:

  Exceeds expectations _____

  Meets expectations _____

  Does not meet expectations _____

  Undetermined at this time _____

EFFORT TOWARD IMPROVEMENT
WHEN NEEDED

Rating:

  Exceeds expectations _____

  Meets expectations _____

  Does not meet expectations _____

  Undetermined at this time _____

EMPATHY FOR PUPILS, EMPLOYEES,
PATRONS

Rating:

  Exceeds expectations _____

  Meets expectations _____

  Does not meet expectations _____

  Undetermined at this time _____

LEADERSHIP

Rating:

  Exceeds expectations _____

  Meets expectations _____

  Does not meet expectations _____

  Undetermined at this time _____

KNOWLEDGE OF, EXPERIENCE IN, AND
TRAINING IN RECOGNIZING GOOD
PROFESSIONAL PERFORMANCE, CAPABILITIES
AND DEVELOPMENT IN SELECTING PERSONNEL

Rating:

  Exceeds expectations _____

  Meets expectations _____

  Does not meet expectations _____

  Undetermined at this time _____

GENERAL COMMENTS:_____

_____

_____

_____

I certify that I have met and discussed the content of this evaluation report with my
supervisor and that I have been given a copy of the report. My signature does not,
however, necessarily indicate agreement with the findings.

_____   _____
Signature   Date

ALABAMA PROFESSIONAL EDUCATION PERSONNEL EVALUATION PROGRAM

SELF-ASSESSMENT FORM

SUPERINTENDENT

Evaluatee: _____   Social Security No: _ _ _ - _ _ - _ _ _ _ .

System/School: _____   Date: _ _ / _ _ / _ _ .
M M   D D   Y Y

This self-assessment instrument should be completed by the evaluatee. The information obtained from the self-assessment should be used by the evaluatee in formulating a professional development plan. The self-assessment results should be used for four purposes: 1) to identify areas which the individual perceives need improvement; 2) to compare individual perceptions of performance with results of evaluation by a superordinate; 3) to determine the basis for personal professional growth activities; and 4) to develop a professional development plan collaboratively with one's supervisor.

Evaluatees should refer to the list of definition items in determining their performance for the indicators and competency areas. *The definition items define each indicator and should be used to formulate a response at the indicator level.* The results from the indicators should be reviewed to formulate an overall rating for each competency area. *The following rating scale should be used to determine the ratings for each of the indicators and competency areas.*

1 - Unsatisfactory	*Indicates the evaluatee's performance in this position requirement is not acceptable. Improvement activities must be undertaken immediately.*
2 - Needs Improvement	*Indicates the evaluatee's performance needs improvement in this position requirement. Improvement activities are required for performance to meet standards.*
3 - Area Of Strength	*Indicates the evaluatee always meets, and sometimes exceeds expectations for performance in this position requirement. Performance can be improved in the area(s) indicated, but current practices are clearly acceptable.*
4 - Demonstrates Excellence	*Indicates the evaluatee does an outstanding job in this position requirement. No area for improvement is readily identifiable.*
L - Limited Responsibility	*Indicates the evaluatee has limited (L) responsibility in this indicator/ competency area. When an "L" is indicated, a numerical rating (1-4) should also be assigned.*

Use Definitional Items to Determine Indicator Ratings
Use Indicator Ratings to Determine Competency Scores

KEY
1 - Unsatisfactory   3 - Area of Strength   L - Limited Responsibility
2 - Needs Improvement   4 - Demonstrates Excellence

1.0 CHIEF EXECUTIVE OFFICER OF THE SCHOOL BOARD	1 2 3 4	L

1.1 Recommends Actions to the School Board and Implements Policies of the School Board — 1 2 3 4 | L

- recommends to the board for approval an education improvement plan, the annual budget, new programs, operations, services, or student requirements — 1 2 3 4 | L
- recommends development and/or adoption of new board policies and modification of existing ones including promotion/retention decisions — 1 2 3 4 | L
- disseminates and interprets board policies to school personnel, parents/guardians, and community — 1 2 3 4 | L
- develops plans, procedures, and timelines for implementation of board policies — 1 2 3 4 | L
- assigns specific implementation responsibilities to appropriate personnel and ensures that they are properly trained for their roles — 1 2 3 4 | L
- monitors implementation efforts — 1 2 3 4 | L

1

1.2 Reports to the School Board the Status of Programs, Personnel, and Operations

1 2 3 4 | L

- prepares and presents to the board an annual written report   1 2 3 4 | L
- reports to the board at the beginning of each school year the certification/licensure status of all professional staff   1 2 3 4 | L
- reports regularly to the board the status of school system operations; e.g., budget, financial conditions, support services, policy implementation efforts   1 2 3 4 | L
- reports to the board school system and school problems of which they should be aware and plans for correcting them   1 2 3 4 | L
- reports and interprets to the board new or modified federal and state laws and State Board policies and regulations   1 2 3 4 | L
- appraises the board of current trends and developments in education   1 2 3 4 | L

1.3 Performs Duties as Chief Executive Officer

1 2 3 4 | L

- ensures that schools are operated in accordance with applicable federal and state laws and the rules and regulations of the state and local boards of education   1 2 3 4 | L
- prepares, when necessary, plans for consolidation of schools and submits them to the board for approval   1 2 3 4 | L
- prepares courses of study in accordance with state board rules and regulations, submits them to the local board for approval and supplies printed copies to all staff and interested citizens   1 2 3 4 | L
- prepares rules and regulations for grading and standardizing the schools and submits them for approval to the local board   1 2 3 4 | L
- visits the schools regularly   1 2 3 4 | L
- directs the taking of the city/county quadrennial school census   1 2 3 4 | L
- prepares and submits the annual report to the state superintendent of education   1 2 3 4 | L
- serves as a liaison between the school board and school personnel   1 2 3 4 | L
- ensures that approved board minutes are maintained and available to the public   1 2 3 4 | L

2.0 EDUCATIONAL LEADERSHIP OF THE SCHOOLS

1 2 3 4 | L

2.1 Communicates Vision/Mission to Staff, Students, and Parents/Guardians

1 2 3 4 | L

- prepares and seeks board approval of a mission and goals statement   1 2 3 4 | L
- disseminates (orally and in writing) the mission and goals of the school system to staff, students, and parents/guardians   1 2 3 4 | L
- speaks regularly to community organizations, civic and church groups, and parent groups about vision, mission, programs of the schools   1 2 3 4 | L

2.2 Provides for Supervision, Evaluation, and Professional Growth of All Personnel

1 2 3 4 | L

- recommends appropriate policies for evaluation of classified and non-classified personnel to the school board and other designated agencies for approval   1 2 3 4 | L
- assigns specific evaluation responsibilities to appropriate personnel   1 2 3 4 | L
- disseminates (orally and in writing) evaluation policies and procedures to all personnel   1 2 3 4 | L
- evaluates all persons directly responsible to the superintendent in accordance with approved policies, rules, and procedures   1 2 3 4 | L
- ensures that all persons responsible for personnel evaluations are trained adequately for their responsibilities   1 2 3 4 | L
- maintains appropriate records of personnel evaluation   1 2 3 4 | L
- ensures that administrative and supervisory personnel are evaluated on their implementation of personnel evaluation policies, procedures, and processes   1 2 3 4 | L
- ensures that personnel evaluation results and needs assessments are used in developing professional development and staff assistance programs   1 2 3 4 | L
- provides fiscal and human resources for a comprehensive staff development program consistent with state and local guidelines   1 2 3 4 | L
- monitors and evaluates the effectiveness of personnel evaluation and staff development programs in the school system   1 2 3 4 | L

232

2.3 Supervises the Planning, Implementation, and Evaluation of Curriculum and Instruction   1 2 3 4   L

- implements a systematic process to promote positive teaching practices which provide for a variety of grouping arrangements and instructional techniques 1 2 3 4   L
- ensures that administrators, teachers, parents/guardians, and students are directly involved in curriculum/instruction planning and evaluation 1 2 3 4   L
- ensures full-time supervision of instructional program 1 2 3 4   L
- ensures that all persons responsible for curriculum/instruction planning, implementation, and evaluation are trained adequately for their responsibilities 1 2 3 4   L
- prepares for the school system a written, sequential curriculum plan which is consistent with state courses of study and ensures that students have equal access to curriculum offerings 1 2 3 4   L
- develops and implements a plan for textbook selection and adoption and for selection and acquisition of supplementary print and non-print materials 1 2 3 4   L
- monitors curriculum/instruction planning, implementation, and evaluation activities 1 2 3 4   L
- maintains appropriate records of curriculum/instruction planning, implementation, and evaluation activities 1 2 3 4   L
- provides appropriate human and financial resources for curriculum planning, implementation, and evaluation activities 1 2 3 4   L

2.4 Establishes Goals for Student Achievement   1 2 3 4   L

- develops and implements a comprehensive, ongoing program of student assessment and a plan for collection of student outcome data (standardized test results, ACT, SAT, criterion-referenced test data, attendance data, attitude surveys, etc.) and monitors data collection 1 2 3 4   L
- establishes procedures for analyzing student achievement data utilizing assessment results consistent with purposes for which designed, and establishing from them achievement goals and objectives 1 2 3 4   L
- identifies strategies and provides human and fiscal resources for attaining achievement goals and objectives 1 2 3 4   L
- monitors and evaluates progress toward achievement goals and objectives annually and reports results to students, parents/guardians, community, and other agencies needing those data 1 2 3 4   L

3.0 PERSONNEL MANAGEMENT   1 2 3 4   L

3.1 Develops and Implements a Comprehensive Personnel Plan   1 2 3 4   L

- identifies long-range and short-range personnel needs and goals 1 2 3 4   L
- ensures that up-to-date job descriptions are developed and maintained for all positions 1 2 3 4   L
- implements strategies for achieving personnel goals, including recruitment of minorities 1 2 3 4   L
- provides human and financial resources necessary to personnel plan 1 2 3 4   L
- monitors and evaluates the effectiveness of the personnel plan and its implementation annually and makes necessary adjustments 1 2 3 4   L

3.2 Assigns, Orients, and Inducts Personnel to Schools and Offices   1 2 3 4   L

- provides lines of authority, responsibility, and accountability for all personnel 1 2 3 4   L
- provides sufficient qualified, trained personnel to schools and programs 1 2 3 4   L
- ensures that all personnel new to their positions receive orientation and induction through meetings, handbooks, orientation materials and programs, and other means 1 2 3 4   L

4.0 FINANCIAL MANAGEMENT   1 2 3 4   L

4.1 Seeks Sufficient Funding for the School System   1 2 3 4   L

- identifies long-range and short-range financial needs of the school system 1 2 3 4   L
- communicates (orally and in writing) specific financial needs of the schools regularly to the local board, local government, community, state board, and state legislature 1 2 3 4   L
- identifies sources of potential funding beyond the state and local budget and applies for them 1 2 3 4   L
- seeks resources and assistance through collaboration with business and industry 1 2 3 4   L

(KEY)	1 - Unsatisfactory	3 - Area of Strength		[L - Limited Responsibility]
	2 - Needs Improvement	4 - Demonstrates Excellence		

4.2 Prepares Budget 1 2 3 4 L

- prepares and submits to the board for approval an annual budget and salary schedule — 1 2 3 4 L
- involves administrative and teaching personnel in budget preparation — 1 2 3 4 L
- prepares for the board and publishes in a newspaper an annual statement of receipts
  and disbursements — 1 2 3 4 L

4.3 Ensures Compliance with Federal, State, and Local Laws and Policies 1 2 3 4 L

- communicates (orally and in writing) to all school personnel federal and state laws and
  policies regarding receipt and expenditures of funds — 1 2 3 4 L
- reviews expenditures by central office personnel and building administrators — 1 2 3 4 L

4.4 Establishes and Maintains Procedures for Procurement and Fixed Assets Control of Equipment and Supplies 1 2 3 4 L

- prepares and disseminates written procedures for procurement and fixed assets control of
  equipment and supplies in accordance with local board policies, state laws, and State
  Board of Education rules and regulations — 1 2 3 4 L
- assigns specific responsibilities for procurement and control to appropriate persons — 1 2 3 4 L
- reviews procurement and control processes regularly and adjusts as necessary — 1 2 3 4 L
- maintains a current fixed assets inventory — 1 2 3 4 L

5.0 COMMUNITY RELATIONS 1 2 3 4 L

5.1 Develops and Implements a System-Wide Plan for Community Relations 1 2 3 4 L

- identifies the segments of the community (individuals, organizations, businesses, industries)
  to which the school system and/or individual schools should relate — 1 2 3 4 L
- develops with appropriate faculty and staff input long-range and short-range goals and related
  objectives for improving community relations, evaluates them annually, and adjusts them when
  necessary — 1 2 3 4 L
- identifies and implements strategies for attaining goals and objectives — 1 2 3 4 L
- ensures that each local school develops and implements a community relations plan compatible
  with that of the school system — 1 2 3 4 L
- provides human and financial resources necessary to planning and implemention of
  community relations program — 1 2 3 4 L

5.2 Utilizes Local Media in Community Relations 1 2 3 4 L

- maintains continuing contact with local media (newspapers, radio, television) — 1 2 3 4 L
- develops materials for use by local media (press releases, articles, audiotapes, videotapes) — 1 2 3 4 L
- uses the local media to communicate the mission, goals for improvement, and progress of
  the schools in meeting stated goals — 1 2 3 4 L

5.3 Models Positive Community Involvement 1 2 3 4 L

- participates actively in civic organizations and community activities — 1 2 3 4 L
- makes school facilities available to the community — 1 2 3 4 L
- invites and provides opportunities for community participation in planning and problem solving — 1 2 3 4 L

6.0 MANAGEMENT OF SCHOOL SYSTEM RESOURCES 1 2 3 4 L

6.1 Manages School Facilities 1 2 3 4 L

- establishes and implements both long-range and short-range plans for financing, construction,
  renovation, maintenance, and demolition of buildings — 1 2 3 4 L
- ensures the protection of school property — 1 2 3 4 L
- monitors and evaluates facilities utilization, construction, and maintenance. — 1 2 3 4 L
- provides adequate human and fiscal resources to ensure the protection of property
  and the adequacy and appearance of facilities — 1 2 3 4 L

234

KEY	1 - Unsatisfactory 2 - Needs Improvement	3 - Area of Strength 4 - Demonstrates Excellence	L - Limited Responsibility

6.2 Manages Pupil Personnel Services — 1 2 3 4 | L

- develops and implements a comprehensive plan for pupil personnel services (counseling and guidance, at-risk students, library media, educational technology, transportation, food services, etc.) and ensures all students have equal access to services — 1 2 3 4 | L
- ensures that an accurate and comprehensive student record system is implemented (to include attendance, health/medical, guidance, psychological, disciplinary, and academic records) — 1 2 3 4 | L
- serves as a liaison between schools and community social agencies — 1 2 3 4 | L
- monitors and evaluates implementation of pupil personnel services — 1 2 3 4 | L

6.3 Implements Policies and Programs Relating to Student Conduct and Discipline — 1 2 3 4 | L

- establishes and communicates policies and procedures governing student conduct — 1 2 3 4 | L
- ensures that student conduct policies and procedures are implemented and consistently enforced — 1 2 3 4 | L
- provides programs for staff and students designed to improve student conduct — 1 2 3 4 | L

6.4 Ensures the Health and Safety of Students — 1 2 3 4 | L

- requires that school personnel establish and enforce appropriate health and safety standards for students — 1 2 3 4 | L
- ensures the safety of personnel and students — 1 2 3 4 | L
- provides adequate human and fiscal resources to ensure the health and safety of personnel and students — 1 2 3 4 | L
- provides programs of health and safety education for students and staff — 1 2 3 4 | L
- monitors the enforcement of health and safety standards through regular visits to schools and program sites — 1 2 3 4 | L

7.0 COMMUNICATION AND INTERPERSONAL RELATIONS — 1 2 3 4 | L

7.1 Speaks Clearly, Correctly, and Coherently — 1 2 3 4 | L

- uses standard speech — 1 2 3 4 | L
- pronounces words correctly — 1 2 3 4 | L
- adjusts rate of speaking when needed/requested — 1 2 3 4 | L
- adjusts speaking volume when needed/requested — 1 2 3 4 | L
- organizes presentations — 1 2 3 4 | L
- uses vocabulary and style appropriate to level of audience — 1 2 3 4 | L
- speaks fluently without hesitations — 1 2 3 4 | L

7.2 Writes Clearly, Correctly, and Coherently — 1 2 3 4 | L

- spells words correctly — 1 2 3 4 | L
- uses correct grammar and mechanics — 1 2 3 4 | L
- writes legibly — 1 2 3 4 | L
- uses vocabulary and style appropriate to level of audience — 1 2 3 4 | L
- organizes written information — 1 2 3 4 | L

7.3 Establishes Effective Communication Processes and Interpersonal Relationships — 1 2 3 4 | L

- develops and maintains systematic, two-way communication with school personnel, students, parents/guardians, board, and community — 1 2 3 4 | L
- brings factions together to resolve issues — 1 2 3 4 | L
- demonstrates skill in conducting conferences and interviews — 1 2 3 4 | L
- listens to other people — 1 2 3 4 | L
- uses nonverbal behaviors to establish positive climate and affect — 1 2 3 4 | L
- demonstrates fair and equitable treatment of all school personnel, students, and parents/guardians — 1 2 3 4 | L
- demonstrates respect and consideration for those with whom he/she interacts — 1 2 3 4 | L
- discusses problems and concerns directly with their sources rather than talking about them to others — 1 2 3 4 | L

F28_0191

KEY	1 - Unsatisfactory 2 - Needs Improvement	3 - Area of Strength 4 - Demonstrates Excellence	L - Limited Responsibility

8.0 PROFESSIONAL DEVELOPMENT AND LEADERSHIP 1 2 3 4 | L

*8.1 Improves Professional Knowledge and Skills 1 2 3 4 | L

- demonstrates knowledge of current developments and trends in curriculum and instruction,
  school management, school organization, and educational leadership 1 2 3 4 | L
- participates in school system and state professional development programs and attends
  state, regional, and national conferences 1 2 3 4 | L
- plans and implements a professional development program to improve job performance 1 2 3 4 | L
- takes formal coursework or obtains advanced degree 1 2 3 4 | L
- uses ideas from books, professional journals, and professional organizations to improve services 1 2 3 4 | L

*8.2 Takes a Leadership Role in Improving Education 1 2 3 4 | L

- provides leadership in identifying and resolving issues and problems facing education 1 2 3 4 | L
- implements systematic procedures to enhance community support and educational improvement 1 2 3 4 | L
- provides leadership in establishing school system goals and achieving them 1 2 3 4 | L
- serves as a catalyst for change 1 2 3 4 | L
- promotes educational improvement in the community 1 2 3 4 | L
- sets high expectations for school personnel and students 1 2 3 4 | L
- takes leadership positions in state/regional/national professional organizations 1 2 3 4 | L
- initiates activities and projects in the school system 1 2 3 4 | L

* *Evaluatees are not expected to exhibit all definitional items in the indicator, but should demonstrate a pattern of them.*

9.0 PROFESSIONAL RESPONSIBILITIES 1 2 3 4 | L

9.1 Implements Federal, State, and Local Laws, Policies, and Procedures 1 2 3 4 | L

- monitors implementation of applicable laws, policies, and procedures 1 2 3 4 | L
- establishes procedures for maintaining up-to-date files of applicable laws, policies, and procedures 1 2 3 4 | L
- communicates relevant information to all personnel to ensure accurate decision making and
  implementation of policies and procedures 1 2 3 4 | L
- seeks clarification of policies, procedures, regulations as needed 1 2 3 4 | L
- makes decisions in accordance with applicable policies and regulations including policies
  and guidelines on student promotion and retention 1 2 3 4 | L
- supports established laws, policies, and procedures to school personnel, students,
  parents/guardians, and others 1 2 3 4 | L

9.2 Performs Duties in a Effective Manner 1 2 3 4 | L

- performs duties in accordance with established job description 1 2 3 4 | L
- selects appropriate channels for communicating/resolving concerns and problems 1 2 3 4 | L
- completes tasks on time 1 2 3 4 | L
- responds to requests for service in a positive manner 1 2 3 4 | L
- considers the interest of all persons when making decisions 1 2 3 4 | L
- makes decisions in a timely manner 1 2 3 4 | L
- performs duties accurately 1 2 3 4 | L
- is punctual for work, meetings, and appointments 1 2 3 4 | L
- provides requested data to school board and other agencies 1 2 3 4 | L

List numbers of no more than three Competencies and a limited number of Indicators identified for the focus of a Professional Development Plan for the next school year:

Competency: Competency: Competency:

Indicator(s):   Indicator(s):   Indicator(s):

Note: If the evaluatee wants to document assigned competency ratings, attach the information on additional sheets.

Superintendent Performance Evaluation

<u>Example of a Checklist</u>

Behavior Checklist

Example 30:
Rock Hill School District 3
Rock Hill, South Carolina   Enrollment: 12,600

SUPERINTENDENT EVALUATION FORM

I. Superintendent's Performance Summary

A. MANAGEMENT SKILLS

1. Management of personnel employment:
   _____(a) Sustained record of employment of top-level employees
   _____(b) Generally able to fill vacancies with able people
   _____(c) Occasionally some positions have to be filled with less able persons
   _____(d) Employment procedures are haphazard and ineffective

2. Utilization of staff personnel:
   _____(a) Outstandingly successful in utilizing services of personnel
   _____(b) Most persons are placed in positions suited to their talents
   _____(c) Some mismatching of persons with positions takes place
   _____(d) Low morale results from poor utilization of personnel

3. Employee relations:
   _____(a) Relations are positive and operating smoothly
   _____(b) Employer-employee relations are on an even keel most of the time
   _____(c) Upheavals in employee relations occur frequently
   _____(d) Strained employer-employee relations go unabated

4. Determining educational needs:
   _____(a) Estimation of educational needs is unusually accurate and far-sighted
   _____(b) Predictions of educational needs are generally accurately calculated
   _____(c) Frequently difficulties are experienced in determining educational needs
   _____(d) Extreme problems are experienced in estimating educational needs

5. Budget preparation:
   _____(a) Budget preparation is an outstandingly effective operation
   _____(b) Preparing the budget is done with care and accuracy
   _____(c) Several problems are usually encountered in preparing budgets
   _____(d) Budget preparation is one of the poorest operations done

6. Budget Management:
   _____(a) Controls over expenditures are extremely efficient and the results are commendable
   _____(b) Budget management procedures are well designed and effective
   _____(c) Several budget management procedures are in need of strengthening
   _____(d) Controls over expenditures are persistently poor

115

Rock Hill School District 3 (continued)

7. Cost-effectiveness in management:
_____(a) This is an area of demonstrated success, year after year
_____(b) Gains are being made in making administrators and supervisors more effective in this area
_____(c) There is still quite a way to go before this can be considered an area of clear success
_____(d) There is practically no evidence that this is a high priority concern in management operations

8. Managing physical facilities:
_____(a) Unusual insight and thoughtfulness are continually exhibited
_____(b) For the most part, facilities management meets needs of district
_____(c) Much needs to be done to upgrade facilities management
_____(d) Most facilities management appears to be "too little, too late"

9. Instructional planning and development:
_____(a) Outstanding initiatives typify instructional planning and development
_____(b) Strides are being made to improve planning and development in curriculum and instruction in the district
_____(c) Several deficiencies exist which should be corrected
_____(d) Very little is being done in instructional planning and development activities

10. Monitoring effectiveness of instructional program:
_____(a) Monitoring results have made a marked and gratifying difference in the effectiveness of the instructional programs
_____(b) Most monitoring procedures are thorough and reasonably effective
_____(c) "Starts and stops" characterize monitoring techniques
_____(d) Minimal concern and attention given to monitoring instructional programs, have little effect upon improvement of instruction

11. Management of attendance:
_____(a) Rigorous standards and persistent efforts to improve attendance have achieved marked results
_____(b) Some gains have been made in the district as a whole
_____(c) Efforts, across the district, are quite uneven
_____(d) Very little direct action to improve attendance has taken place

12. Management of student behavior and discipline:
_____(a) Gains in better behavior have been gratifying and noteworthy
_____(b) Some gains have been achieved in both areas
_____(c) More consistent effort will be required to make desired gains
_____(d) Remains most "unsolved" problem in student affairs

116

Rock Hill School District 3 (continued)

13. Providing for health and safety of students:
_____(a) Results have been extraordinarily successful
_____(b) Moderate improvements have been achieved
_____(c) Some serious difficulties persist
_____(d) Massive resistance prevails in efforts to take vigorous action

14. Developing and implementing comprehensive planning:
_____(a) Results have exceeded expectations
_____(b) Progress in comprehensive planning has been moderate
_____(c) Substantial obstacles continue to stall progress
_____(d) Prospects for ultimate success are very bleak

15. Accountability:
_____(a) Accountability mechanisms have been very successful
_____(b) Gradual acceptance is being experienced throughout the district
_____(c) Accountability is more theory than reality
_____(d) Little or no success has occurred in holding more people accountable

16. Evaluation of planning results:
_____(a) Much deeper commitment to meaningful evaluation is evident
_____(b) Results are reasonably satisfactory
_____(c) There is great unevenness throughout the district
_____(d) Widespread opposition to evaluation of planning results persists

COMMENTS:

B. BOARD/SUPERINTENDENT RELATIONS
1. Materials and reports prepared for the board:
_____(a) Always comprehensive and detailed
_____(b) Usually complete and thorough
_____(c) Sometimes lacking in depth and detail
_____(d) Persistently poorly done

2. Presentation and recommendations to the board:
_____(a) Extremely forthright and convincing
_____(b) Usually thoughtful and sound
_____(c) Occasionally less than carefully prepared
_____(d) Persistently shallow and unreliable

Rock Hill School District 3 (continued)

3. Communications with the board:

_____(a) Always open and forthcoming

_____(b) Generally positive and informative

_____(c) Inconsistent and unreliable, at times

_____(d) Extremely erratic and sometimes devious

4. Fulfilling requests of the board:

_____(a) Consistently.meticulous and responsive

_____(b) By and large, prompt in compliance

_____(c) Many requests are complied with slowly

_____(d) Responses are rarely adequate or on time

5. Periodic communications (reports, newsletters, etc.)

_____(a) Extremely illuminating and well-received

_____(b) For the most part, interesting and attractive

_____(c) Frequently do not reflect high standards of quality

_____(d) Many are dull and ineffective

COMMENTS:

C. SUPERINTENDENT/MEDIA/COMMUNITY RELATIONS

1. Contact with media:

_____(a) Has extremely high credibility with media

_____(b) Is straightforward and cooperative with media

_____(c) Relations with media frequently strained and tenuous

_____(d) Relations are continually negative

2. Interpreting educational programs to community:

_____(a) Always with enthusiasm and conviction

_____(b) Sustains a consistent program of interpretation

_____(c) Stresses some programs; puts less emphasis on others

_____(d) Makes a minimum effort in interpretation

COMMENTS:

Rock Hill School District 3 (continued)

II. Performance Evaluation

_____Exceptional (Results and/or manner in which they were achieved frequently exceed requirements)

_____Meets expectations (Performance consistently conforms to the expected requirements even though there may be variations above and below the standard)

_____Below expectations (Results obtained do not conform to requirements and performance must'improve within a reasonable time)

III. Performance Improvement Plan

IV. Superintendent's Comments:

BOARD OF TRUSTEES
ROCK HILL SCHOOL DISTRICT THREE

_____   _____
Signature   Signature

_____   _____
Signature   Signature

_____   _____
Signature   Signature

_____
Signature

                            _____
                            Superintendent

119

Superintendent Performance Evaluation

Examples of Questionnaires

Open-Ended Questionnaire to be completed by the Board

Superintendent Self-Appraisal Questionnaire

Example 29:
Sioux Falls School District 49-5
Sioux Falls, South Dakota   Enrollment: 14,623

SUPERINTENDENT EVALUATION FORM

1. **Relations with the Board** — Are preparations for board meetings adequate? Are the materials provided sufficient for you to make good decisions? Are recommendations well considered? Does the superintendent respond to your inquiries and requests in adequate fashion? Do you feel that you are kept adequately informed?

2. **Management of Public Relations** — How do we as a district do in handling public relations? What about the superintendent's efforts in this respect?

3. **Management of Curriculum and Instruction** — Is the superintendent adequately informed about curriculum and instruction? Is the district moving in sensible directions? Does the superintendent provide adequate leadership to this program?

4. **Business and Fiscal Management** — Does the district adequately handle business management and fiscal affairs? Does the superintendent provide necessary leadership to this area?

5. **Long and Short Range Planning** — Does the superintendent provide adequate support to the board for long range and short range planning? Are the superintendent's ideas helpful? Is leadership to planning constructive and sound?

Sioux Falls School District 49-5 (continued)

6. Staff Personnel Management—Is personnel management in the district being handled effectively? Does the superintendent provide sufficient leadership?

7. Student Personnel Management — Are we dealing adequately with discipline? What about problems with drugs and alcohol? Is the superintendent providing sufficient leadership in this area?

8. Management of Physical Facilities — Is the building program adequately managed? What about maintenance — appearance of facilities?

9. Personal and Professional Qualities — Is the superintendent respected as a leader in the community? in the state? in the school system?

10. Overall Assessment — What overall suggestions do you have to offer?

Sample

Superintendent's Self-Appraisal

Name _____ Performance Period _____

On separate sheets of paper, please respond to the questions below. Attach the responses to this cover sheet.

1. What do you consider to be your most significant accomplishments during the last school year?

2. Identify goals that were not accomplished during this school year and the factors that you feel prevented completion.

3. What do you feel should be your primary goals for the next school year?

Superintendent's Signature   *Date*

Superintendent Performance Evaluation

Example of Interview Evaluation Form

Structured Interview Evaluation Form

ALABAMA PROFESSIONAL EDUCATION PERSONNEL EVALUATION PROGRAM

SUPERINTENDENT'S STRUCTURED INTERVIEW
FOR COMPLETION BY EVALUATOR(S)

Evaluatee: _____ *Evaluator:* _____ *Date:* _____

This interview instrument is intended to be completed by an evaluator conducting an interview with the superintendent. The interview includes 8 sets of questions. For that reason, the evaluator and superintendent may agree to conduct the interview in more than one session. The superintendent is expected to provide in advance of or at the interview materials which will document the policies, procedures and practices discussed.

The scoring statements on the interview instrument should be used in determining the indicator ratings. Procedures and definitions for scoring the interview appear in the Evaluator and Orientation Manuals. The following rating scale should be used to determine a rating for each item and each indicator assessed:

1 - Unsatisfactory	*Indicates the evaluatee's performance in this position requirement is not acceptable. Improvement activities must be undertaken immediately.*
2 - Needs Improvement	*Indicates the evaluatee's performance needs improvement in this position requirement. Improvement activities are required for performance to meet standards.*
3 - Area of Strength	*Indicates the evaluatee always meets and sometimes exceeds expectations for performance in this position requirement. Performance can be improved in the areas(s) indicated, but current practices are clearly acceptable.*
4 - Demonstrates Excellence	*Indicates the evaluatee does an outstanding job in this position requirement. No area for improvement is readily identifiable.*
Limited Responsibility (L)	*Indicates the evaluatee has limited (L) responsibility in this indicator/competency area. When an "L" is indicated, a numerical rating (1-4) should also be assigned.*

F25_0991

QUESTION SET 1 (INDICATOR 1.1)	DOCUMENTS USED:

QUESTION SET 1
(INDICATOR 1.1)

DOCUMENTS USED:

☐ Board Policy
☐ Administrative Procedures Manual
☐ Board Agendas/Minutes
☐ Staff Handbooks
☐ Memo/Newsletters
☐ Annual Reports
☐ Accreditation Documents
☐ Other _____

How do you go about recommending actions to the school board and implementing board policies once they are established? In your discussion, outline what you do to develop a policy or recommendation to present to the board and what you do after the board has adopted a policy. *Please use actual policy examples in your description.*

LOOK FOR:

KEY

1 - Unsatisfactory	2 - Needs Improvement
3 - Area of Strength	4 - Demonstrates Excellence

[L - Limited Responsibilities]

- Records of implementation efforts
- Systematic dissemination
- Systematic planning for implementation
- Delegation of responsibility
- Appropriate training
- Personal monitoring
- Systematic evaluation of implementation

1. Develops and recommends plans, procedures, and timelines for implementation of board policies   1   2   3   4   L

2. Disseminates/interprets board policies   1   2   3   4   L

3. Assigns and provides training for specific implementation responsibilities   1   2   3   4   L

4. Manages implementation efforts   1   2   3   4   L

MODIFIED SCRIPT OF DIALOGUE:

Indicator Rating: 1   2   3   4   L

QUESTION SET 2 (INDICATOR 2.2)	DOCUMENTS USED:

How do you ensure that all personnel are adequately supervised, evaluated, and provided appropriate professional growth opportunities? *Please share materials which will assist in your explanation.*

LOOK FOR:

KEY

1 - Unsatisfactory   2 - Needs Improvement
3 - Area of Strength ___ ___ 4 - Demonstrates Excellence
[L - Limited Responsibilities]

- Board policies
- Clear administrative procedures
- Delegation of responsibility
- Adequate evaluator training
- Adherence to policy and procedures
- Appropriate records
- Linkage of evaluation results to professional development activities
- Needs assessments
- Allocation of resources to professional development
- Systematic evaluation of professional development programs
- Evaluation of personnel under superintendent

	1	2	3	4	L
1. Recommends board policies for personnel evaluation	1	2	3	4	L
2. Develops and disseminates procedures for evaluation	1	2	3	4	L
3. Assigns responsibilities for personnel evaluation	1	2	3	4	L
4. Evaluates personnel directly responsible to superintendent	1	2	3	4	L
5. Implements personnel evaluation process	1	2	3	4	L
6. Provides training for personnel in evaluation process	1	2	3	4	L
7. Maintains evaluation records and accountability	1	2	3	4	L
8. Uses evaluation results to make staff development decisions	1	2	3	4	L
9. Assesses staff development and personnel evaluation programs	1	2	3	4	L

MODIFIED SCRIPT OF DIALOGUE:

Indicator Rating:	1	2	3	4	L

F25_0991

QUESTION SET 3
(INDICATOR 2.3)

Describe how you plan, implement, and evaluate curriculum and instruction in the school system. Discuss the curriculum plan and activities and responsibilities you have delegated to others. *Share materials which will assist in your explanation.*

DOCUMENTS USED:

☐ Accreditation Documents
☐ Curriculum Guides
☐ Handbooks
☐ Planning Documents
☐ Board Policy Manual
☐ Organizational Charts
☐ Staff Development Agendas
☐ Other _____

LOOK FOR:	KEY	1 - Unsatisfactory 2 - Needs Improvement 3 - Area of Strength 4 - Demonstrates Excellence [L - Limited Responsibilities]

- Board policies
- Administrator/Teacher involvement
- Parent/Guardian/Student input
- Understanding of development processes
- Systematic evaluation of programs
- Systematic textbook and resource
  selection procedures
- Allocation of resources
- Long- and short-range planning
- Appropriate staff development
- Training programs in curriculum/instruction

1. Provides for curriculum and instruction plan, implementation, training, evaluation, and recordkeeping   1   2   3   4   L

2. Demonstrates knowledge of curriculum and instruction development   1   2   3   4   L

3. Involves administrators/teachers/parents/students in planning and evaluating curriculum and instruction   1   2   3   4   L

4. Provides needed resources for curriculum and instruction including full-time supervision   1   2   3   4   L

5. Provides curriculum and instruction staff development and follow-up   1   2   3   4   L

MODIFIED SCRIPT OF DIALOGUE: **Indicator Rating:**   1   2   3   4   L

QUESTION SET 4
(INDICATOR 2.4)

How do you determine academic priorities and student achievement objectives in the school system? Discuss the comprehensive student assessment program, your strategies for the accomplishment and evaluation of achievement objectives and discuss what you do with student achievement data. *Please share any materials which will aid your explanation.*

DOCUMENTS USED:

☐ Accreditation Documents
☐ Annual Reports
☐ Interim Reports
☐ Memos/Letters
☐ Newsletters
☐ Standardized Test Results
☐ Planning Documents
☐ Board Agendas/Minutes
☐ Other_____

LOOK FOR:	KEY	1 - Unsatisfactory 2 - Needs Improvement
		3 - Area of Strength 4 - Demonstrates Excellence
		[L - Limited Responsibilities]

LOOK FOR:

- Definitions of student achievement
- Specific achievement objectives/academic priorities
- Systematic data collection
- Systematic planning for improvement
- Allocation of human and fiscal resources
- Systematic evaluation of system-wide progress

		1	2	3	4	L
1.	Develops and implements plan for improvement of student achievement	1	2	3	4	L
2.	Identifies strategies and provides resources for attaining student achievement goals and objectives	1	2	3	4	L
3.	Monitors and evaluates progress toward student achievement goals and objectives	1	2	3	4	L
4.	Uses student evaluation data	1	2	3	4	L

MODIFIED SCRIPT OF DIALOGUE:

| Indicator Rating: | 1 | 2 | 3 | 4 | L |

F25_0991

QUESTION SET 5 (INDICATORS 3.1 & 3.2)	DOCUMENTS USED:
How do you determine personnel needs of the school system? Discuss your comprehensive personnel plan and the strategies which you use to recruit, induct, and assign employees. How do you determine the effectiveness of your program? *Please provide any documents which will aid your explanation.*	☐ Annual/Interim Reports ☐ Planning/Accreditation Documents ☐ Statistical Reports ☐ Board Agendas/Minutes ☐ Recruiting Materials ☐ System Budget ☐ Job Descriptions ☐ Orientation Materials/Agendas ☐ Staff Handbooks ☐ Other_____

LOOK FOR: (KEY)

1 - Unsatisfactory   2 - Needs Improvement
3 - Area of Strength   4 - Demonstrates Excellence

[L - Limited Responsibilities]

LOOK FOR:	KEY items					
- Needs projections/assessments - Systematic planning/orientation programs - Allocation of human and fiscal resources - Annual evaluation of recruitment program - Job descriptions - Recommendations to the board - Commitment of financial resources	1. Identifies long and short range personnel needs and goals *(3.1)*	1	2	3	4	L
	2. Monitors and evaluates personnel program effectiveness *(3.1)*	1	2	3	4	L
	3. Provides human and financial resources necessary to personnel plan *(3.1)*	1	2	3	4	L
	4. Provides lines of authority, responsibility, and accountability *(3.2)*	1	2	3	4	L
	5. Provides job descriptions and sufficient personnel *(3.2)*	1	2	3	4	L
	6. Provides staff orientation and induction *(3.2)*	1	2	3	4	L

MODIFIED SCRIPT OF DIALOGUE

Indicator 3.1 Rating: 1   2   3   4   L
Indicator 3.2 Rating: 1   2   3   4   L

QUESTION SET 6
(INDICATORS 5.1 & 5.2)

What is your plan for ongoing community relations? What strategies and activities do you use to carry out that plan? Include the use of local media in your discussion. *Please provide any materials which will assist your explanation.*

DOCUMENTS USED:
- ☐ Planning documents
- ☐ Media Reports
- ☐ Annual Reports
- ☐ Budgets
- ☐ Promotional Materials
- ☐ Letters/Memo
- ☐ Newspaper Articles
- ☐ Press Releases
- ☐ Videotapes
- ☐ Audiotapes
- ☐ Other: _____

LOOK FOR:

KEY

1 - Unsatisfactory 2 - Needs Improvement
3 - Area of Strength 4 - Demonstrates Excellence
[L - Limited Responsibilities]

- Systematic planning for community relations
- Assignment of personnel
- Expectations for local schools
- Allocation of financial resources
- Involvement of local school personnel/media/community
- Systematic evaluation of community relations efforts
- Interactions with newspapers, radio, television stations
- Materials produced for media use
- Efforts to publicize staff and student accomplishments

1. Develops community relations plans at the system and school levels (5.1)   1 2 3 4 | L

2. Implements strategies for attaining community relations goals and objectives (5.1)   1 2 3 4 | L

3. Provides human and financial resources for implementation of community relations program (5.1)   1 2 3 4 | L

4. Evaluates community relations goals and objectives (5.1)   1 2 3 4 | L

5. Develops media materials (5.2)   1 2 3 4 | L

6. Uses local media to communicate mission, goals for improvement, and progress of schools (5.2)   1 2 3 4 | L

MODIFIED SCRIPT OF DIALOGUE:

Indicator 5.1 Rating: 1 2 3 4 | L
Indicator 5.2 Rating: 1 2 3 4 | L

F25_0991

QUESTION SET 7
(INDICATORS 6.2 & 6.3)

How do you develop and carry out plans for implementing and managing programs and services relating to students? In your discussion, include your plan and how you manage pupil personnel services (i.e., counseling/guidance, at-risk students, transportation, food services, etc.), how you maintain a comprehensive student record system, and how you ensure appropriate student conduct and discipline. *Please provide materials which will assist your explanation.*

DOCUMENTS USED:

☐ Accreditation Documents
☐ Board Agendas/Minutes/Manuals
☐ Planning Documents
☐ Annual Report/Budget
☐ Staff Meeting Agendas/Minutes
☐ Student/Parent Handbooks
☐ Program Agendas
☐ Policy List
☐ Other:_____

LOOK FOR:	KEY	1 - Unsatisfactory 2 - Needs Improvement 3 - Area of Strength 4 - Demonstrates Excellence [L - Limited Responsibilities]

- Needs assessments
- Systematic planning
- Assignment of responsibilities
- Personal monitoring
- Presence of systems for attendance, student achievement, guidance/psychological reporting
- Regular, systematic evaluation of records systems
- Board Policies
- Administrative procedures
- Communication efforts
- Student development programs

1. Plans and uses implementation strategies for pupil personnel services (6.2) 1 2 3 4 L

2. Ensures and uses student records management system (6.2) 1 2 3 4 L

3. Develops relationships and services with community social agencies (6.2) 1 2 3 4 L

4. Monitors and evaluates pupil personnel programs (6.2) 1 2 3 4 L

5. Implements and consistently enforces student behavior policies and procedures (6.3) 1 2 3 4 L

6. Provides staff/student development programs for improving student conduct (6.3)

MODIFIED SCRIPT OF DIALOGUE:

Indicator 6.2 Rating: 1   2   3   4   L

Indicator 6.3 Rating: 1   2   3   4   L

QUESTION SET 8
(INDICATOR 6.4)

What measures are taken to ensure the health and safety of all employees and students? **Also discuss how you provide for any health and safety education programs in the school system.** *Please provide related materials.*

DOCUMENTS USED:

- ☐ Accreditation Documents
- ☐ Curriculum Guides
- ☐ Staff Handbooks
- ☐ Planning Documents
- ☐ Board Policy Manual
- ☐ Annual Reports
- ☐ Memos/letters
- ☐ Student/Parent Handbook
- ☐ Incident/Report Forms
- ☐ Other_____

LOOK FOR:	KEY	1 - Unsatisfactory 2 - Needs Improvement 3 - Area of Strength 4 - Demonstrates Excellence [L - Limited Responsibilities]

LOOK FOR:
- Board policies
- Written rules and procedures
- Allocation of human and financial resources
- Regular visits to schools and service sites
- Procedures for reporting accidents/ problems
- Programs of health and safety education

1. Establishes and enforces policies/procedures for health and safety of personnel — 1 2 3 **4** | L

2. Establishes and enforces policies/procedures for health and safety of students — 1 2 3 **4** | L

3. Provides resources and programs of education for health and safety of personnel and students — 1 2 3 **4** | L

4. Monitors health and safety standards — 1 2 3 **4** | L

MODIFIED SCRIPT OF DIALOGUE: Indicator Rating: 1 2 3 **4** | L

F25_0991

Superintendent Presentation Performance Evaluation Forms

Example of Evaluation Forms for Superintendent Presentations

Structured Presentation Analysis Form

Structured Presentation Rating Form

ALABAMA PROFESSIONAL EDUCATION PERSONNEL EVALUATION PROGRAM

SUPERINTENDENT'S STRUCTURED PRESENTATION

Evaluatee: _____ Evaluator: _____ Date: _____

This presentation instrument is intended to be completed by members of the local board of education or other evaluators during a scheduled board meeting or a called meeting specific to the presentation. The presentation with the superintendent includes 8 sets of questions. For that reason, the board members and superintendent may agree to conduct the presentation in several different sessions. For example, the board may wish to conduct the interview across several meetings by addressing only those questions which focus on a specific competency. The superintendent is expected to provide in advance of or at the interview materials which will document the policies, procedures and practices discussed.

The scoring statements on the separate Superintendent's Structured Presentation Rating Form should be used to determine the indicator ratings. Procedures and definitions for scoring the presentation appear in the Evaluator and Orientation Manuals.

258

QUESTION SET 1 (INDICATOR 1.1)	DOCUMENTS USED:

QUESTION SET 1
(INDICATOR 1.1)

How do you go about recommending actions to the school board and implementing board policies once they are established? In your discussion, outline what you do to develop a policy or recommendation to present to the board and what you do after the board has adopted a policy. *Please use actual policy examples in your description.*

DOCUMENTS USED:

☐ Board Policy
☐ Administrative Procedures Manual
☐ Board Agendas/Minutes
☐ Staff Handbooks
☐ Memo/Newsletters
☐ Annual Reports
☐ Accreditation Documents
☐ Other _____

LOOK FOR:

- Records of implementation efforts
- Delegation of responsibility
- Systematic evaluation of implementation

- Systematic dissemination
- Appropriate training

- Systematic planning for implementation
- Personal monitoring

NOTES/RESPONSE:

QUESTION SET 2
(INDICATOR 2.2)

How do you ensure that all personnel are adequately supervised, evaluated, and provided appropriate professional growth opportunities? *Please share materials which will assist in your explanation.*

DOCUMENTS USED:

- ☐ Accreditation Documents
- ☐ Personnel Evaluations and Results
- ☐ Board Policy Manual
- ☐ Evaluation Orientation Manuals
- ☐ Training Manuals
- ☐ Professional Development
- ☐ Reports/Assessments
- ☐ Other _____

LOOK FOR:

- Board policies
- Adequate evaluator training
- Linkage of evaluation results to professional development activities
- Systematic evaluation of professional development programs

- Clear administrative procedures
- Adherence to policy and procedures
- Needs assessments
- Evaluation of personnel under superintendent

- Delegation of responsibility
- Appropriate records
- Allocation of resources to professional development

NOTES/RESPONSE:

<table>
<tr><td colspan="2">

QUESTION SET 3
(INDICATOR 2.3)

Describe how you plan, implement, and evaluate curriculum and instruction in the school system.   Discuss the curriculum plan and activities and responsibilities you have delegated to others. *Share materials which will assist in your explanation.*

</td><td>

DOCUMENTS USED:

☐ Accreditation Documents
☐ Curriculum Guides
☐ Handbooks
☐ Planning Documents
☐ Board Policy Manual
☐ Organizational Charts
☐ Staff Development Agendas
☐ Other _____

</td></tr>
</table>

LOOK FOR:

- Board policies	- Administrator/Teacher involvement	- Parent/Guardian/Student input
- Understanding of development processes	- Systematic evaluation of programs	- Systematic textbook and
- Allocation of resources	- Long- and short-range planning	resource selection procedures
- Long- and short-range planning	- Appropriate staff development	- Training programs in
		curriculum/instruction

NOTES/RESPONSE:

QUESTION SET 4 (INDICATOR 2.4)	DOCUMENTS USED:

QUESTION SET 4
(INDICATOR 2.4)

How do you determine academic priorities and student achievement objectives in the school system? Discuss the comprehensive student assessment program, your strategies for the accomplishment and evaluation of achievement objectives and discuss what you do with student achievement data. *Please share any materials which will aid your explanation.*

DOCUMENTS USED:

☐ Accreditation Documents
☐ Annual Reports
☐ Interim Reports
☐ Memos/Letters
☐ Newsletters
☐ Standardized Test Results
☐ Planning Documents
☐ Board Agendas/Minutes
☐ Other_____

LOOK FOR:

- Definitions of student achievement
- Systematic planning for improvement

- Specific achievement objectives/academic priorities
- Allocation of human and fiscal resources

- Systematic data collection
- Systematic evaluation of system-wide progress

NOTES/RESPONSE

QUESTION SET 5 (INDICATORS 3.1 & 3.2) How do you determine personnel needs of the school system? Discuss your comprehensive personnel plan and the strategies which you use to recruit, induct, and assign employees. How do you determine the effectiveness of your program? *Please provide any documents which will aid your explanation.*	DOCUMENTS USED: ☐ Annual/Interim Reports ☐ Planning/Accreditation Documents ☐ Statistical Reports ☐ Board Agendas/Minutes ☐ Recruiting Materials ☐ System Budget ☐ Job Descriptions ☐ Orientation Materials/Agendas ☐ Staff Handbooks ☐ Other_____

LOOK FOR:

- Needs projections/assessments - Annual evaluation of recruitment program - Commitment of financial resources	- Systematic planning/orientation programs - Job descriptions	- Allocation of human and fiscal resources - Recommendations to the board

NOTES/RESPONSE:

QUESTION SET 6
(INDICATORS 5.1 & 5.2)

What is your plan for ongoing community relations?
What strategies and activities do you use to carry out that plan? Include the use of local media in your discussion. *Please provide any materials which will assist your explanation.*

- [ ] Planning documents
- [ ] Media Reports
- [ ] Annual Reports
- [ ] Budgets
- [ ] Promotional Materials
- [ ] Letters/Memo
- [ ] Newspaper Articles
- [ ] Press Releases
- [ ] Videotapes
- [ ] Audiotapes
- [ ] Other: _____

LOOK FOR:

- Systematic planning for community relations
- Allocation of financial resources
- Interactions with newspapers, radio, television stations

- Assignment of personnel
- Involvement of local school personnel/media/community
- Materials produced for media use

- Expectations for local schools
- Systematic evaluation of community relations efforts
- Efforts to publicize staff and student accomplishments

NOTES/RESPONSE

F2509918

264

QUESTION SET 7
(INDICATORS 6.2 & 6.3)

How do you develop and carry out plans for implementing and managing programs and services relating to students? In your discussion, include your plan and how you manage pupil personnel services (i.e., counseling/guidance, at-risk students, transportation, food services, etc.), how you maintain a comprehensive student record system, and how you ensure appropriate student conduct and discipline. *Please provide materials which will assist your explanation.*

- [ ] Accreditation Documents
- [ ] Board Agendas/Minutes/Manuals
- [ ] Planning Documents
- [ ] Annual Report/Budget
- [ ] Staff Meeting Agendas/Minutes
- [ ] Student/Parent Handbooks
- [ ] Program Agendas
- [ ] Policy List
- [ ] Other: _____

LOOK FOR:

- Needs assessments
- Personal monitoring
- Presence of systems for attendance, student achievement, guidance/ psychological reporting

- Systematic planning
- Regular, systematic evaluation of records systems
- Communication efforts

- Assignment of responsibilities
- Board Policies
- Administrative procedures
- Student development programs

NOTES/RESPONSE

QUESTION SET 8 (INDICATOR 6.4)	DOCUMENTS USED:

QUESTION SET 8
(INDICATOR 6.4)

What measures are taken to ensure the health and safety of all employees and students? Also discuss how you provide for any health and safety education programs in the school system. *Please provide related materials.*

DOCUMENTS USED:
- ☐ Accreditation Documents
- ☐ Curriculum Guides
- ☐ Staff Handbooks
- ☐ Planning Documents
- ☐ Board Policy Manual
- ☐ Annual Reports
- ☐ Memos/letters
- ☐ Student/Parent Handbook
- ☐ Incident/Report Forms
- ☐ Other_____

LOOK FOR:

- Board policies
- Regular visits to schools and service sites
- Programs of health and safety education

- Written rules and procedures
- Procedures for reporting accidents/ problems

- Allocation of human and financial resources

NOTES/RESPONSE

266

ALABAMA PROFESSIONAL EDUCATION PERSONNEL EVALUATION PROGRAM

SUPERINTENDENT'S STRUCTURED PRESENTATION RATING FORM

Evaluatee: _____ Evaluator: _____ Date: _____

The scoring statements on the Superintendent's Structured Presentation Rating Form should be used in determining the indicator ratings. Procedures and definitions for scoring the presentation appear in the Evaluator and Orientation Manuals. The following rating scale should be used to determine a rating for each item and each indicator assessed:

1 - Unsatisfactory

Indicates the evaluatee's performance in this position requirement is not acceptable. Improvement activities must be undertaken immediately.

2 - Needs Improvement

Indicates the evaluatee's performance needs improvement in this position requirement. Improvement activities are required for performance to meet standards.

3 - Area of Strength

Indicates the evaluatee always meets and sometimes exceeds expectations for performance in this position requirement. Performance can be improved in the areas(s) indicated, but current practices are clearly acceptable.

4 - Demonstrates Excellence

Indicates the evaluatee does an outstanding job in this position requirement. No area for improvement is readily identifiable.

Limited Responsibility (L)

Indicates the evaluatee has limited (L) responsibility in this indicator/competency area. When an "L" is indicated, a numerical rating (1-4) should also be assigned.

RATING FORM FOR
SUPERINTENDENT'S STRUCTURED PRESENTATION

KEY

1 - Unsatisfactory 2 - Needs Improvement
3 - Area of Strength 4 - Demonstrates Excellence
[L - Limited Responsibilities]

QUESTION SET 1 (INDICATOR 1.1)		1	2	3	4	L
How do you go about recommending actions to the school board and implementing board policies once they are established? In your discussion, outline what you do to develop a policy or recommendation to present to the board and what you do after the board has adopted a policy.	1. Develops and recommends plans, procedures, and timelines for implementation of board policies	1	2	3	4	L
	2. Disseminates/interprets board policies	1	2	3	4	L
	3. Assigns and provides training for specific implementation responsibilities	1	2	3	4	L
	4. Manages implementation efforts	1	2	3	4	L
	Indicator Rating:	1	2	3	4	L

QUESTION SET 2 (INDICATOR 2.2)		1	2	3	4	L
How do you ensure that all personnel are adequately supervised, evaluated, and provided appropriate professional growth opportunities?	1. Recommends board policies for personnel evaluation	1	2	3	4	L
	2. Develops and disseminates procedures for evaluation	1	2	3	4	L
	3. Assigns responsibilities for personnel evaluation	1	2	3	4	L
	4. Evaluates personnel directly responsible to superintendent	1	2	3	4	L
	5. Implements personnel evaluation process	1	2	3	4	I
	6. Provides training for personnel in evaluation process	1	2	3	4	L
	7. Maintains evaluation records and accountability	1	2	3	4	L
	8. Uses evaluation results to make staff development decisions	1	2	3	4	L
	9. Assesses staff development and personnel evaluation programs	1	2	3	4	L
	Indicator Rating:	1	2	3	4	L

QUESTION SET 3 (INDICATOR 2.3)		1	2	3	4	L
Describe how you plan, implement, and evaluate curriculum and instruction in the school system. Discuss the curriculum plan and activities and responsibilities you have delegated to others.	1. Provides for curriculum and instruction plan, implementation, training, evaluation, and recordkeeping	1	2	3	4	L
	2. Demonstrates knowledge of curriculum and instruction development	1	2	3	4	L
	3. Involves administrators/teachers/parents/students in planning and evaluating curriculum and instruction	1	2	3	4	L
	4. Provides needed resources for curriculum and instruction including full-time supervision	1	2	3	4	L
	5. Provides curriculum and instruction staff development and follow-up	1	2	3	4	L
	Indicator Rating:	1	2	3	4	I

11

F2509918

QUESTION SET 4
(INDICATOR 2.4)

How do you determine academic priorities and student achievement objectives in the school system? Discuss the comprehensive student assessment program, your strategies for the accomplishment and evaluation of achievement objectives and discuss what you do with student achievement data.

		1	2	3	4	L
1.	Develops and implements plan for improvement of student achievement	1	2	3	4	L
2.	Identifies strategies and provides resources for attaining student achievement goals and objectives	1	2	3	4	L
3.	Monitors and evaluates progress toward student achievement goals and objectives	1	2	3	4	L
4.	Uses student evaluation data	1	2	3	4	L

Indicator Rating: 1   2   3   4 | L

QUESTION SET 5
(INDICATORS 3.1 & 3.2)

How do you determine personnel needs of the school system? Discuss your comprehensive personnel plan and the strategies which you use to recruit, induct, and assign employees. How do you determine the effectiveness of your program?

		1	2	3	4	L
1.	Identifies long and short range personnel needs and goals (3.1)	1	2	3	4	L
2.	Monitors and evaluates personnel program effectiveness (3.1)	1	2	3	4	L
3.	Provides human and financial resources necessary to personnel plan (3.1)	1	2	3	4	L
4.	Provides lines of authority, responsibility, and accountability (3.2)	1	2	3	4	L
5.	Provides job descriptions and sufficient personnel (3.2)	1	2	3	4	L
6.	Provides staff orientation and induction (3.2)	1	2	3	4	L

Indicator 3.1 Rating: 1   2   3   4 | L
Indicator 3.2 Rating: 1   2   3   4 | L

QUESTION SET 6
(INDICATORS 5.1 & 5.2)

What is your plan for ongoing community relations? What strategies and activities do you use to carry out that plan? Include the use of local media in your discussion.

		1	2	3	4	L
1.	Develops community relations plans at the system and school levels (5.1)	1	2	3	4	L
2.	Implements strategies for attaining community relations goals and objectives (5.1)	1	2	3	4	L
3.	Provides human and financial resources for implementation of community relations program (5.1)	1	2	3	4	L
4.	Evaluates community relations goals and objectives (5.1)	1	2	3	4	L
5.	Develops media materials (5.2)	1	2	3	4	L
6.	Uses local media to communicate mission, goals for improvement, and progress of schools (5.2)	1	2	3	4	L

Indicator 5.1 Rating: 1   2   3   4 | L
Indicator 5.2 Rating: 1   2   3   4 | L

QUESTION SET 7
(INDICATORS 6.2 & 6.3)

How do you develop and carry out plans for implementing and managing programs and services relating to students? In your discussion, include your plan and how you manage pupil personnel services (i.e., counseling/guidance, at-risk students, transportation, food services, etc.), how you maintain a comprehensive student record system, and how you ensure appropriate student conduct and discipline.

	1	2	3	4	L
1. Plans and uses implementation strategies for pupil personnel services (6.2)	1	2	3	4	L
2. Ensures and uses student records management system (6.2)	1	2	3	4	L
3. Develops relationships and services with community social agencies (6.2)	1	2	3	4	L
4. Monitors and evaluates pupil personnel programs (6.2)	1	2	3	4	L
5. Implements and consistently enforces student behavior policies and procedures (6.3)	1	2	3	4	L
6. Provides staff/student development programs for improving student conduct (6.3)					
Indicator 6.2 Rating:	1	2	3	4	L
Indicator 6.3 Rating:	1	2	3	4	L

QUESTION SET 8
(INDICATOR 6.4)

What measures are taken to ensure the health and safety of all employees and students? Also discuss how you provide for any health and safety education programs in the school system.

	1	2	3	4	L
1. Establishes and enforces policies/procedures for health and safety of personnel	1	2	3	4	L
2. Establishes and enforces policies/procedures for health and safety of students	1	2	3	4	L
3. Provides resources and programs of education for health and safety of personnel and students	1	2	3	4	L
4. Monitors health and safety standards	1	2	3	4	L
Indicator Rating:	1	2	3	4	L

F250991E

Superintendent Performance Evaluation

<u>Examples of Professional Activities Descriptions</u>

Inventory of Superintendent and District Issues/Events

Professional Development and Leadership Summary

DES MOINES PUBLIC SCHOOLS

SUPERINTENDENT AND DISTRICT ISSUES/EVENTS
1988 - 1993

The following is an inventory of school district issues and events the superintendent has been involved in since beginning his role on July 1, 1988, and extending through May 1993. Items shown in **Bold Print** have been addressed since the annual evaluation for 1991-92 was completed. The list includes:

SETTING EDUCATIONAL DIRECTION

✓ *Focus on teaching for learning and management issues/events*

- Annual State of the Schools Report (4).

- Voter issues approved (3) . . . Central Campus, Bond/10 Year Capital Improvement Levies, and 10 Year Instructional Improvement Levy.

- Legislative issues involvement . . . Urban Education Network, BEST Coalition, At-Risk Programs (e.g., Youth-Based Services Grants and Youth At-Risk Coalition), Greater Des Moines Chamber of Commerce (e.g., state and federal lobbying), and **National Urban Reform Network (CTAC).**

- School-community Issues/Events:
  Boundary changes (elementary, middle and high school), religion in the curriculum, elementary, middle, and high school class size, **staffing formula**, central campus evaluation, high school 7-period day, standardized test scores, Smoother Sailing Program, JROTC, special education/ neighborhood placement, elementary

departmentalization v. self-contained classrooms, **open enrollment**, voluntary transfer program, Dowling recruitment, Partners for Progress, Business/Education Alliance, **International Summer Institute, Success Program,** Minority Achievement Program, elementary traditional school policies, opening Samuelson (early childhood and staff development center), 16-Member Athletic Conference realignment, school-based management, **waiver process, extended school year, district report card (Annual Report),** facility renovations and new construction, **property transactions (public library and warehousing),** Hoover fire, **Hoover student allegations,** Brody fire, bomb threats, racism claims, student discipline, inclement weather decisions, **media involvement** and **VISION 2005: Stakeholders Forum.**

- Human Resource Issues:
  Wright School (race and politics), Lincoln High School (theft), Roosevelt High School (279 Proceedings), transfer and dismissals, no smoking process, **central staff reorganization,** and staff development activities.

- Relationships with DMAA:
  Expulsion policy, **written employee agreement,** salary and TSA clarification, business leaves, and recruitment, hiring and placement procedures and **Administrative Excellence Program.**

- Relationships with Board:
  Department of Board and Community Relations restructured, Board meeting agenda format development (e.g., issue statement, background, and recommendation), work sessions, **retreats, board**

updates, CIPP reports, strategic planning report, property matters, district improvement plan (e.g., goals), **withdrawal and enrollment reports**, legal and policy issues, budget and employee bargaining procedures, **cable television, and contacts with individual board members.**

* Relationships with Civic and Professional Organizations:
  Service on boards -- **Community Focus**, Chamber of Commerce, **Boy Scouts, Junior Achievement, United Way, City Superintendents,** HMO Iowa, Junior League, **Center for Research and Accountability on Teacher Evaluation (advisory panel chair),** AEA 11 (chair of superintendents), Mayor's Task Force on Drugs and Alcohol Abuse, **Steering Committee (chair of) for State Outcomes and Assessment.** -

In addition, the following professional development tasks were completed from 1988 - 1993.

* Taught School Superintendency course at Drake University (1991).

* Speaker at Midwest Regional Educational Research Association Convention (Chicago) and Iowa Educational Research Association Convention (Cedar Rapids) (1991).

* Co-authored chapter titled "Financial Services" in the book School System Administration: A Strategic Plan for Site-Based Management (1991)

* Authored chapter on "Creating Partnerships with the Private Sector to Support Children" in the book Meeting the Needs of At-Risk Students (1991).

- Speaker at Rotary Teacher-of-the-Year meeting (1992 and 1993).

- Speaker at Kiwanis Student Recognition ceremony (1993).

- Conducted workshop at Center for Research Educational Accountability/Teacher Evaluation on "School Evaluation Models", Snowmass, CO. (1992).

- Attended IBM Executive Training Institute, Palisades, NY (1992).

- Conducted workshop in Norman, Oklaholma, on program evaluation (1993).

- Assisted district team with National Educational Reform Network Convention: CTAC, Boston, MS. (1992).

- Selected as one of "100" of North America's Best and Brightest School Executives by the Executive Educator magazine (1993).

SETTING PERSONAL DIRECTION

✓ *Focus on family and career*

A continued involvement with family (including a teenage son), church activities, favorite recreational pursuits, Rotary, and ties with friends and colleagues provide personal satisfaction to life beyond the role of superintendent. In nearly ten years as an Iowa superintendent, I have been involved in significant educational change ranging from closing schools (Waterloo), to the aforementioned issues in Des Moines. The superintendent's role requires continued reflection on professional, as well as personal goals in order to maintain perspective. At this time both my professional and personal growth needs are being met. Des Moines continues to be a fine community to meet the challenging issues that face the urban superintendency. Des Moines is also a great place to raise a family and call "home."

GLW:jd
5/10/93

F82-0891

ALABAMA PROFESSIONAL EDUCATION PERSONNEL EVALUATION PROGRAM
PROFESSIONAL DEVELOPMENT AND LEADERSHIP SUMMARY

Evaluatee: _____ Evaluator: _____

Year Beginning: _____ Year Ending: _____

The Professional Development and Leadership Summary reports activities undertaken and completed for an evaluation cycle. For *non-tenured* personnel, the cycle is *annual*; for *tenured* personnel, the cycle may be *annual, two years, or three years* depending on the option of the local school system. If the form is being completed by a tenured staff member on a multi-year evaluation cycle, the form should be updated during May of each year. *More detailed instructions concerning completion of this form are found in the Orientation Manual.*

To complete the form:
1.) Check whether the activity is related to the indicator, *Improves Professional Knowledge and Skills,* or to the indicator, *Takes a Leadership Role in Improving Education.*
2.) Check the box which describes the basis for the activity: Was it part of a required local inservice training program? Was it self-initiated? Was it included as part of a Professional Development Plan? Was it included as part of a Goal Accountability Plan?
3.) Complete the box marked "ITEM" by indicating the definition item the activity matches. A complete listing of definition items is located in the *Orientation Manual.* (Do *not* complete the section marked *Definition Item Score.*)
4.) In the space provided: a) describe the activity(ies); b) list the year(s); c) list the time spent in the activity(ies) by approximate hours; and d) describe the benefit of the activity(ies) to self, students, personnel, or school system.
5.) Duplicate this form if additional space is required to report activities for the evaluation cycle. (When more than one page is submitted to an evaluator, list the number of pages used to report all activities completed during the evaluation cycle in the space provided at the bottom of the page.

Directions:

This section is for the evaluator's use only:

The evaluator should review the scores assigned to activities submitted for each indicator and determine the overall score for each indicator. This score should be recorded by the appropriate indicator in the column, *Indicator Ratings.* Notes for justification of scores should be written in the space provided. The overall indicator ratings should be recorded in the appropriate spaces on the evaluatee's Evaluation Summary Report (ESR).

Professional Development and Leadership Summary Ratings

	Indicator Ratings
Improves Professional Knowledge and Skills	1 2 3 4
Takes a Leadership Role in Improving Education	1 2 3 4

Notes for Justification of Scores

(Check the indicator which the activity addresses)
[ ]   Improves Professional Knowledge and Skills
[ ]   Takes a Leadership Role in Improving Education

Check the Basis for the Activity:

[ ] Required Inservice   [ ] Self-Initiated Activity   [ ] Professional Development Plan   [ ] Goal Accountability Plan

(Write in the definition item being addressed by this activity)
Item: _____

Description:

Year: Time Spent *(approximate hours):*

Benefit:

1   2   3   4
Definition
Item Score

(Check the indicator which the activity addresses)
[ ]   Improves Professional Knowledge and Skills
[ ]   Takes a Leadership Role in Improving Education

Check the Basis for the Activity:

[ ] Required Inservice   [ ] Self-Initiated Activity   [ ] Professional Development Plan   [ ] Goal Accountability Plan

(Write in the definition item being addressed by this activity)
Item: _____

Description:

Year: Time Spent *(approximate hours):*

Benefit:

1   2   3   4
Definition
Item Score

Superintendent Performance Evaluation

<u>Example of a Summary Evaluation Form (For a-Multiple-Data-Collection Model</u>

Evaluation Summary Report

ALABAMA PROFESSIONAL EDUCATION PERSONNEL EVALUATION PROGRAM

EVALUATION SUMMARY REPORT
SUPERINTENDENT

Evaluatee: _____ Social Security No: _ _ _ - _ _ - _ _ _ _ .

Evaluator: _____ Social Security No: _ _ _ - _ _ - _ _ _ _ .

School
System: _ _ _ . _____ School: _ _ _ _ . Date: _ _ / _ _ / _ _ .
    Code No.   Code No.   M M   D D   Y Y

This evaluation summary form should be used to combine information from the various data collection instruments: Structured Interview/Structured Presentation (SI/SP), Superintendent Questionnaire (QT), and Professional Development and Leadership (PDL) Summary. First, scores from these instruments should be listed in blank space(s) by indicator. If 'L' for Limited Responsibility has been assigned an indicator, record only the numerical rating on the ESR. Second, this information should be reviewed to determine a competency score. Third, competency scores should be listed in the blank space designated for competency ratings. Fourth, documentation is required on this report for each competency area. The following rating scale should be used to determine indicator scores and the overall score for each competency area:

1 - Unsatisfactory	Indicates the evaluatee's performance in this position requirement is not acceptable. Improvement activities must be undertaken immediately.
2 - Needs Improvement	Indicates the evaluatee's performance needs improvement in this position requirement. Improvement activities are required for performance to meet standards.
3 - Area Of Strength	Indicates the evaluatee always meets, and sometimes exceeds expectations for performance in this position requirement. Performance can be improved in the area(s) indicated, but current practices are clearly acceptable.
4 - Demonstrates Excellence	Indicates the evaluatee does an outstanding job in this position requirement. No area for improvement is readily identifiable.
L - Limited Responsibility	Indicates the evaluatee has limited (L) responsibility in this indicator/competency area. When an 'L' is indicated, a numerical rating (1-4) should be assigned.

COMPETENCIES Indicators	SI/ SP	QT	PDL
1.0 CHIEF EXECUTIVE OFFICER OF THE SCHOOL BOARD	RATING		
1.1 Recommends Actions to the School Board and Implements Policies of the School Board			
1.2 Reports to the School Board the Status of Programs, Personnel, and Operations			
1.3 Performs Duties as Chief Executive Officer			

Competency Documentation:

F40_0991

280

COMPETENCIES Indicators	SI/ SP	QT	PDL
2.0 EDUCATIONAL LEADERSHIP OF THE SCHOOLS	RATING		
2.1 Communicates Vision/Mission to Staff, Students, and Parents/Guardians			
2.2 Provides for Supervision, Evaluation, and Professional Growth of all Personnel			
2.3 Supervises the Planning, Implementation, and Evaluation of Curriculum and Instruction			
2.4 Establishes Goals for Student Achievement			
Competency Documentation:			

COMPETENCIES Indicators	SI/ SP	QT	PDL
3.0 PERSONNEL MANAGEMENT	RATING		
3.1 Develops and Implements a Comprehensive Personnel Plan			
3.2 Assigns, Orients, and Inducts Personnel to Schools and Offices			
Competency Documentation:			

COMPETENCIES Indicators	SI/ SP	QT	PDL
4.0 FINANCIAL MANAGEMENT	RATING		
4.1 Seeks Sufficient Funding for the School System			
4.2 Prepares Budget			
4.3 Ensures Compliance with Federal, State, and Local Laws and Policies			
4.4 Establishes and Maintains Procedures for Procurement and Fixed Assets Control of Equipment and Supplies			
Competency Documentation:			

COMPETENCIES *Indicators*	SI/ SP	QT	PDL
5.0 COMMUNITY RELATIONS	RATING		
5.1 Develops and Implements a System-Wide Plan for Community Relations			
5.2 Utilizes Local Media in Community Relations			
5.3 Models Positive Community Involvement			
Competency Documentation:			

COMPETENCIES *Indicators*	SI/ SP	QT	PDL
6.0 MANAGEMENT OF SCHOOL SYSTEM RESOURCES	RATING		
6.1 Manages School Facilities			
6.2 Manages Pupil Personnel Services			
6.3 Implements Policies and Programs Relating to Student Conduct and Discipline			
6.4 Ensures the Health and Safety of Students			
Competency Documentation:			

COMPETENCIES *Indicators*	SI/ SP	QT	PDL
7.0 COMMUNICATION AND INTERPERSONAL RELATIONS	RATING		
7.1 Speaks Clearly, Correctly, and Coherently			
7.2 Writes Clearly, Correctly, and Coherently			
7.3 Establishes Effective Communication Processes and Interpersonal Relationships			
Competency Documentation:			

3

F40_0991

COMPETENCIES Indicators	SI/ SP	QT	PDL
	RATING		
8.0 PROFESSIONAL DEVELOPMENT AND LEADERSHIP			
8.1 Improves Professional Knowledge and Skills	░	░	
8.2 Takes a Leadership Role in Improving Education	░	░	
Competency Documentation:			

COMPETENCIES Indicators	SI/ SP	QT	PDL
	RATING		
9.0 PROFESSIONAL RESPONSIBILITIES			
9.1 Implements Federal, State, and Local Laws, Policies, and Procedures	░		░
9.2 Performs Duties in an Effective Manner	░		░
Competency Documentation:			

List numbers of no more than three Competencies and a limited number of Indicators identified for the focus of a Professional Development Plan for the next school year:

Competency: Competency: Competency:

   Indicator(s):   Indicator(s):   Indicator(s):

Evaluatee's Signature _____   Evaluator's Signature _____

Other Data Collectors' Signature: _____   _____

NOTE: Signature indicates that information from other instruments has been shared and evaluation results have been discussed.

Superintendent Performance Evaluation

<u>Example of Post-Evaluation Development Plans</u>

Professional Development Plan

Goal Accountability Plan (for professional and organizational development)

.

284

PROFESSIONAL EDUCATION PERSONNEL EVALUATION PROGRAM
PROFESSIONAL DEVELOPMENT PLAN
(NON-TENURED AND TENURED PERSONNEL)

EVALUATEE: _____ POSITION: _____ EVALUATOR: _____ DATE: _____

DIRECTIONS: This plan should be developed from the evaluatee's evaluation results. List three areas identified for the focus of a Professional Development Plan for the next school year.

AREA NUMBERS	PROFESSIONAL DEVELOPMENT RELATED GOALS/OBJECTIVES	PROPOSED ACTIVITIES	TIME LINE	ASSESSMENT METHOD(S)	MID-YEAR REVIEW	END-OF-YEAR ASSESSMENT
Competency Area: Indicator(s):						
Competency Area: Indicator(s):						
Competency Area: Indicator(s):						

We, the undersigned, agree upon the Goals/Objectives, Activities, Timelines, and Assessment Method(s) listed

Evaluatee _____ Date _____   Evaluator _____ Date _____

We, the undersigned, have discussed the Assessment Results described

Evaluatee _____ Date _____   Evaluator _____ Date _____

(Attach additional sheets if more space is needed.)

* All non-tenured and tenured personnel must develop a Professional Development Plan annually

F37-0691

PROFESSIONAL EDUCATION PERSONNEL EVALUATION PROGRAM
GOAL ACCOUNTABILITY PLAN
**(TENURED PERSONNEL ONLY)

EVALUATEE: _____ POSITION: _____ EVALUATOR: _____ DATE: _____

DIRECTIONS: The evaluatee and evaluator should select and mutually agree upon specific, measurable objectives, activities, timelines, and the method of assessing attainment of goals/objectives for the professional development plan, as well as for student achievement/development or program improvement, and personal/professional areas.

GOALS/OBJECTIVES	PROPOSED ACTIVITIES	TIME LINE	ASSESSMENT METHOD(S)	MID-YEAR REVIEW	END-OF-YEAR ASSESSMENT
Student Achievement/Development or Program Improvement:					
Personal/Professional: (Education - Related)					

We, the undersigned, agree upon the Goals/Objectives, Activities, Timelines, and Assessment Method(s) listed.

Evaluatee _____ Date _____   Evaluator _____ Date _____

We, the undersigned have discussed the Assessment Results described

Evaluatee _____ Date _____

Evaluator _____ Date _____

(Attach additional sheets if more space is needed.)

** If so designated by the Superintendent, tenured personnel may be placed on a multi-year evaluation option which includes full evaluation one year and Goal Accountability (including a Professional Development Plan) during the other year(s).

F37-0961

INDEX

.